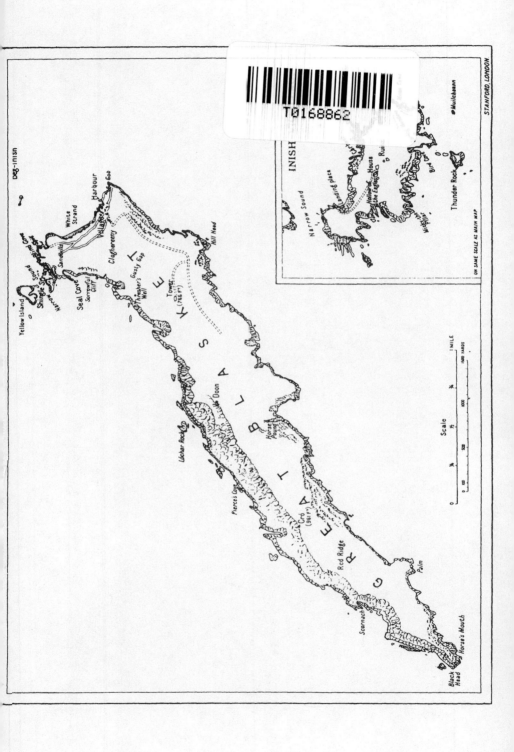

Dog-Inish

Yellow Island

Shingle Sound · Pints Cove

Sandhills

Maroon Sound

Seal Cove · Sorrowful Cliff

White Strand

Whiskey Harbour

Clogheraroy

Thresher's Well

Gusty Gap

Tower (765 Ft)

Hill Head

Goo

Long Doon

Uiobar Rock

Pierce's Cove

Horse Pound

Cro (961 Ft)

Red Ridge

Scarnach

Palm

Black Head · Horse's Mouth

KYSALT BAY

GREAT

INISH

Narrow Sound

Landing place

Hallowell House · The Expedition

Ruin

Mullaghmore

Bird Rock

Thunder Rock

Muilcheann

ON SAME SCALE AS MAIN MAP

STANFORD, LONDON

Scale

0   ¼   ½   ¾   1 MILE

1600 YARDS

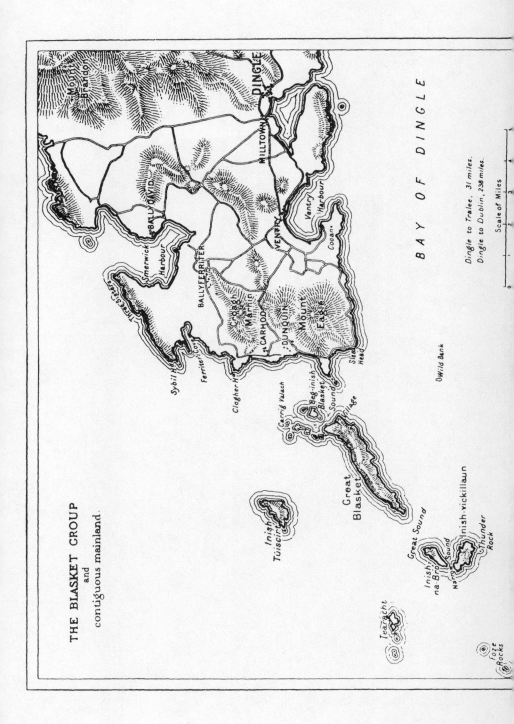

THE BLASKET GROUP
and
contiguous mainland.

BAY OF DINGLE

Scale of Miles

Dingle to Tralee, 31 miles.
Dingle to Dublin, 238 miles.

Mount Brandon

DINGLE

MILTOWN

BALLYDAVID

Smerwick Harbour

BALLYFERRITER

VENTRY

Ventry Harbour

Croagh Marhin

Three Sisters

Sybil Head

Ferriter's Cove

Clogher Ho.

CARHOO

DUNQUIN

Mount Eagle

Cooaan

Sleah Head

Carrig Valach

Beg-inish

Blasket Sound

Wild Bank

Village

Great Blasket

Great Sound

Inish Tuiscirt

Inish na-Bro

Narrow Sound

Inish-vickillaun

Thunder Rock

Tearacht

Foze Rocks

TWENTY YEARS A-GROWING

*The publishers would like to thank the following
individuals for their kind assistance in
preparing this edition:*

Mrs. Maura O'Sullivan Kavanagh and
Ms. Gráinne Kavanagh;

Mr. Mícheál de Mórdha and everyone at
the Blasket Centre, Dún Chaoin,
County Kerry.

MAURICE O'SULLIVAN

TWENTY YEARS A-GROWING

With an Introductory Note by E. M. Forster

Translated from the original Irish
by Moya Llewelyn Davies
and George Thomson

J.S. SANDERS & COMPANY
NASHVILLE
1998

First published in Irish in 1933
English translation published in the same year
by Chatto and Windus, London, and
the Viking Press, New York

First J.S. Sanders & Company edition published 1998
Reprinted by permission of Mrs. Maura O'Sullivan Kavanagh

ISBN 1-879941-39-2

LIBRARY OF CONGRESS CATALOGING-IN-PUBLICATION DATA

O'Sullivan, Maurice.
[Fiche blian ag fás. English]
Twenty years a-growing / Maurice O'Sullivan;
with an introductory note by E.M. Forster;
translated from the original Irish by
Moya Llewelyn Davies and George Thomson.
Originally published: London: Chatto and Windus, 1933.
ISBN 1-879941-39-2 (pbk: alk. paper)
1. O'Sullivan, Maurice—Homes and haunts—Ireland—Blasket Islands.
2. Blasket Islands (Ireland)—Social life and customs.
3. Blasket Islands (Ireland)—Biography I. Title
DA990.B6508 1998
941.9'6—DC21   98-36227

Published in the United States by:
J.S. Sanders & Company
Post Office Box 50331
Nashville, Tennessee 37205

1 3 5 7 9 10 8 6 4 2

CONTENTS

Contents

Note.—á is pronounced like aw in shawl, é like ay in bay, í like ee in bee, ú like oo in cool. The Irish peasant is usually known among his own people by his Christian name followed by that of his father or mother, whichever is the more notable character, sometimes by that of his grandfather (like Tomás Owen Vaun). Nicknames are very common.

INTRODUCTORY NOTE

T HE best introduction to this autobiography is its own first chapter. If the reader laughs at the schoolmistress and the matrons, and is moved by the dream of the butterfly inside the horse's skull—then he is assured of amusement and emotion to come. He is ready to go on to Ventry Races, and to make the great journey from Dingle east, where O'Connor and the girl were so unreliable. He is ready, furthermore, to make another journey: to steal out on Hallowe'en and catch thrushes above waves of the living and the dead, and see the Land of the Young in the west, and hear the mother-seal saying to the hunter, "If you are in luck you will leave this cove in haste, for be it known to you that you will not easily kill my young son." All this—both the gaiety and the magic—can be sampled in the opening chapter, and the reader can decide for himself quickly, so that there is no need to say to him "This book is good."

But it is worth saying "This book is unique," lest he forget what a very odd document he has got hold of. He is about to read an account of neolithic civilization from the inside. Synge and others have described it from the outside, and very sympathetically, but I know of no other instance where it has itself become vocal, and addressed modernity. Nor is a wiseacre speaking for it; we are entertained by a lively young man, who likes dancing and the movies, and was smart at his lessons. But he is able to keep our world in its place, and to view it only from his own place, and his spirit never abandons the stronghold to which, in the final chapter, his feet will return. "When I returned home, the lamps were being lit in the houses. I went in. My father and grandfather were sitting on either side of the fire, my grandfather smoking his old pipe." With these words the story closes, and it is as if a shutter descends, behind which all three generations disappear, and their Island with them.

The book is written in Irish, and the original is being published in Dublin. As regards the translators, one of them is in close and delicate touch with the instincts of her country-side, the other, a scholar, teaches Greek through the medium of Irish in the University of Galway. I know the author, too. He is now in the Civic Guard in Connemara, and though he is pleased that his book should be translated, his main care is for the Irish original, because it will be read on the Blasket. They will appreciate it there more than we can, for whom the wit and poetry must be veiled. On the other hand, we are their superiors in astonishment. They cannot possibly be as much surprised as we are, for here is the egg of a sea-bird—lovely, perfect, and laid this very morning.

E. M. Forster
1933

TRANSLATORS' PREFACE

THE Blasket Islands lie off the Kerry Coast, in the extreme south-west corner of Ireland. The largest of them, the only one now inhabited, is about five miles long, and for the most part less than half a mile broad, rising to not quite a thousand feet at its highest point—a treeless ridge of bog and mountain pasture descending in the west to a wind-swept headland of bare rock. The village is huddled under the shelter of the hill at the eastern end, nearest the mainland, where there is enough soil to yield a scanty crop of potatoes and oats. There is no harbour, and the only kind of boat in use is the curragh, a canoe of wicker framework and canvas covering, light enough for two men to carry on their backs. The distance from the mainland, quay to quay, is three and a half miles—an easy journey in good weather, but impossible in bad. The present population of the Island is about a hundred and fifty. Before the European War it was two hundred. The decrease is mainly due to emigration to America. It is recorded that the population doubled during the Great Famine (1840–50) when the starving and evicted peasantry of the interior flocked to the coasts in search of food.

The other islands, similarly featured but smaller and even more exposed, lie to the west and north of the main island. The most fertile of them, Inish-vick-ilaun, was inhabited till the end of the last century, and one house still stands, being used in the summer for the lobster-fishing. Inish-na-Bró is a rugged hog's-back with a remarkable headland perforated by the sea, like the arches of a Gothic cathedral. Tearacht, the most westerly, is a pyramid of naked rock, about six hundred feet high, with a lighthouse on the seaward side. Inish Túiscirt, to the north, has the remains of an oratory of Saint Brendan, the patron saint of the district.

Some of the Islanders own cows and sheep, and the pasture yields delicious mutton. Turf is plentiful at the western end. The main industry is fishing—lobster in the summer and mackerel in the winter—a dangerous and precarious livelihood. The nearest market is the town of Dingle, twelve miles east of Dunquin, the mainland village opposite the Island.

The houses are of the usual west-of-Ireland type—long, low, and narrow. Many of them are dug into the steep slope of the hill, for shelter from the wind. They contain a living-room, with a floor of boards or beaten mud, and an open hearth at the west end. The sleeping-room is usually at the east end, but in some houses there is another small room behind the hearth. There is a loft, but no upper story, and when an Islander speaks of going up or down in the house, he means that he is going towards or away from the hearth. The roof is of tarred canvas, the same material which is used for covering the curraghs. There are a number of spinning-wheels on which the women spin their wool, but the old local dyes are going out of use. There are no shops of any kind. The nearest chapel is at Dunquin, where the men of the Island go to hear Mass every Sunday when the sea is calm.

Only Irish is spoken and little English is known. Reading is a habit only recently acquired and seldom practised. The pastimes are singing, dancing, story-telling and conversation. The literature, which has been preserved entirely by oral tradition, includes ancient legends, some of them older than Beowulf, poems and songs dating from the seventeenth and eighteenth centuries, and a wealth of folklore, still only partly collected. The people are fond of poetry and music. The art of impromptu verse composition in intricate metrical forms survived within living memory, and in recent years they have shown considerable skill in making and playing violins. The dances are the hornpipe, jig, four-hand reel, various country figures, and most popular of all, the "sets," a descendant of the old quadrille.

The language, like the life, is largely medieval—vigorous, direct, rich in oaths and asseverations, and delighting in neat and witty turns of phrase which are largely lost in translation. In these respects it resembles the speech of other peasantries, but it also possesses an elegance and grace which is due to its peculiar history; for, when the clan system on which Irish culture was based finally broke down in the seventeenth century, the poets and scholars were scattered among the common people.

This book is the story of one of the Islanders, written by himself for his own pleasure and for the entertainment of his friends, without any thought of a wider public. In the first part of the book he gives an account of his childhood in the Island; in the second he goes on to describe how he left his native place and went to Dublin in order to join the Civic Guard, the new Irish police force. It is the first translation into English of a genuine account of the life of the Irish peasants written by one of themselves, as distinct from what has been written about them by the poets and dramatists of the Anglo-Irish school. He was subject to only one literary influence. When he was a boy, a copy of Gorky's *My Childhood* found its way into the Island. He read it, and it made a deep impression on him.

A few words may be added about the translation. The English language, as commonly spoken in Ireland, differs considerably from standard English, and these differences are mainly due to memories, conscious or unconscious, of Irish speech. The new language has been twisted to fit the moulds of thought and idiom peculiar to the old. Hence we have freely used the Irish dialect of English as being the nearest to our original, and in this respect we are following the example of Synge, who of all writers in English had the deepest understanding of the Irish-speaking peasantry. But rich and highly coloured as this English is, its range is less than that of Irish, and since its literature is mainly in prose and entirely modern, it lacks the stamp of an ancient poetical tradition which is a marked feature of Irish. The range of vocabulary in the translation is less than that of the original, and there is not a word or phrase in the original which is not current in ordinary conversation.

With regard to the spelling of proper names, we have sought rather to facilitate the English reader than to be consistent. Some Irish names have an English form, others have not; and we have used one or the other, whichever seemed the more convenient.

We have omitted some passages of the original.

MOYA LLEWELYN DAVIES
GEORGE THOMSON
1933

One

IN DINGLE

T HERE is no doubt but youth is a fine thing though my own is not over yet and wisdom comes with age.

I am a boy who was born and bred in the Great Blasket, a small truly Gaelic island which lies north-west of the coast of Kerry, where the storms of the sky and the wild sea beat without ceasing from end to end of the year and from generation to generation against the wrinkled rocks which stand above the waves that wash in and out of the coves where the seals make their homes.

I remember well, when I was four years old, I was in the town of Dingle in the care of a stranger woman, because I was only half a year old when my mother died, dear God bless her soul and the souls of the dead. So there was no one to take care of me. I had two brothers and two sisters, but at that time they had little more sense than myself. So, as I have said, my father sent me to Dingle to be cared for by a woman there.

Very great indeed was the control that was over us, for there were many others like me, and as everyone knows, whenever there is a crowd of young children together they do be troublesome and very noisy at times. We had a great dislike for school, but that is not one man's disease in my opinion. There was teaching us as schoolmistress, a woman who was as grey as a badger with two tusks of teeth hanging down over her lip, and, if she wasn't cross, it isn't day yet. She was the devil itself, or so I thought. It was many a day I would be in terror when that look she had would come over her face, a look that would go through you.

I remember the first day I went to school. Peg de Róiste brought me, holding my hand, and it was with great plámás[1] she coaxed me to go. "Oh," she would say, "it is to a nice place I will take you today." "Are there any sweets there?" "There are and plenty and nice books full of pictures." She was for ever coaxing me that way until I went in with her.

Shyly I sat on the bench alongside of Peg. There were many, many children there making a power of noise. "Where are the sweets, Peg?" said I, and I had hardly said it when the mistress noticed me and beckoned me to go up to her. "Go up, now," says Peg, "she's for giving you the sweets."

Well, I had a drowning man's grip of Peg for fear of the mistress. "Leave go of me," said she. "Come up with me," said I. "Come on, then," said she, getting up and taking me by the hand.

Shamefaced I stood before the mistress. "Who are you and what is your name?" "They call me Maurice." "Maurice what?" said she sourly. "Maurice," said I again, my voice trembling. "All right," said she.

She went to a cupboard and took out a big tin and put it down before me. Then I saw a sight which put gladness into my heart—sweets in the shape of a man, a pig, a boat, a horse, and many another. I was in many minds, not knowing which I would choose. When I had taken my choice she gave me a book and put me sitting on the bench again. "Be a good boy,

---

1. Soft, coaxing talk.

now," said she, "and come to school every day." "I will." "You will surely," said she, leaving me and going up again to the table. So there I sat contentedly looking at the book while I was not forgetting to fill my mouth.

Soon, hearing a very pleasant sound, I lifted my head, and what would I see but a bell in the mistress's hand and she was shaking it: "Playtime," said she (in English). And so out with us all together.

"What are we to do now, Peg? Is it home we are going?"

"Not at all, but half an hour's ree-raa out here."

(But one thing I must say before I go on with my story. There was not a word of Irish in my mouth at that time, only English entirely.)

When we were out in the field, the boys began kicking a football and myself tried to be as good as another. But faith, if so, I did not do well for long, for a big, long gawk of a lad gave a kick to the ball and hit me neatly in the face the way I fell on the flat of my back without a spark of sight in my eyes or sense in my head. As I fell I heard Peg crying that I was dead, and I remember no more till I awoke inside the school to see the boys and girls all round me and the tears falling from Peg.

"Good boy!" said she, "sure nothing ails you. How are you now?"

"I am finely."

"Maybe you could eat an orange?" said the mistress.

She brought me a big one and soon my headache went away, it is so easy to coax the young.

I was going to school every day from that out. But it was not long before the sweets and the gentleness began to grow cold. So I became disgusted with school—the seven tasks of the mountain on me as I thought, when I was carrying my bag of books, and obliged to learn this and that. Before long it seemed to me there was nobody in the world had a worse life than myself.

Near the school was the poorhouse, full of people, each with his own affliction. There was one set of them we were always pursuing—the blind men. Many a fine evening we went up to play games on them—games for our own advantage. They used to be given supplies of sugar done up neatly in bags and we would wait for the chance to snatch them, which came easy since they were unable to see us.

But the thief does not always prosper. One evening we went up—five or six of us—and got a good haul, filling our pockets, upon which we darted away, thinking to be down in a ditch and swell ourselves out with the sugar. But we had not gone far when we saw the matron coming after us, a strap in her hand, the gate closed behind her, and a poisonous haste on her.

"Och, God be with us, boys," said I, "we are done for now or never, what will we do at all?"

"Faith," said Mickil Dick, "better a good run than a bad standing."

"But where shall we turn our faces?" said I.

"To the Hill of the Cairn," said Mickil.

Off we went, one to the east, another to the west, the matron pursuing us. It is then there was a roaring among the boys who had no substance in them, getting it heavy from the strap whenever she got hold of them.

I was lithe of limb myself at that time and I was not long making the top of the hill. As soon as I was safe I stopped to look back, and who should I see coming up the hill but Mickil, panting for breath. When I got my own breath back again I asked him where were the others. I got no answer. He sat down on a tuft of grass, stretched himself out his full length, and tightly closed his eyes. My heart leapt. I jumped towards him. There was not a puff in him. I screamed and caught him by the waist, but I couldn't get a stir or a move out of him. I was too weak. At last I seized him by the two feet and dragged him after me down the slope of the hill to a boghole about five

yards below. There I baptized him well but that was all I got
for my pains. Ne'er a breath was coming into him. Then I
thought of thrusting his head into the water, and when I had
given him a good dipping he began to come round. I pulled
him out again, white foam on his mouth, and went on beating
him till he opened his two eyes.

"Come safe, Mickil," said I. "Where am I?" said he. "You
are in a good place, my boy." But even then for half an hour
he was as dumb as a baker.

We remained on the top of the hill till darkness came, for we
were afraid to start for home in the daylight in case the matron
would see us. But what good was that? There was a thrashing
waiting for us whenever we would go home, because it was the
rule of the place to be in bed by six o'clock.

"Mickil," said I, "it is going from bad to worse for us to stay
here. Let us be going."

Off we went, slowly and reluctantly, till we strolled in
through the door. I was seized at once by the hair and Mickil
the same. The clothes were stripped off us. Blow after blow
fell till they had us half dead, and then not a bite nor a sup, but
threw us into the bed. There was no sleep for us that night for
the aches and pains darting through us.

Next morning we set out slow and heavy-hearted for school.

"I wonder what would you say for us to go mitching?" said
Mickil.

I leaned my back against the wall, thinking. While I was
thinking, what did I see up through the passage but a man and
two women looking at me and smiling. I wondered why they
were not looking at Mickil. They came straight towards me,
but I was afraid of them and began to run. As I ran I could hear
one of the women calling me by name. I ran on till I lay down
in a hole behind a gate where I found a way of peeping at them
through a chink.

I could see Mickil there, and they talking to him, and I was
not long peeping when I saw them giving him an apple and

orange. With that I didn't give a second glance, but back I ran as hard as I could till I was within a yard of them.

One of the women came over to me. "Why did you run away just now?"

"Nothing," said I bashfully.

"Do you know who I am?"

"I do not."

"I am your aunt," says she, taking me up in her arms and kissing me. The other woman did the same. "That is another aunt, too," said the first woman, "and this is your uncle," says she, pointing to the man who was standing behind us.

With that the man spoke out in Irish for he had no knowledge of English, or, if he had, he did not let on.

"What sort of talk has that man?" said I to the woman who had me in her arms.

"That's Irish."

"What's Irish?"

"Oh, wait now," says she, "till you go home, that is the time you will have the Irish."

"Where is my home? We have no Irish at all in this home here."

"This is not your home, Maurice, but the Blasket."

But I was as blind to what she said about the Blasket as the herring leaping in the Bay of Dingle.

"Your father is for coming out the next day to take you home. Would you like that, Maurice?"

"Who is my father?"

"Isn't it often your father was talking to you? You should have known him long ago."

"I don't know which of the men he is," said I, "for many come."

At that she gave a great laugh. "Ah, musha² youth is a queer thing," said she to the other woman.

___
2. Indeed.

I began putting questions to her about the Blasket now that my courage was coming back to me, and feeling well contented with my fill of the bag of sweets, the apples and the oranges, and she answered every question readily.

"And has my father sweets at home?" said I, after devouring a fine apple.

"Oh, he has indeed, and everything else."

After a while she let me down. Then they all kissed me, gave a farewell and a blessing to the two of us, and went away.

My uncle turned back and came up to me. He began talking, though neither of us could understand him. Then he let out a great rush of talk, and another rush after it. I looked at Mickil, Mickil looked at me, we making great wonder of him. When he was going, he put his hand in his pocket and gave me half a crown, and a shilling to Mickil.

"I never saw a penny as bright as that," said Mickil; "where is yours?"

"Look," said I, "mine is bigger."

"I don't know what we had better buy with them."

"Apples and sweets, and it is the fine life we will have with them. But oh, Mickil, we are forgetting. What about school! The devil take it, let us make haste!"

Off we ran as hard as we could until we reached the school. In we hurried, panting. We were an hour late. We thought, my son, we had our feet clear and we were about to sit down on the bench at our ease when the mistress called us. Heavily and unwillingly we went up and stood before her. She was in a posture, staring at us from under her brows. At last she spoke. "Where were you? What kept you so late?" said she sourly.

I looked at Mickil. His lips were pouting, getting ready to cry.

"Have done with your snivelling," said she angrily, "and answer my question."

"We weren't in any place," said I, "but when we were coming to school we met some kinsfolk of mine and they kept us talking."

"Isn't it a fine excuse you make up! Go out now and cut a good fat rod and bring it in to me, my good boy, the way I won't hear any more of your blather."

I went out and cut the worst rod I could find and brought it in to her.

"Stretch out your hand." I did; and I got it hard. "Now the other hand." I got the same again. Three blows on each hand she gave me before she was done, and Mickil the same. I winked at him not to cry so as to give her no satisfaction. Then she took us to the far end of the school. There were two posts there, coming down from the roof to the floor, on which we were accustomed to drill. She tied one of us to each post. But, if so, we were well content, as no lessons were being put on us and that is what we wanted.

We were there about half an hour when there was a knock on the door. The mistress jumped from her chair and began walking to and fro without any sense. We were tied too fast for her to release us in a hurry. The knock was made again sharply. She could wait no longer to open the door. Who was there but the parish priest!

"It is with us now, my boy," I whispered to Mickil. "You will soon see sport."

The priest walked in, a tin of sweets in his hand as was the way with him, and he began talking to the children. The mistress was as white as death. "The devil take you," said Mickil, "do you see the look on the mistress?" It is then we had the bright smiles.

It wasn't long before the priest was asking where were Mickil and Maurice.

"Here we are, father," said we with one voice.

He came over to us looking knives. "Oh, what is the meaning of this?" said he. "Who tied you here?"

"The mistress, father," said I.

"Why?"

"I will tell you, father. When Mickil and I were coming to

school we met some kinsfolk of mine and they kept us talking, the way we were an hour late."

He beckoned to the mistress to come down. "What is this you are after doing to the poor little children?"

"Oh, father, I beg your pardon, I was for putting a little fear into them."

"Look, father," said I, showing him my hands, which were blistered with the blows.

"Oh, my shame," said the priest. Then turning to the mistress: "I will make short delay," said he, "of putting you out of the school if you go on with this work. Untie them at once, and if I find that you set hands on them again you will have news to tell."

That was the first time I ever saw anger on a priest and I said to myself that it comes on them as on any other man. The end of it was that we had the evening under the hedge, for we got the rest of the day off.

I remember another fine day long afterward when I was on my way to school. There was a bell over the hall door, a bell to let the people know what would be going on—Mass, Mary's Crown,[3] or maybe dinner or supper for the poor people. It was not to be sounded except when there was need and there was a chain hanging down to pull it.

It happened that I had not much knowledge of it at that time, and so I took hold of the chain and began to play with it. I gave it a gentle pull which sent music all over the place. I liked it well, so I gave it another and a better pull which sent out the music louder still. I had five good pulls at the chain.

In a minute there wasn't an old person, not a cripple nor a sick person, but they were falling over each other's heels to the hall, a crowd from below, another crowd from above, a man from the east, another from the west. Young though I was, I realized my mistake.

---

3. The Rosary.

I went among them. I could hear the old people discussing excitedly together. "It is no dinner, anyway," one would say to another. Some of them made for the chapel, the rest following. I let on nothing. If I were found out, said I to myself, it is likely I would be tied to the post again.

By this time the hall was full of chatter, gibberish, and confusion. Looking back, whom should I see but the mistress, her brood in her wake, making for the chapel. I let on to be as surprised as anyone. She beckoned me to her. "What is it, Maurice?"

"I don't know in the world, mistress," said I.

She went in, we behind her. We went down on our knees. The chapel was full from end to end. But there was no priest coming, and well I knew that no priest would come.

After a while a nun came in and spoke to the congregation. "What brought ye here," said she, "and who set the bell going?"

With that the mistress got up and said it was a strange business for any man to do such a thing, especially to take old people who could not walk from their corners and to put the day astray on herself. When she had finished speaking, the nun ordered the people to depart. A cold sweat was coming out on me by this time, and my heart leaping. Whenever anyone looked at me, it seemed to me he could tell I was guilty.

In the end we got the rest of the day off on account of it.

One winter's night, very wild, with the patter of snow on the window-panes, the wind blowing with a lonely whistle among the trees, an ass braying far away with the coldness of the night, and myself stretched out on the flat of my back in the fine cosy bed, I was thinking and ever thinking of the Blasket. When would the day come when I would be a man, free from the control of the matrons, no school to sicken me and the mistress beating me no more? Then the driving snow against the window-pane would put the Island out of my head, and I would hear with pity the poor ass braying in the distance. Oh, if I were where you are now, my assaleen, said I to myself, isn't it I would be terrified of the pooka![4]

At that moment, I heard a knock at the door.

"Who's there?" said the matron.

"Let me in," said a voice plaintively.

As soon as the door was opened a strapping, middle-aged woman stumbled into the room, two children at her feet, all of them in rags, looking as if they had walked far, water dripping from them from head to heel.

"God save all here," said she.

"God and Mary save you," said the matron.

"For the love of God, can you find room for us within till morning from the cold of the night?"

"You will have it and welcome."

Three chairs were set for them. I kept watching the woman. Tea was made and they sat in to the table. There was not another word out of her, but she kept giving a side glance at the door like someone who had committed a great crime.

They had only taken a couple of bites when there came another loud knock. The matron ran to the door.

"Who's there?"

"Constabulary," said a voice outside, answering her at once. At that the poor woman jumped up from the table.

"Oh, God save my soul," she cried, "they have me."

Two constables leapt in—fine men, clean above six feet high and as straight as a candle, a wild look on them. Anyone could tell they were in pursuit of the poor woman.

"What brought you in here?" said one of them to her angrily.

She made no answer. She was trembling hand and foot.

"I charge you with breaking the panes in the chapel to make your way in," said he in a loud, rough voice.

Then the constables caught her by the hands and led her away.

---

4. Hobgoblin.

All this time I was watching them and I began thinking again, as I listened to her going away from the house shouting and crying, that it was a queer world—a full-grown woman like her to be under control the same as myself. I could still hear an odd cry from her now and again. As she went farther away, the shouting grew weaker till I fell into a heavy slumber.

Before long I was dreaming that Mickil Dick and I were walking through a fine green meadow, gathering flowers. When we had gathered our fill of them, we sat down, talking of school and brilla-bralla,⁵ as is the habit of children.

After a while it seemed that Mickil fell asleep. I was looking at him, he snoring fine and easy. While I sat thinking what a strange thing was that same sleep, what would I see come out of his mouth but a pretty white butterfly. It began to walk down over his body. I stopped and reflected that it was a queer thing to come out of his mouth. Down went the butterfly through the meadow, I after it, ever and ever, till it came to an iron gate. It began to climb the bars of the gate, from bar to bar, slowly and easily, I watching. When it came to the top of the gate, down it went on the other side. I stood watching every turn it was taking. It came down into another meadow where there was an old skull of a horse which looked as if it had been there for years. In went the butterfly through the holes of the eyes, I still watching intently.

It must have been five minutes before I saw it coming out again through the mouth of the skull. Back it came to the gate, up each bar and down the other side, just as it had done before, then up through the meadow, I following it ever and ever till it went back into Mickil's mouth.

At that moment he awoke.

"Where am I?" said he looking round.

"Don't you know the place?" said I, not letting on to him yet about the butterfly.

---

5. Childish nonsense.

"Oh, Maurice," said he, "sit down till I tell you the fine dream I am after having. Would you believe it, I dreamt we went astray on each other when we were gathering the flowers, and that I walked on for a long, long way till I came to some railway tracks which crossed each other like the threads of a stocking. I didn't know where in the world I was. I kept shouting and calling to you, but that was all the good I got out of it. When I came to the end of the railway line, I saw a big bright house. I went up to it. There was a big round doorway with no door in it. I stopped and looked. God save my soul, said I, what place is this? Shall I go inside? Oh, there is not a lie in what I am saying, Maurice."

"I believe you well," said I. "Go on with your story."

"Well, in I went. But, if so, there was no one alive or dead to be seen. I was passing from room to room, but upon my word, Maurice, my fill of fear was coming over me."

"It was no wonder for you."

"Well, faith, I thought I was going astray in the rooms and that I would never be able to find the way out. I was groping my way, ever and ever, till at last I reached the doorway, and, the devil if I didn't come back again over the same railway tracks, and just as I found myself in the meadow again, I awoke."

"Safe be your storyteller,"[6] said I. "It seems," I said, looking up at the sun, "when a man dreams, a white butterfly does be after coming out of his mouth and walking away; and when it comes back again, it is then he awakes."

"Why do you say that?" says Mickil.

"Because I saw it coming out of your own mouth when you were asleep, and it walked down through the meadow, up through that gate below, and from there into the old skull of a horse in the field beyond. Out it came again, up through the same place, and back into your mouth. It was then you awoke,

---

6. A blessing at the end of a story.

and as sure as you are alive that was the big house you were in."

At that moment I was awakened by a shout of laughter. There was Mickil beside me, bursting his sides to hear the way I was talking in my sleep.

We got up, made ready for school, and went away.

And I spent that day without learning anything but telling my dream to Mickil.

Two

MY FIRST JOURNEY HOME

I REMEMBER a day in July, in the year 1911. I wasn't long in school when a lad came in and spoke to the mistress, saying I was wanted by someone in the hall.

On going out whom did I see but my father, my uncle, and my two aunts. My aunt ran towards me and without saying a word she took me in her arms and kissed me. My other aunt did the same.

"Would you like to go home with me today?" said my father.

"I would indeed," said I, my heart snatching at it. "What sort of place is it?"

"Oh, a fine nice place."

"Will we be going now?"

"If we were ready, as soon as we have eaten our dinner, we will be moving in the name of God."

"I will go in now so," said I, "and say good-bye to Mickil."

An egg would not have broken under my feet with the lightness and gladness in my heart. I stretched out my hand. "Good-bye, Mickil," said I, "I am going home today, and I hope I shall see you again in health and happiness."

"The same to you," said he, his tears falling.

When I turned to speak to the mistress, I noticed that her two eyes were in lumps. It is not much good to speak to yourself, I thought, but I went up and spoke to her nicely. "I am going home today," said I.

"What is that you are saying?" said she, jumping up angrily.

"I am going home today," I repeated softly.

"Who came for you?"

"My father."

"Where is he?"

"He is outside."

She said no more but went out, I following her, till we reached the place where my father was. She gave him a thousand welcomes and spoke gently at first; but looking at her I could see that she had no good intentions. It was not long before she spoke her mind.

"Arra, musha, you ought to know what you are doing," said she, "taking the child home when he is just learning his scholarship, and if you left him here he would have a livelihood for ever."

"Och, my pity for your head," replied my father, "I don't know what livelihood he would get but only to let him follow his nose in the end of all."

"Well, Shaun," said she, "I always thought you had some sense until today, and you to do such a thing to the poor boy. In the first place he will lose his English, and so he will be a fool when he grows up a stripling, if he lives so long. Where will he go, and how will he get work without the English?"

"Isn't it better still for him to have the two languages?" said my father. "And another thing, you don't know what way will Ireland turn out yet. Maybe the foreign tongue will go under foot," said he with a laugh.

"Och," said she, "the way with you is, live horse and you will get grass."

"That is the thing I was going to say myself referring to the child, for that will be the way with him. But it is no good spending the day so. Come along," said he to me.

We gave the mistress a farewell and a blessing and departed.

"We must go up to the Institution now," said my father, "to dress you up, for I have bought you a nice suit of clothes."

When I heard that I was so delighted it seemed as if there was no one in the world but myself, especially as I had never worn trousers yet. Wouldn't it be a great change for me in another half-hour! I a grown man, leaving behind the distress of the world and the oppression of the matrons!

On our way up the sun was shining. It was very hot, not a cloud in the sky, the birds singing sweetly in the trees. Indeed, little bird, said I in my own mind, there was a time when I thought I could never be so happy and contented as you.

"I think," said my father, "you are sorry to leave."

"Sorry!" said I. "Indeed I am not, but in a hurry to put on the trousers and to see my native village."

A nun was standing before us in the doorway. She gave my father a welcome and questioned him about me kindly and courteously. When she had left us, I saw a parcel on the table and I thought at once of the new suit. I kept watching until my father opened it. He took out a pair of breeches and a jacket, then a shirt, a collar, a cap, slippers and a pair of black stockings.

"Now," said he, "cast off from you the child's clothes."

When I was ready, my father looked at me laughing. "Faith, you are a grown man, God bless you. Turn round till I see the back. They fit you as well as if the tailor had made them. Wait till I get you the looking-glass. Look at yourself now," said he.

When I saw the form in which I was, all thought of Mickil and of everything else went out of my mind. "Oh, dad," said I, "I am a great sport for fineness."

Out we went and down the road again, and before long I struck up a whistling tune, every step as long as my father's the way people would know I was a man.

In a little while we met my two aunts. They tore me asunder with kisses, for women are the very devil for plámás, so that I did not like to meet them at all. Why wouldn't they take it fine and soft like a man? Not at all, they must be fawning on you every time they come across you.

When my aunts were satisfied, each of them put a half-crown in my pocket, with a good deal more I had got from others, and now I had my two hands down in my pockets, making music out of the coins with my fingers. It was a custom in the district, when a boy was wearing his first suit, for him to go from house to house through the village, and it is he would be puffed up with pride coming home in the evening with all the money he was after getting during the day.

We were soon in the town, the three in front of me and I behind, looking at myself and taking a good, long stride to give myself the look of a man. We went into the shop of Martin Kane in the big street.

"God bless your lives," said Martin.

"Long may you live," said my aunt.

"Who is the lad along with you?"

"It is a son of mine," said my father.

"I would never have known him. Do you like to be going to the Blasket?" said he to me.

"I do, indeed."

"Upon my word," said Martin, "the day will come when you will turn your back on the place, my boy."

"It will never come," said I.

"By my arm," said Martin, "if you take after your grandfather, I am doubting you will never leave it. Maybe you would make a good fisherman yet. But come inside; I dare say you are hungry."

We sat in to the table and they began conversing in Irish. I sat listening to them shyly, like a dog listening to music, but I could not make any sense out of it. I slipped across to my aunt and gave her a nudge in the back. "What sort of talk is that going on between my father and the other man?" said I.

"That's Irish, astór[1]," said she, putting her arms round me and kissing me.

---

1. My treasure.

I would rather the frost than that to be done to me. When I got myself free of her I slunk away to the door, where I watched the people passing up and down, thinking still of the silly ways of women that you can't speak to them without their leaping at you.

My father, uncle, and Martin were now pretty merry with the drink. "Wait here till I get a car," said my father. "I won't be long."

In half an hour he came back with it. We were ready waiting, and I longing for the road in order to see the country, for I had no knowledge of it, and so my father was giving me the name of every place. Before long I could see the sea, ever and ever, till we came to Slea Head.

"Now, Maurice, see your native place!" said my father, stretching out his hand north-west to a small island which had been torn out from the mainland. I could not speak: a lump came in my throat when I saw the Island.

"But how can the horse get in there?" said I at last.

"We will go in with a curragh[2]," said my father.

"What sort of a thing is a curragh?" said I.

I stopped questioning, and went on thinking and looking out. I saw little white houses huddled together in the middle of the Island, a great wild hill straight to the west with no more houses to be seen, only a tower on the peak of the hill and the hillside white with sheep. I did not like the look of it. I think, said I to myself, it is not a good place. While those thoughts were passing through my mind, the car stopped, the people got out, and my father lifted me down.

"Where are we going now?" said I.

It was a week-day, and, as soon as we reached the top of the cliff, the King of the Island came up with his post-bag on his back. He spoke to my father, but not a word could I understand. There were many others round the place and they

2. A canoe of wicker covered with canvas and tarred.

all with their own talk. I don't know in the world, said I in my own mind, will the day ever come when I will be able to understand them.

The King turned to me. "Musha, how are you?" said he, stretching out his hand.

I looked at him—a fine, courteous, mannerly, well-favoured man.

"Thank you very much," said I (in English).

"The devil," said he. "I think you have no understanding of the Irish?"

"I have not," said I.

But he himself had the two languages, fluent and vigorous. "How does it please you to be going into the Island?" he asked me.

"I don't know," said I. "It does not look too nice altogether."

"Upon my word, Shaun," said the King, turning to my father, "it is time for us to be starting in." And he began to move down.

I was watching the white crests on the sea below. A good gale of wind was blowing from the south-west. We moved down through a great cliff, a rough, narrow little path before us. When I came in sight of the quay, what did I see but twenty black beetles twice as big as a cow!

"Oh, dad," said I, "are those beetles dangerous?"

The King gave a big, hearty laugh which took an echo out of the cliff, for he was a fine strong man with a voice without any hoarseness.

"Indeed, my boy," said he, "it is no bad guess you made, and you are not the first that gave them that name."

When we got down to the quay, I looked up at the height of the cliff above me, yellow vetchling growing here and there, a terrible noise from the waves breaking below. I saw a big black bird up in the middle of the cliff where it had made its nest. Oh Lord, said I to myself, how do you keep your senses up there at all!

Then I turned my eyes towards the slip and what did I see

but one of the big black beetles walking out towards me. My heart leapt. I caught hold of my aunt's shawl, crying, "Oh, the beetle!"

"Have no fear," said she, "that is a curragh they are carrying down on their backs." And she snatched another kiss from me. I thought of telling her that it was a nasty habit of women, but I held my tongue.

The curragh was now afloat, like a cork on the water, as light as an egg-shell. In went my uncle, and the way he set her rocking I thought every moment she would overturn. In went the King, and, faith, I was sure she would go down with the weight that was in the man. I was the last to be put in. The King was seated at his ease on the thwart, his pipe lit. My aunts were in the stern, I at their feet sitting on a tin of sweets.

"Now," said the King, "let us move her out in the name of God."

Soon the curragh was mounting the waves, then down again on the other side, sending bright jets of foam into the air every time she struck the water. I liked it well until we were in Mid-Bay. Then I began to feel my guts going in and out of each other, and as the curragh rose and fell I became seven times worse. I cried out.

"Have no fear," said my father.

"Oh, it isn't fear, but something is coming over me which isn't right."

"Lift up your head, my boy," said the King, "and take a whiff of the wind."

I did so, but it was no help. Before long a streak of pain ran across my chest. I wanted to throw up. I tried, but I could not.

"Heave it up," said the King, "and nothing more will ail you."

Seven attempts I made, but with no success.

"Put your hand back in your throat," said my father, "as far back as it will go, and then you will have it."

I did as he said, but I did not like it.

"Have no fear," said my father.

"But isn't it the way I am worst when I put my hand back in my mouth?"

"Don't mind that, but leave it well back until the burden comes up."

I tried again and again. Every time I pushed my hand back the desire to retch would run through my body. I kept my hand back patiently, ever and ever, till at last I felt my belly beating against the small of my back. Then up came the burden and I threw it out.

My uncle was on the thwart in the bows rowing hard. He looked at me and gave out a great rush of talk. But, alas, I no more knew what he was saying than the oar in his hand.

We were only a quarter of a mile from land now, with a fine view of the Island before us. The wind had dropped. There was not a breath in the sky, a dead calm on the sea, a wisp of smoke rising up straight from every chimney on the Island; the sun as yellow as gold shining over the Pass of the Hillslope from the west; a curragh towards us from the north, and another from the south; an echo in the coves from the barking of the dogs, and, when that ceased, the corncrake crying "Droach, droach, droach!" The beauty of the place filled my heart with delight. Soon I saw people running down by every path—two, three, four! At last it was beyond me to count them. They were coming like ants, some of them running, others walking slowly, till they were all together in a crowd above the quay.

We went in through a narrow creek no wider than the curragh. My eyes opened wide as I looked at the pool within. Not an inch of the slip but was covered with children and grown men. You would think it was greed was on them to tear the curragh asunder, and they chattering and clamouring like a flock of geese a dog would send scattering.

The curragh stretched up alongside the slip. I got out. The crowd closed round, all but the children who gathered round myself, every one of them staring at me, some with a finger in their mouths, others coming up behind me. A shamefaced feeling came over me with the way they were peering at me. When I looked at them they would smile and hide their faces one behind another.

"Be off!" said the King to the children who were in his way. They scattered in fear. And now the men had the curragh on their backs and were putting her on the stays. I was standing on the top of the slip, a little afraid, for before me was a stout little lad as plump as a young pig. He kept staring at me out of his big blue eyes, his nose dripping, his finger in his mouth and he chewing it. He looked at my head and then at my feet. Then he moved round to examine me behind. I could feel his warm breath on the back of my neck. I put my hand in my pocket and gave him some sweets so that he would take his close face away from me, upon which he ran off to the others. But when they saw the sweets they all came round again pressing in upon me.

At that moment down the path came an old man. He looked at me smiling. Coming up he embraced and kissed me and began to talk to me in fine English.

"Who are you?" said I.

"Och, isn't it a strange thing that you would not know your own grandfather?" said he with a laugh. "Come up with me now," said he, taking me by the hand. But, oh Lord, it was a good half-hour before we reached the house on account of all the old women who came out to welcome me. "The devil take you," said an old man who was standing near, "don't choke the child!"

The house put great wonder on me. I had never seen the like of it before. It was small and narrow, with a felt roof, the walls outside bright with lime, a fine glowing fire sending warmth into every corner, and four súgán³ chairs around the hearth. I sat down on one of them. A dog was lying in the cinders. When I patted him with my hand he leapt up with a

---

3. Rope made of hay used for seating chairs.

growl, drew his tail between his legs, and slunk away into the corner.

I had two sisters and two brothers in the house, so I did not feel lonesome. When everything was ready we sat in to the table. And a fine, wholesome table it was for good, broken potatoes and two big plates of yellow bream—the custom of the Island at the fall of night. My father and my grandfather and my two sisters were talking in Irish, but I could not understand them. Now and then they would look at me and smile. After a while two boys came in, then three girls, and so on until the house was full.

When supper was over my sister swept the floor and shook sand over it. I was sitting on the chair, watching all that was going on. In another little while the lamp was lit. I could see the dry sand sparkling on the floor in the lamplight. Then a sound behind me made me turn round. It seemed to be within the hearth. I turned to my father:

"What is it," said I, "making music in the hearth?"

"Did you never hear that? It is a cricket."

Meanwhile a young man had come in with a melodium under his arm and now he struck up a tune. Two boys and two girls came out on the floor, and it would raise the dead from the grave to watch them dancing the four-handed reel.

I looked at the clock. To my surprise it was midnight. I had not felt the time passing. Musha, said I to myself, if I were in Dingle now, it is long since I would have been in bed with Mickil beside me, and great talk we would have had together!

The dance was getting wilder and wilder. A soft drop of sweat was coming out on the boys. When it was over they sat down and all clapped hands.

"Why are they doing that?" said I to my grandfather.

"They are urging Eileen to sing," said he.

At that moment she began. It was delightful to listen to her in the stillness of the night, everyone silent, with their chins on their hands, not a word out of them save now and then, at the end of the verse, when my grandfather would cry, "My love for ever,[4] Eileen," and that was the first bit of Irish I picked up that night.

When the song was finished everyone clapped again and the clamour spread through the house, a couple here and a couple there whispering together, all of them full of bright laughter.

After a while, my father whispered in my ear, "Ask your grandfather to sing. He has a fine voice."

"Won't you give us a song yourself now, grandfather?" said I.

"I will not refuse you," said he, smiling.

Leaning his cheek on his hand, he struck up "Éamonn Mágáine," and there is no doubt but he was a fine singer in those days. Listening to him as he came to the end of each verse, I would feel a shiver of delight in my blood, and it is no wonder, with the sweetness of the song and the tremor of his voice. Every word came out clearly. I did not understand the meaning of the words, but the other part of the song was plain to me—the voice, the tremor, and the sweetness. There was not a sound from anyone, only the cricket, which had not ceased its own music in the hearth.

When he came to the end: "My love for ever!" I cried aloud in Irish. Everyone laughed and clapped their hands.

It was now very late. The people began to scatter homeward to the white gable.[5] Soon we were all asleep.

---

4. A blessing signifying praise.
5. That is, to bed.

Three

—————◄►◄————

THE ISLAND

"WOULD you like to go up to the hill with me?" said my grandfather, putting the straddle on the ass to bring home a load of turf.

It was a fine, calm, sunny day. My father had gone at the sparrow's chirp lobster-fishing to Inish-vick-ilaun in the west and was not to return till Saturday.

"I would," said I.

We went up the road, my grandfather with a stick in one hand, the other holding his pipe in his mouth for lack of teeth.

When we reached the top of the road we had a fine view between us and the horizon to the south—the Great Skellig and Skellig Michael clearly to be seen, Iveragh stretched out in the sunshine to the south-east, not a puff of air nor a cloud in the sky, herring-gulls in hundreds around the trawlers which were fishing out in the bay, larks warbling sweetly over the heather, young lambs dancing and playing tricks on one another like school children who would be let out in the middle of the day.

We walked on until we reached Hill Head. "Look where your father is lobster-fishing," said my grandfather, pointing west towards the Inish. "Oh, it is grand to be up in that Island on such a day as this. Do you see the house?"

I stopped and looked. "I do not," said I.

"Look carefully at the middle of the Island and you will see the sun sparkling on something."

"Oh! Is that it? I dare say you were often there."

"My sorrow, I spent a great part of my life going out to it, and it is little the shoe or stocking was worn in those days, not even a drop of tea to be had, nor any thought of it."

"What used you to have?"

"Indian meal, oatmeal, potatoes, and fine fish from the sea; and they left their mark on the people. Little sickness or infection came to them. Arra, man, it is the way with them now that they have shoes on them as soon as they can crawl, not to mention all the clothes they wear, and for all that they are weak, and will be. Would you believe that it is many a day I left the house at sunrise, myself and Stephen O'Donlevy, Pad Mór, and Shaun O'Carna, for we were the crew of the one boat, dear God bless their souls, they are all on the way of truth now."

As he spoke, the tears fell from the old man and he stopped for a while as if to put from him the catch at his heart.

"Well," said he, drawing a long sigh, "would you believe it, we would have nothing on leaving the house but five or six cold potatoes and we would not come home until the blackness and blindness of the night? Where is the man who would stand such hardship now? Upon my word he does not exist."

"I doubt he does not. And what used you to be doing in the run of the day?"

"Killing seals and hunting rabbits. And if so, my boy, we used to be envied when we came home with our spoils, for I tell you, little Maurice, there were many here at the time who could not stand that hardship."

We were shortening the way in this manner until we came to where the road ended. "Isn't it a great wonder," said I, "the road was not continued all the way to the west?"

"I will tell you why, since one story draws another. Do you see that tower above? At first it was to be built on the summit of the Cró to the west and the road was to be made up to it. But when they got as far as this they were overcome with laziness, so the head man said it was too costly to make the road all the way to the Cró and they went no farther with the road but built the tower up there instead."

"I suppose you don't remember it being made?"

"Scarcely. But my father, God have mercy on his soul and the souls of the dead, was working on it. His wages were only fivepence a day."

"Musha," said I with a laugh, "wasn't it very small pay?"

"Upon my word, Maurice, it wasn't too bad for that time. There was no flour to be bought, no tea or sugar. We had our own food and our own clothes—the gathering of the strand, the hunt of the hill, the fish of the sea and the wool of the sheep. The devil a bit was there to buy, Maurice, save tobacco, and you could get a bandle of that for threepence. So where was the spending?"

We were silent then for a while until we reached Gusty Gap, with a view now of the north coast of the Island, where the waves were thundering in from the ocean and breaking against the rugged, upstanding cliffs, sending jets of foam as far as you could see into the sky.

"Isn't it a wild place, daddo[1]?"

"It is indeed. Do you see that rock below? It is called the Lóchar Rock, and I will tell you how it got the name."

He sat down on a tuft of grass, took off his hat and passed his hand back over his grey hair. "I was only four years old, but I remember well the day when a sailing-ship called the *Lochar* struck that rock below. Five sailors came safe out of her. They swam ashore and climbed up the cliff and not much of the morning was spent when they walked down into the village,

---

1. Name for grandfather.

not a stitch of clothes on them but the same as when they were born. The wonder of the world was on the people of the village as to where they had come from, and they could not understand their speech. My father brought two of them to our house, Pad Mór took in another two, and it was Tomás O'Carna, I think, who took in the fifth man. It was, indeed; I remember now. My father asked them where they were from and what was their cargo. One of them had a few words of English and he gave my father to understand that it was wheat they had on board. The place they had left was Halifax and they had spent three months on the sea, tossed east and west until the gale threw them in on that rock below. Soon afterwards the storm broke up the ship and the coves and strands were filled with wheat. We lived the lives of gentlemen while it lasted. My father had so much gathered in that we had enough for a whole long year."

"Well, now, that is a wonderful story," said I.

My grandfather got up and we walked on towards the Doon to the turf-stack. I didn't notice the time passing until we had both panniers full and were on our way back across the hillside. My grandfather was teaching me Irish all the way home, and I was well pleased with all the knowledge I was getting from him.

I had a brother and sister, Michael and Eileen, going to school at that time.

"What about coming to school with us?" said Eileen.

"I don't know. What sort is the teacher?"

"A very nice man."

"I am glad to hear it is a man, for the women are the devil," said I.

I went along with her at last. The master had not come yet so we sat down on the ditch. A crowd of boys were kicking a stocking football. I had never seen the like of it before—the heel of a stocking full of crushed straw and the mouth sewn up. There was a head of sweat on the players, and no wonder; the top of the village against the bottom of the village and the bottom always winning. They were giving each other a terrible pounding, with bruises and cut shins in plenty, sparks flying from nailed boots and everyone panting and groaning.

"The master is coming," said Eileen.

I looked up and saw him walking down through the glen—a short, stout man with a big belly out before him. He opened the door, rang the bell, and we went in.

It was not long before he noticed me. "What is your name?" I told him. "Where were you till now?" "In Dingle." "Were you going to school?" "I was, master." "What class were you in?" "The fifth class." "Good boy," said he, opening the roll-book and writing down my name.

I sat down on a bench beside a fine gentle lad, a sturdy little lump of a fellow. An arithmetic lesson was going on. I soon had my sums done and put down my pen and looked around. All had their heads bent except two, who were already finished like myself. The stout little fellow nudged me. "I see you are very quick at your tables. Will you help me?"

"I will," said I. I looked at them and soon had them done.

"Would you be my companion every day now?" said he shyly.

"I would like it very much. Where is your house?"

"I will show it to you when we go home."

"Very well. What is your name?"

"Tomás Owen Vaun."[2]

"Whist, Tomás, here is the master."

Tomás and I were together every day now, going to and coming from school. I was picking up Irish rapidly, getting to know the boys and girls and becoming a fine talker dependent on no one but as good as another at the language.

One day I was at school, Tomás on one side of me and Michael Peg Mór[3] on the other. The master walked out to the yard. We began playing tricks on each other. But he had only

2. Thomas (grandson of) fair-haired Owen.
3. Michael (son of) big Peg.

gone down behind the school and he put in his head through the bottom of the window where we could not see him. We were having a great ree-raa when everyone began to laugh and look at us. We wondered, guessing something must be wrong. Looking round, we began to tremble hand and foot when we saw the master.

"Ha! ha! when the cat's away the mice will play."

That is the only time they have for it, said I in my own mind. "Your soul to the devil, Michael, we are done for."

The master came in as white as the wall, his two nostrils wide open.

A blow across the legs, another across the back and then across the legs again. But though the pain was going to our hearts we let on there was nothing in the world we liked better. Then he caught me by the shoulder and put me in the corner with a long hard sum to do on my slate. The same with Michael. When I had finished I saw Michael making a sign to me that his sum was beyond him. The devil, said I to myself, I will give you succour by hook or by crook. When the master strolled out as far as the ditch I darted across and handed Michael my slate. "Take mine," said I, seizing his. I was scarcely back in my corner when the master returned. I had only finished Michael's sum when he came across to me, scowling. "Have you done it?"

"I have, master," said I, handing him the slate.

He didn't say a word and it seemed to me he wasn't too pleased that I had been able to do it. He went over to Michael, and his of course was done too.

When all the others went home we were kept in. The door was locked as though we were in prison. Michael began telling me of all the ghosts that had ever been seen in it.

"Whist," said I, "isn't it easy for us to get out through the window?"

We climbed out and away home with us.

The next day was Saturday and no school, so my heart was in my mouth for joy and delight. I walked out on to the ditch.

There was a fine burst of sunshine, my feet up on the ditch and I considering where I would turn my face.

I saw Shaun Fada coming towards me, the old man with the loud voice.

"Isn't it a fine day, Shaun?"

"There wasn't a day like it this year, praise and thanks to the King of Glory! Don't you see him to the east, my boy?" said he, pointing towards the old man they nicknamed White. A stooped figure was standing under the gable of the house. "If you want to foretell the weather, look at that fellow. If you see his head out, it will be sultry, but if you don't, you had better make for cover."

The man in the east had not spoken yet though he was not looking too kindly at Shaun.

"It seems we shall have sultry weather so," said I.

"You may be as sure of it as there's a cross on the ass."

"Oh, musha," said White, "I was never so bad as I am today."

"Bad, the devil," said Shaun; "aren't you always bad?"

"Musha, the killing of the castle on you[4] if you haven't a noisy windpipe and it is no lie for the man who first called you Junie of the Scroggle[5]," said White, leaving the gable and going into the house.

"He is in a temper now," said Shaun.

"It looks like it," said I.

"I swear by the devil you are making great progress with the Irish."

"Ah, there's nothing like youth for picking it up."

"That's true. Praise youth and it will prosper. How do you like the Island?"

"I like it well."

"My heart from the devil, you will tire of it some day."

"I don't know that yet."

---

4. An old curse.
5. Name for the heron, in reference to its long neck.

"On my oath, you will," said he, leaving me.

I sat down on the ditch again, nothing to be heard but a woman east calling her son Tigue, another woman west calling her daughter Kate, and a dog barking far away.

"Your dinner is ready, Maurice," said my grandfather, coming out.

"Isn't the sea very calm today, daddo?"

"It's a fine sight, praise to God on high," said he, baring his head. "Come in now before the potatoes get cold."

Four

———⟞⦿⟝———

A DAY'S HUNTING

THE next day, a Sunday, was very fine, the sea calm, and not a sound to be heard but the noise of the waves breaking on the White Strand and the footsteps of men walking down to the quay on their way out to the mainland to Mass.

There were six or seven curraghs out in Mid-Bay by this time, the men in them stripped to their shirts. Soon I saw Tomás coming down.

"God be with you, Tomás."

"The same God with you. Wouldn't it be a fine day on the hill? Would you have any courage for it?"

"Your soul to the devil, let us go," said I.

We went up the hill-road together, sweet music in our ears from the heath-hens on the summit. Each of us had a dog.

"Maybe," said Tomás, "we would get a dozen of puffins back in the Fern Bottom and another dozen of rabbits. I have a great dog for them."

We reached Horses' Pound, the heat of the sun cracking the stones and a head of sweat on us. We sat down on a tuft of grass. The devil if Tomás had not a pipe and tobacco. He lit it and handed it to me. "I don't smoke," said I. "Try it," said he.

When I had had my fill of it, I gave it back to him and stretched myself out on my back in the heat of the sun. But, if so, I soon began to feel Horses' Pound going round me. I was frightened. Tomás was singing to himself.

"Tomás," said I at last, "something is coming over me."

He looked at me. "It is too much of the pipe you have had. Throw up, and nothing will ail you."

I would rather have been dead than the way I was, wheezing and whinnying ever and ever till at last I threw up.

When we got to our feet we could not find the dogs. We whistled but they did not come.

"Beauty, Beauty, Beauty," I cried aloud, for that was the name of my dog.

"Topsy, Topsy, Topsy," cried Tomás.

At that moment my dog appeared with a rabbit across her mouth. "My heart for ever, Beauty!" I cried. Then Topsy returned with her mouth empty. "You can see now which is the better dog," said I.

We went on to the Fern Bottom and soon my dog had scented a puffin. We began digging the hole, but the ground was too firm and we had to give it up. Off with us then as far as White Rocks.

"We have a good chance now for a dozen of rabbits, for the burrows are very shallow here."

"Look," said I, "Beauty has scented something."

Down we ran. I thrust my hand into the burrow and drew out a fine fat rabbit.

"Your soul to the devil, Topsy has scented another," shouted Tomás, and away with him down to the hole. Before long we had a dozen and a half.

"We had better take a rest now," said Tomás, sitting down on the grass. He took out the pipe again and offered it to me. "Musha, keep it away from me," said I; "I have bought sense from it already."

It was midday now, the sun in the height of its power and a great heat in it. While we were talking, Tomás rose up on his elbow. "Do you know where we will go for the rest of the day?"

"Where?"

"Gathering sea-gulls' eggs in the Scornach."

Away we went till we reached its mouth. Looking down at the cliff, a feeling of dizziness came over me.

"What mother's son could go down there, Tomás?"

"Arra, man," said he with a laugh, "you only lack practice. I was the same way myself when I came here the first day with Shaun O'Shea. He was for ever urging me till I agreed to go down with him."

"Maybe you are right. We had better hide the rabbits here on top and not be carrying them down and up again."

We began to search for a suitable hole.

"There is a good one here, Tomás."

"The devil, the black-backed gulls would find them out there."

At last we found a place and we did not leave as much as a pinhole without covering it with fern and sods of earth. Then we turned our faces towards the cliff.

Tomás was down before me leaping as light as a goat through the screes, and no wonder, for it is amongst them he had spent his life. "Take it fine and easy," he said to me, "for fear your foot would loosen a stone and hit me on the head as it went down the hill. It is then you would be raising a clamour, Maurice, when you would see me falling over the cliff."

"Don't be talking that way, Tomás. You make me shiver."

A cold sweat was coming out on me with the eeriness of the place. I stopped and looked up. When I saw the black rugged cliff standing straight above I began to tremble still more. I looked down, and there was nothing below me but the blue depth of the sea: "God of Virtues!" I cried, "isn't it a dangerous place I am in!"

I could see Tomás still climbing down like a goat, without

a trouble or care in the world. There was a great din in the gully, it shining white with the droppings of the sea-birds— kittiwakes, herring-gulls, puffins, guille-mots, sea-ravens, razor-bills, black-backed gulls and petrels—each with its own cry and its own nest built in the rock.

I was looking at them and watching them until before long the dizziness left me, while I thought what a hard life they had, foraging for food like any sinner.

As I was thinking, I saw a puffin making straight towards me in from the sea. It was quite near me now, and I saw that it had a bundle of sprats across its mouth. It came nearer and nearer until it was only five yards away. It was likely going to land on the rock, I thought, so I lay down in the long heather which was growing around. It came in fearlessly and I made a grab at it with my hand. But it had gone into a burrow beside me. The entrance was covered with bird dung. I began digging it out, and it was easy enough, for I had only to thrust my hand back and lift up the ledge of a stone. There was a fine fat whippeen[1] in it. I thrust my hand in to draw it out, but, if so, I wished I had not, for it gave me a savage bite with its beak. When I caught it by the throat it dug its claws into me so that my hand was streaming with blood. At last I drew it out and killed it.

I arose and looked down. Tomás was nowhere to be seen.

"Tomás," I cried.

"Tomás," said the echo, answering me.

"Well," came up from Tomás far below.

"Well," repeated the echo, the way you would swear by the book there were four of us on the cliff. It seemed to me that he was miles below me. God of Virtues, said I to myself, he will fall over the cliff as sure as I live. I will go no farther myself anyway.

I was wandering backwards and forwards among the screes until I came across another burrow with dung at its mouth.

---

1. Young puffin.

Faith, I have another, said I, taking courage. I began to dig. Soon I had drawn out a fine fat puffin. At the end of my wanderings I had three dozen.

I was now the happiest hunter on the hills of Kerry. I sat down on a stone and drew out the bundle of bread I had brought with me for the day. I ate it hungrily. When I got up and looked at the whippeens I had thrown in a heap in the hollow beside me, I wondered how I would carry them home. Then I remembered I had a rope round my waist. Untying it, I took hold of a dozen of the birds, put their heads together and tied up the dozen in a single knot. I did the same with the second dozen and the third, till I had them all on the rope.

The sun was now as round as a plate beyond the Teeracht to the west, and a path of glittering golden light stretching as far as the horizon over the sea. I looked down, but Tomás was not coming yet, for he was a man who never showed haste or hurry so long as plunder was to be had. I gave a whistle. The echo answered me as before. Soon after I heard him shouting, "I am coming!"

Hundreds of birds were flying round, rabbits leaping from one clump of thrift to another, a sweet smell from the white heather and the fern, big vessels far out on the horizon you would think were on fire in the sunlight, a heat haze here and there in the ravines, and Kerry diamonds lying all around weakening my eyes with their sparkle.

Now I could see Tomás climbing slowly up, his face dirty and smeared with earth and no jersey on him. I laughed aloud when I saw the look of him. He was climbing from ledge to ledge till he was within a few yards of me. He had taken off his jersey, tied a cord round the neck of it and thrown it over his back with whatever booty he had inside it. Coming up to me he put down the jersey carefully on the ground.

"The devil take you, Tomás, what have you got?"

"I have guillemots' eggs, razor-bills' eggs and sea-gulls' eggs, my boy," said he, wiping the sweat from his forehead with his cap.

"By God, you have done well!"

"Your soul to the devil, why didn't you come down, man, and we would have had twice as many?"

"I was too frightened," said I, pretending I had got no plunder myself. "I dare say it is as well for us to be starting now." And going across to my bundle I threw it over my back.

"What have you there?"

"Puffins in plenty."

"Where did you get them?"

"Here in the scree without stirring out of it."

"By God, you are the best hunter I ever met."

We were moving on now up to the head of the cliff. We went on from ledge to ledge and from clump to clump. When we were up at last we lay down to rest.

"Wait till you see the eggs I have," said Tomás, opening his jersey.

They were a lovely sight, covered with black and red spots. "We have had a great hunt," said I.

"Very good indeed. Have you many whippeens?"

"Three dozen."

"Och, we will never carry them all home. But it is where the trouble will be now if the eggs are not clean after all our pains."

"Can't you see for yourself they are clean?" said I, laughing.

"Ah, that is not the cleanness I mean; but come with me and we shall soon know."

We went down to the south to a big pool of water in a bog-hole. "Look now," said he, taking up an egg, "if this egg is hatching it will float on the water, but if it is clean it will sink."

He threw in the egg. It remained floating.

"Och, the devil take it, there is a chick in that one."

He took it out and broke it against a stone and sure enough there was a chick in it. "Faith," said he, "it is a good beginning." He put in another in the water and it was the same way again. "The devil a clean one among them," said I. "I am afraid you are right," said he, throwing in another and not one of them sinking.

He lost heart then after all his walking in the run of the day and all for nothing. Seeing how despondent he was on account if it: "Don't mind," said I; "haven't we enough, each of us with a dozen and a half rabbits and a dozen and a half whippeens?"

We divided the spoils, and when we had all done up in bundles we were ready for the journey home. I looked at Tomás again and laughed.

"I don't know in the world why you are laughing at me since morning."

"Because anyone would think you were an ape you are so dirty."

"Faith, if I am as dirty as you are, the yellow devil is on me."

"What would you say to giving ourselves a good dip in the pool?"

"It is a good idea."

We stripped off all we had and went in, and when we were dressed again we felt so fresh we could have walked the hill twice over.

"The devil, that was a grand dip."

"Arra, man, I am not the same after it. Now in the name of God let us turn our faces homewards."

It was growing late. The sun was sinking on the horizon, the dew falling heavily as the air cooled, the dock-leaves closing up for the night, sea-birds crying as they came back to their young, rabbits rushing through the fern as they left their warrens, the sparkle of the Kerry diamonds gone out and a lonesome look coming over the ravines.

"It is night, Tomás."

"It is. Isn't there a great stretch on the day?"

"There is, and my people will likely be anxious about me for they don't know where I am. They will say it is into some hole I have fallen."

"Ah, mo léir,² it is often I was out and it is only mid-night would bring me home."

"But I am not the same as you."

"Why not? Amn't I a human being the same as yourself?"

"Ah, you are an old dog on the hill and your people are used to your being out late and early. It is the first time for me."

We were now in sight of the village, lamps lit in every house, dogs barking, the houses and rocks clearly reflected in the sea which lay below them without a stir like a well of fresh water, the moon climbing up behind Cnoc-a-comma, big and round and as yellow as gold.

We said good-bye and parted, Tomás to his house and I to mine.

---

2. Literally, my woe, my ruin—alas!

Five

VENTRY RACES

O NE fine day in the month of August the King was after coming in from Dunquin with the post-bag. It is the custom of the Island for everyone to be on the quay for his coming, young and old, and often he would have enough to do to draw breath with the crowd around him, thrusting in their heads and chattering.

"I dare say you have no news from outside?" said Shaun Fada.

"Musha, it is little news you would get at this time, only the people to be hard at work," replied the King, fingering the letters.

"Oh, long work on them," said Shaun Fada, turning out towards the sea, "there are people here, too, and the devil a bit of work is sickening them and they are living as well as any sinner in Ireland, though it's a strong word to say."

"Indeed, you were ever talking nonsense."

"Your soul to the devil, it's no nonsense. Don't you see them yourself as lazy as any cripple from here to Belfast?"

"Any man now who has any spirit," said the King, getting

up, "let him take a curragh south to Ventry next Sunday. There is going to be a great race in it."

"They won't go—no fear of it. Did you hear of any curragh to be going in for it?" asked Shaun, turning to the King.

"Indeed there are—a curragh from the Cooas, one from Ballymore and another from Leitriúch."

There was now no talk in the village of anything else but the races. Everyone I met on road, hill, or strand, his first greeting was "Are you going to the races?" "I am. Are you?" "I am."

On the Saturday night before they took place the boys and girls were gathered in together gossiping about the morrow. I met Tomás Owen Vaun. "The devil, Tomás, what about going to the races?"

"The devil, let us go."

"Does your father know?"

"Arra, man, I told him today I was going and all I got was a clout on the back which threw me out on my mouth."

"It is the same with me, but we will creep out unknown to them. If we could get ourselves inside any curragh all would be well."

"Oh, it would, man."

"Be up with the chirp of the sparrow, so, and we will make off in the first curragh we can get."

When I went in, Eileen, Shaun, and Michael were polishing their shoes for the races. I said nothing but sat by the fire, with a lip on me. Eileen was running around in a flutter. She came up and took the iron from the fire. "Go to bed now," said she to me, "and have the kettle boiling for us in the morning." She annoyed me so that I gave her a slap on the cheek. Then I ran down to the room and went to bed. But, believe me, my two eyes never closed. I lay listening to the tick-tock, tick-tock of the clock all night long till it struck five.

I got up unknown to the others, washed and dressed myself, and an egg would not have broken under my feet for the lightness of my tread for fear I might be heard on the floor. I made the fire and put on the kettle. Then I put my head out through the door, and indeed it would have raised the dead from their graves—an edge of golden cloud over Mount Eagle from the sun that was climbing in the east, a calm on the sea, not a stain in the sky and the lark singing sweetly above my head.

When I had eaten my bread and tea I went off for Tomás and found him ready before me. "Shaun Tigue and Shaun Tomás are gone down to the quay. Hurry on and they will take us out."

They had the curragh afloat. "Hurry, hurry," I cried, "or they will be gone."

We raced down the slip. "Shaun, will you take us?"

"Where are ye going?"

"To the races."

"Very well, jump in."

In we leapt, joy in our hearts, the two of us seated in the stern, the happiest creatures on the earth of the world. When we were a little distance out from the quay I looked back at the village and saw the boys and girls walking down. "Look, Tomás, what good luck we had to leave the quay in time!" Laughing, he gave me a pinch in the thigh. "Musha, it's true. If we were on the quay now we would never get away."

The sea was like a pane of glass, a stream of ebbing tide out through the Sound to the north, guillemots, razor-bills and petrels on the water, the four men stripped to their shirts rowing hard.

Shaun Tigue spoke out in the bows, "Do you see the loon?"

We looked south and saw a big, white-breasted bird floating down with the tide.

"Isn't it a fine bird, Tomás? Wouldn't you think it was a young gannet?" said I.

"It is very like one."

An old man, Shamus Kate, was in the middle. "That is a bird never stepped on dry land," said he.

"And where do they lay?" asked Shaun Tomás.

"Out on the sea."

"And wouldn't you say the sea would carry off the egg?" asked the other man.

"On my oath it does not, for she lays it between her two thighs and keeps it there till the chick is hatched."

We were approaching Great Cliff. It was a low ebb-tide. "By God," said Shamus, "we'll have great work taking the curragh upon to the shore." Everyone took off his shoes and drew his trousers up over his knees. Leaping out, we drew the boat up through the stones till we had her above high-water. As soon as we found ourselves on dry land, Tomás and I ran up the Cliff and made neither stop nor stay till we reached the chapel in Bally-na-houn.

We sat down to wait for Mass, very shy, for we knew no one in the place. "The devil, isn't there a great difference between this place and the Island?" said Tomás. It was his first day on the mainland and it was a great wonder to him.

When the priest arrived we went into the chapel. As we went down on our knees Tomás whispered to me: "Oh, isn't it a big house! How was it built at all?"

"Whist," said I, "or the priest will hear you."

Soon he was prodding me again. "Oh, I'll be killed, for my father is down behind and he looking at me," he whispered.

I glanced back and saw my brother Shaun shaking his fist at me. "Oh, they will kill us," said I.

"Don't mind. We'll steal away south unknown to them."

We moved up more into the crowd till we were by the wall so that they could not see us. Then we crept along slowly till we were near the door. As soon as Mass was over we ran out and up through the fields to the Hill of Clasach.

The day was very sultry.

"The devil, Tomás, let us throw off our shoes and we'll be as light as a starling for the road."

"A great thought," said he, and we sat down on the roadside. We tied our shoes together and flung them over our shoulders.

Half-way up the Clasach I looked back and saw the crowds ascending the road from the chapel.

"Oh, Lord, look at all the people coming to the races!"

"Oh, mo léir, aren't there many people in the world!"

When we came in sight of the parish of Ventry, Tomás was lost in astonishment.

"Oh, Maurice, isn't Ireland wide and spacious?"

"Upon my word, Tomás, she is bigger than that. What about Dingle where I was long ago?"

"And where is Dingle?"

"To the south of that hill."

"Oh, Lord, I always thought there was nothing in Ireland, only the Blasket, Dunquin, and Iveragh. Look at that big high hill beyond! Wouldn't it be grand for us to have it at home? What sport we would have climbing to the top of it every evening after school! I wonder what is the name of it!"

"Don't you know it and you looking at it every day from the Blasket? That's Mount Eagle."

"Is that so, indeed? In the Blasket it seemed as if it were in Dunquin."

We had a brilliant view before our eyes, southwards over the parish of Ventry and the parish of Maurhan and north to the parish of Kill, green fields covered in flowers on either side of us, a lonely house here and there away at the foot of the mountain, Ventry habour to the south-east, lying still, three or four sailing-boats at anchor, and a curragh or two creeping like beetles across the water, the mountains beyond nodding their heads one above the other.

We were leaping for mirth and delight. "Your soul to the devil, Tomás, it is a grand day we will have."

"Arra, man, think of the boys at home. Won't they be envious when they hear the two of us are gone to the races!" And he took a goat's leap down the road and I after him panting.

"But one thing only, Tomás," said I when I caught him up. "We haven't a penny to buy anything."

"Don't mind that. I promise you when we meet our own people they will give us pennies."

"Maybe."

"And what's more, when my father is drunk, believe me it is easy to get money out of him."

We were down at White Mouth now. On our way through the village Tomás stopped again.

"The devil, Maurice, look at the shop and the nice things in the window."

"Musha, if we had money, isn't it nice and comfortably we would buy those fine apples?"

"Do you know what we'll do? Let us wait here till they come. You know they won't kill us now."

We sat down outside the shop.

"The devil, isn't it grand for the boys who live here?" said Tomás. "Isn't it they have the fine life compared with us who are stuck in the Island?"

"Musha, it's true for you. Any time they like they can go down to Dingle."

"Arra, man, can they not go down to the place where the liners leave for America? What is to stop them? There is no sea before them."

"I don't know about that. You imagine now if you were living on the mainland that you could go anywhere you pleased, but upon my word you couldn't, my boy."

"Why not?" said he with his two eyes thrust in to the window of the shop.

"What about the long road and the empty pocket?"

"Musha, when I got hungry I would go into a house and get food, and away I would go again."

"That's talk in the air, my boy. Wait now till I tell you a story I heard from my grandfather about his own father. My people were living at that time at the Cooan. Do you see that place to the south?" I said, pointing towards it. "Well, that is where I would be today only for my great-grandfather going to the Island."

"Wasn't he a strange man to go there?"

"Ah, what could the poor people do at that time when the

rotten landlords threw out all the tenants at the Cooan and scattered them like little birds? However, that is not the story I have to tell you, but about my great-grandfather. When he was living at the Cooan they used to go to Cork selling their firkins of butter, and one day when he happened to be going there and was within three miles of Cork there fell the heaviest rain that ever fell. He walked on, wet to the skin. After a while whom should he meet on the road but the great poet of long ago, Egan O'Rahilly, and would you believe it, Tomás, they were closely akin to each other!

"'God save you, Micky,' said Egan.

"'God and Mary save you, Egan,' said my great-grandfather.

"'I dare say you are hungry as well as wet since leaving the Cooan?'

"'Faith, I am a little.'

"'And so am I.'

"It happened there was a farmer's house by the road-side which had a very bad name, for the farmer had a heart as hard as a stone and the world knew it as a house where no man ever got food to eat or drink to drink. But, if so, the barony that time was trembling in fear of the poets."

"Why?"

"Arra, man, wouldn't they shame you alive in those days with the satires they would write! Anyone who displeased them they would cover him with abuse to be read by the big world.

"Soon they were approaching the farm-house. 'Let us go in here now and I tell you we'll get food and drink,' said Egan. My grandfather looked at him. 'Arra, man, isn't it time you should know that house where no man ever got either?' 'Don't mind that,' said the poet, 'he is the devil himself if I can't manage him.'

"They went inside dripping with water. The farmer was seated at the hearth. My great-grandfather stood in the doorway. 'God bless all here,' said Egan, walking over and giving his heels to the fire. The farmer did not speak a word at first or ask if they had a mouth on them. Then at last he spoke: 'Should you not know your manners not to be wetting the floor that way.'

"Egan gave him no answer, but after a while when he saw the churlishness there was in his heart he winked at my great-grandfather and gave a shout of laughter.

"'God give us cause to laugh,' said the farmer with a start, 'what is amusing you, you buffoon?'

"'Musha, I am thinking of the crow I came across today on my road from the west and what it said.'

"'And what did it say?' said the farmer, sticking out his lip.

"'It came over my head, following me for a quarter of a mile, and this is what it was saying: Egan, Egan, Egan O'Rahilly; Egan, Egan O'Rahilly! Look how the crows themselves do know me.'

"Arra, Tomás, when the farmer knew whom he had in the house he leapt from his chair.

"'A hundred thousand welcomes to you! Maura!' he shouted to his wife, 'come in here. Musha, isn't it God who guided him to us?' 'Who?' said she. 'Arra, the noble Egan O'Rahilly!'

"She ran up to him with outstretched hands. 'A thousand welcomes to you!'

"The farmer gave the same welcome to my great-grandfather and led him up to the fire. He went down to the room and brought out a couple of chairs. Neither he nor his wife could do enough for them; they got the choice of all food and a bed to sleep in, for the farmer would not let them go without spending the night in his company, a thing he had never done before."

"Wasn't Egan very cunning?" said Tomás.

I stretched myself and glanced back along the road. "The devil, Tomás, they are coming."

"Is it so?" said he, looking back, a flush spreading on his cheek.

"Don't mind. Think of Egan and how cunning he was. Let

on we are perished with the hunger and they will give us something."

We were thinking now that they would beat the life out of us. But as they came nearer I saw they were smiling. "All's well, Tomás," I whispered. We remained with our heads bent till they were before us.

"Musha, look where the two changelings are," said my sister Maura. They all laughed. "Well, it's no good talking. They would do anything they liked," said Maurice Owen Vaun. "Don't mind about that," said my brother Shaun, "don't you know that youth does be gay." "Let them go now," said Maurice.

"Come in here with us," said my brother.

I gave Tomás a prod, and indeed we soon had all we wanted, the two of us sitting on a stool drinking tea. My brother gave me ten shillings and a crown to Tomás, and Tomás's father likewise.

"When ye go down now to the strand keep back from the horses," said Maurice Owen Vaun. "Off with you now and spend the day as ye please."

Out and away with us down the road to the east.

"I wonder, Tomás, what shall we buy?"

"Do you know what we'll buy?" said he in a whisper; "we will have a drink."

"Maybe it would make us drunk."

"Ah, we won't drink much."

"Did you ever drink?"

"Arra, man, I did, that night they had the barrel in the house of Dermod O'Shea. I drank a pint and never got drunk."

In the course of our talk we were walking on till we found ourselves outside the public-house in Ventry.

"Your soul to the devil," said Tomás, "we'll get it in here."

We went in and sat down on a long settle stretched beside the wall. There was a tall, grey-headed woman inside the counter and a cross look on her face. She spoke in English.

"Are ye going to the races?"

"We are," said I.

Tomás laughed. I winked at him. He understood at once what I had in mind and put on a dignified expression. At last I got up.

"Give us two pints, if you please."

She looked at me and laughed. Then she looked at Tomás. We looked at each other.

"Two pints?" said she in surprise.

"Two pints," I repeated sourly.

"Where are ye from?"

"From City-cow-titty[1]," said I, with a glance at the door to see if my brother Shaun was coming.

"And have ye money?"

"We have," said I.

"We have," said Tomás.

She turned in and filled two pints.

I took hold of one and handed it boldly to Tomás. Then I took my own pint and sat down to drink it. I could not help laughing when I saw the impudent look on the face of Tomás as he raised the glass to his mouth. He took five sips. Then he stopped, looked at me, shook his head and frowned.

"It is good," said I.

"Oh, it has a foul taste. I will never drink it."

"You want courage, my boy," said I, raising my own glass again. "I will tell you," said I, putting it down, "why you get a foul taste in it. It is because you are only sipping it. When you raise your glass to your mouth make no stop till you have to draw your breath."

He raised his glass and took a good pull out of it. "I think you are right," said he.

We finished our pints and Tomás wiped his lips with his hand.

"Let us have another."

---

1. A village east of Dingle.

"The devil, we have our fill now."

"Don't mind that," said he, turning to the counter and calling for two more.

I whispered to him: "I am thinking we don't look like men yet, the way that scraggy woman is laughing at us, and we had better clear out of this before your father and Shaun come in."

"Drink that," said he, "and don't be talking. Isn't it a day out of sixty days, as the old man said the night they had the barrel in Dermod's house?"

I saw he was getting merry. I raised my pint to my mouth and we went on till we had the glasses drained again. I began to feel my head in a whirl. I looked at Tomás and his two eyes were sunk back into his head. He laughed and laughed again without any cause.

"Come on," said I.

At that moment I felt the house beginning to go round me. I began to sweat. I stood up and went out. No sooner had I passed the door than I was thrown down on the back of my head. I looked round. No one was to be seen. "All's well," said I, groping along the wall till I reached the yard. I sat down on a stone and tried to throw up. Putting my fingers back in my throat I threw it up as clean as I had drunk it. I lifted up my head, and, by God, I felt as well as ever but I tell you I cursed the man who first thought of porter.

I don't know in the world where is Tomás, said I to myself. Isn't it a great wonder the desire to retch hasn't come over him as it did with me. I walked out whistling, letting on nothing. When I approached the door I heard talking inside and I knew by the voice it was Tomás. I could hear him saying there wasn't a man in Ventry good enough for him. I went in. He was standing in the middle of the floor, without his cap, a big new pipe in his mouth at which he was puffing. He was running with sweat.

"The devil take you, where did you get the pipe?"

"I bought it, as I am well able to do."

"Isn't it he who has the sauce now?" said the woman.

Tomás leapt up to the counter and struck his fist on it.

"If it is fight you want come on out here. I am the man for you and for any man in Ventry."

"Come, Tomás, or we will miss the races."

"The devil. I had forgotten all about them talking to that scarecrow of a woman."

At last I got him away.

"By God, Tomás, you are drunk," said I, and we went down the road to the east.

"Arra, man, I am not," said he with a laugh. "I could drink a barrel of it yet."

With those words he fell against the wall. I lifted him up and lead him into the yard. "Try if you could throw up now, Tomás, and you will be all right after it."

He put his hand back into his mouth and before long he threw up all he had drunk.

Raising his head he looked at me sorrowfully. "Musha, isn't it great folly for any man to be drinking?"

"It is true."

"I feel well now but for the nasty taste in my mouth."

"That is easy to cure." And I ran back to the shop and bought some sweets.

We walked on, eating the sweets, without stop or stay till we reached Ventry Strand.

"Oh, Lord, where will food be found for them all?" said Tomás.

"Isn't it a wonderful crowd?"

"Oh, it passes understanding."

The two of us now did not know was it on earth or air we were walking with the delight in our hearts, such a tumult and confusion were on the strand, every sort of party each with its own trick going on.

Before long we noticed a big bulk of people together and the laughter of the world on them.

"There is sport back here," said Tomás.

We ran towards them. There was a terrible big man standing

in their midst with a little table and a pack of cards, the four aces on the table. I had no other thought but that the veins in his neck would burst the way he was shouting. "Hello, hello, hello! Come on, ladies and gentlemen! Someone for the lucky club! Hello, hello, hello!"

"What is he saying?" asked Tomás.

"If you put a penny on any club or on an ace and it turns up, you get threepence and a penny for himself."

We stood watching him, getting the fun of the world. It was not the game we were watching but the man himself and the strain he was putting on the veins of his neck with his bawling.

"Come on," said I; "maybe we would see a better trick than that."

We had not gone far when we came upon a cripple playing a banjo and singing to the music. "The devil," whispered Tomás, "isn't it well he is able to stand on the two feet that are under him?"

As soon as he finished, a lanky fellow who was along with him came round with his cap in his hand gathering pennies which he got in plenty. We gave him one, the same as the rest. Then the cripple began to sing "Danny Boy," and a good hand he made of it.

There was a "Hello" here and a "Hello" there, the two of us running round like a hen after laying an egg, till we came to a barrel and a man down inside it and everyone making shots at him. He would stick his head up and put out his tongue. Then someone threw one of the blocks, two of them, three, but did not hit him. Another man was attending the crowd, shouting, and neither of them with a word of Irish. "Hurray, hurray, here is Sammy in the Barrel willing to keep his head for any man. Three chances for a penny. Come on! Come on, lads! Sammy is prepared to die if he gets a severe blow."

At that moment Sammy showed his head and let out a roar, the two of us there and our hearts broken with laughter.

"Your soul to the devil, Tomás, let's try it," said I.

I went up to the man. "Give me three blocks."

He handed them out. "Come on, my lads," he cried.

I went up to the mark. A big crowd was gathered round. Sammy showed his head. "Pooh! Pooh!" he shouted.

I could not help laughing when I saw the way he was bent. Then I threw a block and just hit the edge of the barrel.

"A great shot, my hearty," cried an old man beside me.

I took courage and let the next one go before Sammy showed his head. Just as the block was making for the edge of the barrel he bobbed up and got it straight on the bridge of the nose. His companion ran over and took him up. He was streaming blood.

When the crowd saw what I had done they pressed round from all sides, embracing me. "Musha, my love for your hand for ever!" cried one. "Oh, musha, may God save you! Isn't he the sprightly lad?" said another.

An old man leapt towards me. "Arra, musha, where are you from?"

"From the Island."

"Musha, my love for you for ever from the village far west!" he cried, putting his hand in his pocket and giving me half a crown.

I was senseless with the clamour all round me and I was frightened, too, that Sammy would come up to get satisfaction for the blow.

When I got myself extricated from them, we ran down the strand leaping as lightly as goats for sheer delight until we noticed four curraghs drawn up in a line, the men stripped and their oars stretched forward.

"Your soul to the devil, Tomás, look at the curraghs ready to race."

"Oh, Lord! won't it be great sport watching them!" And he leapt into the air for joy.

We sat down on our heels.

It is there was the clatter and clamour, the disputing and gnashing of teeth, the praise and the disparagement, each man with the people in the race according to his ancestors, like a swarm of bees buzzing on a fine day of harvest.

"Isn't it a great pity, Tomás, we don't know the curraghs?"

"It's true. We won't get any pleasure in the race since we don't know them."

"Wait now and I will ask someone," said I, going up to a man seated above us.

"Where are those curraghs from that are going to race?"

"Well, do you see the curragh that is nearest to you?" he said. "That is from my own place, a crew in whom I have confidence."

"What place is that?"

"The Cooas. And do you see the curragh with the white shirts? That is from Ballymore. And the one with the red shirts is from Leitriúch. And the curragh with the black shirts is from Ballydavid."

"Thank you," said I, returning to Tomás and telling him what I had heard.

"I wonder who is that splendid, big man in the middle of the curragh from the Cooas?" said Tomás.

"Isn't he a wonderful man for size?"

I turned to the old man above us and asked him who was the big fellow.

"Arra, man," said he, laughing, "you must have heard mention of Tigue Dermod, the man who would draw the devil himself in the wake of the curragh."

"Ah, is that he?"

"It is indeed. They will soon be racing now," taking a slice of tobacco out of his pocket, putting it into his back-teeth, and chewing it.

At that moment a gun-shot was fired and off they started. The old man let out a roar:

"Boo, boo, boo! Pull Tigue, Tigue, Tigue!"

Tomás and I burst out laughing to see the old man standing up on the rock without his hat and heedless of everyone.

There was shouting and whistling all over the strand and the old man beating the rock with his boot.

"Your soul to the devil, Tigue, take the victory to the north!" he cried. "Remember you never lost yet! Remember your ancestors!" with his mouth open from ear to ear and a long yellow streak of tobacco down his chin.

He was losing his wits now and the hoarseness choking him. He slid down the rocks with his capering and slipped up to his knees in the sea. But, my sorrow, he took no heed of the water. There he was, striking his palm with his fist. "Bravo, bravo, bravo to you, Tigue!"

A middle-aged woman came down, her shawl in her hand, her voice cracked with shouting. We knew from the way she was praising them that she was from Ballymore.

"Musha, my love to you for ever, oh flower of men!" cried the old man.

"Yé, what's that you are saying?" cried the woman, her hair flying in the wind.

"Look at them winning, my girl." And he threw his hat into the air.

The curragh from the Cooas was now turning the last post.

"Bravo, bravo, bravo, flower of men!" roared the old man again, his feet stretched into the water unknown to him, his mouth covered in tobacco stains, while he kept putting in a fresh slice every minute.

When the curragh from the Cooas was approaching the quay, the man in the bows lifted up his two oars in the air to show they were the victors.

"Up Cooas!" roared hundreds of voices together. "Up Cooas! Up Cooas!"

"Oh, Lord! they have my head split," cried Tomás.

"Come down to the slip till we see how they look after the race," said I.

People were up to their waists in the sea, stretching out their hands and welcoming the crew. I had no thought but that they would drown themselves in the crush. There was no understanding what they were saying with the hundreds of mouths all shouting together.

"Don't go too far down, Tomás, or you will be drowned."

At that moment he startled me with a laugh.

"Why are you laughing?"

"Look! Do you see the old fellow below trying to keep his grip?"

I looked down. I was anxious for him, for I was sure he would be drowned. He was giving his hand to the man in the stern. "Musha, son of a good mother, I knew you would do it," he shouted. Then he went up to Tigue Dermod and gave him his hand. "Man beyond all men, if you could not do it, who could?" Then to the second man, giving him his hand: "Musha, son of him who lives not, didn't I see it was in your muscles?" And last of all to the stroke: "Musha," he sang, "love of my heart, my little jug, may it be full!"[2]

At that moment the curragh and all inside it was lifted out of the water on to the green grass above. Then away with them all to the public-house.

"Come on up, Tomás. It is there will be the sport."

"The devil," said he when we reached the door, "this is the house we were in before. We have no need to go in again."

"Don't mind that," said I, and we went in boldly.

Tigue Dermod was standing in the middle of the floor, as tall as a giant. The old man who had done the roaring was standing at his side talking hoarsely and looking up at him like a child asking his father to take him in his arms.

Tomás and I never took our eyes off the giant. His neck was as thick as a bull's, God bless the man. They were calling for gallons, one after another, till they were blind drunk.

"Musha, your soul to the devil, Tigue, isn't strength a fine thing! Up Cooas! Up Cooas!"

At that moment a man from Ballymore leapt up to him.

---

2. Snatch of an old song.

"What the devil is that talk!" said he, catching the old man by the hair.

Tigue leapt out to the man from Ballymore and raised his fist above his head. "If I let down this sledge-hammer, you will be as dead as a stack."

Everyone laughed.

"If he strikes him," said Tomás to me, "he will make a dead stone of him."

Soon songs began about the house and everyone raging-red with drink, as is the habit at such times.

"I wonder, Tomás, where is your father and my brother Shaun. Maybe they would be looking for us. We had better go out and see if we can find them."

We went out and in the course of our search we came across a tall, lanky fellow on the strand with a stick stuck in the sand and he shouting. We went down to him. He came towards us with three rings in his hand.

"Three shots for a penny. Come on, my boys!"

"Try it," said I to Tomás.

He went up and got the rings.

"Take it fine and easy," I advised him when he was standing on the mark. "If you get the three rings down on the stick you will win threepence."

He threw one and got it down on the stick.

"Musha, my heart for ever!" I cried. "Now the second one! Take it easy."

He let go another but did not get it down.

"The third now!"

He threw the third and got it down.

"You went very near it."

The lanky fellow ran round gathering up the rings. "All but!" he shouted. "Try again!"

Tomás took up the rings, stood on the mark, threw one and got it down on the stick. "My heart for ever, again!" I cried. He threw another and got it down. The lanky fellow was watching with his eyes starting out of his head.

"Easy now, Tomás! Keep your arm in the same position it was before."

He did not reply but let fly the third ring.

It went straight down on the stick.

I gave a shout of applause. But the lanky fellow was not shouting any longer. Tomás leapt up to him. "My sixpence, my boy!"

The lanky fellow gave a cry, pointing down the strand to the west. "Oh, my God! there is something up." He went off at a run, and at first we thought something wonderful had happened. But a man came up to us. "Listen, my lads, nothing has happened, but that fellow wants an excuse for not paying you."

"I swear by the devil I will drag it out of his pocket," said I to Tomás.

"As sure as there's a cross on the ass."

We ran after him. He was a lean, worn-out fellow, his two jaws jutting out through his skin and his legs bending under him. "Arra, man, what is he but a skeleton!" said Tomás.

We watched him till he had the stick standing again on another part of the strand, and was shouting shrilly.

"Go up to him and ask for the sixpence."

Tomás went over. "Are you going to give me my sixpence?" said he, with a shake in his voice.

He took no notice of Tomás but went on with his "Hello! Hello! Hello!"

"Are you going to give me my sixpence?" said Tomás again, but, getting no attention, he ran up to the stick, pulled it out of the sand and swept off the rings along with it. At that the lanky fellow let out a yell. "Where are you going with them, you rascal?"[3] he cried, seizing him by the throat.

Tomás's blood was up now and I behind him cheering him on in the name of his ancestors. That was enough. Tomás struck him in the chest and sent him staggering, his legs

---

3. In English.

shaking beneath him. Then the lanky fellow made for him again, but Tomás put his head down and dived into him. He had a great grip of him now, pushing and pounding the way you would hear them a mile away and I behind Tomás urging him to battle. He was a stout, solid block of a lad and he was getting the upper hand of the skinny fellow. People were gathering in ones and twos around the warriors while I was growing hoarse giving Tomás the prick of youth. There was now a big crowd round us.

"What the devil is going on here?" said one man.

"Don't you see the little boy," replied another, "and he too much for Cosey." (That was the name of the lanky lad.)

Then another man spoke who seemed to know Cosey well. "The devil take you, Cosey, have you no shame for that little babe of a boy to be getting the upper hand and the whole barony looking on?"

A tremble came into my blood. "Your soul to the devil, Tomás, don't spend the day with that scarecrow! Make one effort and strike him down beneath you! Think of all who are looking on! Play your strength on him! Bring the victory to the west, man!" I cried, my blood boiling.

I had hardly finished when the lanky lad went head over heels, Tomás on top of him, his knees on his belly and his hand on his throat.

"Oh," cried Cosey, "I am dead."

"By God, you will be dead indeed if you don't give up the sixpence," cried Tomás.

"Ah, it is a great pity to see a man killed before your eyes," said one in the crowd, and he ran in to part them.

I went up to Cosey and told him to give up the sixpence. Putting his hand in his pocket he gave it to me. "All right, now," said I, "you can keep it. We only wanted to let you know that you can't bluff boys from the west."

Then turning to Tomás: "Come on," said I, "maybe we would get a flip from someone on account of this."

We went up the strand. "Faith," said Tomás, "a good word does not break a tooth."

"Do you know what I was thinking when I saw you and the other fellow fighting, especially on Ventry Strand? I was thinking of the duel between Dáire Donn and the King of France long ago,[4] for Dáire Donn was a big, long fellow and the King of France a sturdy little block of a man like yourself."

"By God!" said Tomás, rubbing his hands with delight, "we were like enough to them."

Before long we met Shaun, Maura, Eileen, and Tomás's father. They were making ready for the road.

"Musha, where were you since morning?" said Shaun.

"Faith, we spent the day strolling among the crowd."

"Your soul to the devil," said Tomás, giving me a nudge, "let us stay here tonight. We'll have grand sport."

"Musha, my pity for your pate," said his father, "isn't it youth that's foolish!"

"Let us be moving west while we have the day," said Shaun.

"It is as well," said Maurice Owen Vaun. "There is no need to let the night overtake us."

We started off on our road. The sun was sinking behind Mount Eagle in the north and the evening fine and warm; mirth and merriment, laughter and shouting here and there after the day; every man merry with drink, children with cheeks stained from ear to ear from eating sweets, tricksters hoarse with shouting, racers exhausted from all the sweat they had shed, tinkers at the roadside sound asleep after two days' walking to the races; here a pair singing, there a pair fighting; groups of people in the distance as far as the eye could see and they staggering from side to side; all of them making for home and talking of nothing but Tigue Dermod and his crew, a melodium at every cross-road making the hillsides echo in the stillness of the evening; groups of boys and girls dancing to the

---

4. The reference is to the *Battle of Ventry*, an old Irish legend.

music and the boys shouting "Up Cooas!" at the end of every tune.

"Musha, aren't we unfortunate," said Tomás, "that we can't stay among them and take a turn in the dance because of the long road we have to travel, and, worst of all, with three miles of sea to cross! Oh, isn't it heartbreaking entirely?" said he, looking pitifully into my face.

"And maybe the sea rough," said I.

"Oh, it is true for you, and if I live to grow a beard I will bid farewell to the Island and build a house for myself out here."

"Think of the poor old men over there who cannot make merry as they made merry here today."

"Musha, I don't know in the world who was the poor fool who went over there first," said he with a laugh.

"Whoever he was, he hadn't a spark of sense."

We were approaching the top of the Clasach and were unable to keep up with the others we were so weak.

"Faith, I am done for with the hunger," said I.

"You took the word out of my mouth. I don't know what we will do."

We could hardly put one foot before the other.

"What we will do is, the first house we meet, we will go inside."

We wandered on slowly until we saw a house far away down in a lonely valley, a wisp of smoke rising from the chimney, trees growing around and a steep hill above it. Whatever hunger was on us before, the sight of the house made us ten times worse.

"Let us go to it," said Tomás.

"Ah, it's too far. Maybe we can make our way to Dunquin."

We started off again, our knees bending under us with fatigue. We dragged on, step after step, till we came to Ballykeen. The house of Pádrig Éamonn was before us at the side of the road.

"Come in here, Tomás. It is a good house, man."

"I will do it if you say so," said he, blushing.

The door was open. Tomás looked in through the window. "Faith, there is no one inside, and I see a loaf of bread on the table."

"Is that so?" said I, going in and Tomás following me.

We looked up and down the house. There was no one to be seen and nothing to be heard save the crickets singing in the hearth. We looked at each other. "Since we are here we had better stay our hunger with the loaf," said I.

I took it, struck it against the edge of the table and halved it. I gave the other half to Tomás.

When we had eaten our fill, we set off again but we were hardly outside the door when we were caught from behind and dragged back to the middle of the floor. I looked up to see Pádrig Éamonn with a grip of me and his wife with a grip of Tomás.

"What devil or demon brought ye in here to take off that loaf of bread?"

"Oh, hold your hand, strong man," said I, for Pádrig was a big giant of a man and he was looking vicious.

With those words he let me go and looked at me between the eyes.

"We are from the Island," said I, "and when it goes hard with the hag she must run, and that is the way we were with the loaf, for we did not taste a bite of food since we left home at the chirp of the sparrow. So as we came up the Clasach our guts were twisted together with hunger and faintness."

"Oh, God help ye," said Pádrig, looking pitifully at us now. "Go out, Kate, and bring in a tin of milk. That is the best for them. I thought at first ye were lads from this parish."

Kate went out with a can in her hand.

Tomás and I were seated on two chairs still biting lumps out of the loaf. Pádrig was talking to us, but I tell you it was little desire we had for talk. "Take it easy," said he, "till you get the milk."

Kate came back and handed me a big saucepan and another to Tomás. Pádrig was questioning us about the races, but it was little heed we gave him with our greed for the food and drink. When we had the loaf finished we would have liked another, but we had already taken too much and so who would have had courage to ask for more. I tried to ask for another but something spoke inside my heart, saying: "Don't ask. Don't disgrace yourself. Aren't the people of the house amazed at ye enough without asking for more?"

"I suppose," said Pádrig, "ye won't go over tonight."

"Upon my word, we will."

"And where are the rest of the Islanders?" said he, stirring in his chair.

"They were down the hill before us."

"Faith, I am thinking it is they we saw down the road to the cliff an hour ago," said Pádrig, looking at his wife.

"There was no one else to be there," said she.

"On my word, if so they will be gone over before you."

"Maybe you are right," said I, getting up. "Good-bye now and a thousand thanks for your generosity."

"The blessing of God be with ye," said the two together.

Away we went down the roads, leaping now as light as goats, we were so fresh after the meal. The sun had gone down in the west after bidding farewell to the big world, sheep-shearings in the sky overhead, the old men of the parish stretched out on the top of the cliff giving their breasts to the fragrant sea air and talking together after the day, a heat-haze here and there in the bosom of the hills moving slowly among the valleys, a colt whinnying now and then and asses braying.

As we reached the top of the cliff we met Shamus Beg.

"God save you, Shamus," said I.

"God and Mary save ye, my treasures," said Shamus Beg softly. "Where were ye since morning?"

"At the races, Shamus. Did you see any man from the Island going this way?"

"Musha, my treasures, ye had better step out or they will be gone over before you."

We hurried on, but only to see the curragh out past the Cock. I whistled through my hand. Tomás shouted.

"The devil a turn will they make," said he.

I gave another whistle. They stopped and turned back.

"Your soul to the devil, I thought we would be out tonight," cried Tomás with a leap into the air.

"Well, if we were itself, it is not a stranded stone we would be. Think of what you said yourself this morning: 'Isn't Ireland wide and spacious?'"

We went down to the slip. "What the devil was keeping you?" shouted Maurice Owen Vaun.

"We went for food, and we needed it," said I.

"What house?"

"Pádrig Éamonn."

"A good house," said my brother Shaun. "You did well."

We sat behind in the stern. The sea was very still, a little sickle of a moon over in the south-west and the lights of the Island plain to see.

"The devil, Maurice, strike up a song for us," said I, for he was pretty merry at that time.

He gave us "Éamonn Mágáine" fine and slowly. We were now in as far as Mid-Bay. Maurice's voice was growing stronger. "My love for your voice, Maurice," said Shaun now and then, and when he would hear the praise he would surpass himself.

As soon as the song was finished he began "Skellig's Bay" without any inducement, and there was no stopping him now till we reached the quay. He was taking an echo out of the coves, and when the dogs on the Island heard his voice they raised their own. You would swear by the book, in the strangeness of the night with forty dogs or more raising an olagón, that living and dead were gathered on the shore. And when the people heard the clamour, not a man, woman, or child but came out from their houses. We burst into laughter to see them. They crowded down to the quay. We moved into the pool, Maurice shouting "Up Cooas! Tigue Dermod for ever!"

The curragh was backed in. Soon she was being dragged up the slip, everyone lending a hand and shouting "Ho-lee-ho-hup! Ho-lee-ho-hup!"

Now Tomás and I were standing at the top of the slip. We were full of pride and conceit, and why not—home from the races like any man.

When we went into the house—my brother Shaun, Maura, Eileen, and myself—my father and my grandfather were at the fireside before us and they proud, as is the wont of parents, to see their children returning to them full of bright laughter.

"Well, Maurice, I suppose you had a great day?"

"Musha, I never had the like of it before."

"I believe you, my heart, for you ate nothing leaving the house. Did you see the Srool?"

"What is the Srool?"

"Is that the way with you after your fine long day on the Strand of Ventry?" said my grandfather with a laugh.

"I never heard mention of the Srool, so it was hard for me to notice it."

"It is a stream of water which runs down the strand and the whole world can see it bursting up and down again, up and down, up and down without ceasing."

"I wonder why it does be bursting up and down in that way continually."

"Did you never hear tell of the duel between Oscar and the foreign warrior on that strand during the Battle of Ventry? Whenever Oscar threw the foreigner the water would burst up through the sand; when he got up again the water would sink back; and it has remained so ever since."

"I don't know at all. It is hard to believe it."

"No doubt it is hard to believe, but we have to believe many things we never saw."

"Ah, but there are things and things."

"Och, you with your 'things and things'! Wasn't it the same

way with us the first time we heard that the Germans had made a ship to fly in the sky. I tell you it is many times the man who wrote that nonsense story in the paper was called a fool."

"It is true for you."

"Well, no more of that, but tell me, did you see anything to interest you?"

"Musha, I didn't, but the number of people that was there—you would say there were not as many in the whole world."

"Ah, God pity you, aren't there twice as many people in the city of London as there are in the whole of Ireland?"

Before long I was dozing in the chair, no longer heeding what my grandfather was saying. I began to dream that I was fighting Tomás and that he thrust a spike into my ear. I leapt up from the chair. It was my grandfather. He was tickling my ear with a wisp of straw, and burst out laughing when he saw the leap I gave.

"Ah, musha," said he, "you are beaten by the sleep at last. Leave the chair and go to bed."

Six

PIERCE'S CAVE

My grandfather and I were lying on the Castle Summit. It was a fine sunny day in July. The sun was splitting the stones with its heat and the grass burnt to the roots. I could see, far away to the south, Iveragh painted in many colours by the sun. South-west were the Skelligs glistening white and the sea around them dotted with fishing-boats from England.

"Isn't it a fine healthy life those fishermen have, daddo?" said I.

I got no answer. Turning around I saw that the old man was asleep. I looked at him, thinking. You were one day in the flower of youth, said I in my own mind, but, my sorrow, the skin of your brow is wrinkled now and the hair on your head is grey. You are without suppleness in your limbs and without pleasure in the grand view to be seen from this hill. But, alas, if I live, some day I will be as you are now.

The heat was very great, and so I thought of waking him for fear the sun would kill him. I caught him by his grey beard and gave it a pull. He opened his eyes and looked around.

"Oh, Mirrisheen[1]," said he, "I fell asleep. Am I long in it?"

"Not long," said I, "but I thought I had better wake you on account of the sun. Do you see those trawlers out on the horizon? I was just saying that it's a fine healthy life they have."

"Musha, my heart," said my grandfather, "a man of the sea never had a good life and never will, as I know well, having spent my days on it, and I have gone through as many perils on it as there are grey hairs in my head, and I am telling you now, wherever God may guide you, keep away from the sea."

"Musha, it seems to me there is no man on earth so contented as a seaman."

I looked south-east to the Macgillicuddy Reeks. They looked as if they were touching the sky.

"Musha, aren't those high mountains?"

"They are indeed, if you were down at their foot."

At that moment a big bee came around murmuring to itself. My grandfather started to drive it away with his hat. "There is no place under the sun is finer than that," said he, stretching his finger south towards the harbour of Iveragh. "When you would be entering that harbour you would have the Isle of Oaks on your right hand and Beg-Inish out before your face."

"I dare say the water is very still there."

"A dead calm. The creek runs three miles up through the land to Cahirciveen. And do you see, on the east of the creek, there is another harbour? That is Cooan Una. And east again is Cooas Cromha, and east again the place they call the Rodana."

"It seems you know those places well, daddo."

"Ah, my sorrow, it is many a day I spent in them."

. He put his hand in his pocket and drew out a pipe. When he had it lighted, he got up. "Come now and I will take you into Pierce Ferriter's Cave."[2]

---

1. Little Maurice.
2. Pierce Ferriter, lyric poet, leader of the Kerrymen in the Rising of 1641, when he was captured and hanged at Killarney.

We moved down through the Furrows of the Garden, up to our ears in fern and dry heather.

"Look now," said he, pointing down, "do you see that ledge of rock? That's the Cave."

"Isn't it a great wonder he went down so far?"

"Sure that's the place he wanted, my boy, where he could cut down the soldiers of England."

"How?"

"Don't you see the ledge? The entrance is under the overhanging cliff. He used to be inside with a big stick. Then the first soldier who would come down to the mouth of the cave, Pierce would just give him a thrust with the stick and send him over the cliff."

"Wasn't he a wonderful man?"

"Oh, he did great destruction on the English at that time."

We were down at the Cave now. My grandfather crept in on all-fours and I behind him, for the entrance was not more than two feet high. Once inside, there was room to stand up for it was above seven feet. I looked around. "Musha, isn't it a comfortable place he had, but I dare say he used never to leave it."

"Indeed he did, whenever the soldiers left the Island."

"And how would he know that?"

"The people here used to be coming to attend upon him whenever they got the chance. Look at that stone. That's where he used to lay his head."

"It was a hard pillow."

"No doubt. Did you ever hear the verse he composed here when he was tired of the place, on a wild and stormy night? It is only a couple of words."

He sat down on the stone and, taking off his hat, he recited:

"O God above, dost Thou pity the way I am,
    Living alone where it is little I see of the day;
    The drop above in the top of the stone on high
    Falling in my ears and the roar of the sea at my heels."

As he spoke the last words, the tears fell from the old man.

"Musha, daddo, isn't it a nice lonesome verse? And another thing, it is many the fine learned man the English laid low at that time."

"Ah, Mary, it is true. I tell you, Maurice, Pierce suffered here if ever a man did. Have you the verse now?" said he.

"I think I have, for it went to my heart." And I repeated it to him.

"You have every word of it."

"Isn't it wonderful the way you would keep in your head anything you would take an interest in?"

"That is very true, for when I was young like yourself there is not a word I would hear my father saying, dear God bless his soul, but it would stay in my memory. It is time for us to be making for the house now in the name of God."

I looked up at the cliff and then down where the waves were breaking angrily. "There's no doubt, daddo," said I, "but he had the roar of the waves at his heels.

The sun was fading in the west, yellow as gold, the birds singing in the heather, hundreds of rabbits out on the clumps of thrift, some of them, when they saw us, running off with their white tails cocked in the air, others with their ears up looking hard at us.

"Wait now, till you see them scatter in a moment," said my grandfather, picking up a stone. He threw it, but they did not stir. "Upon my word but they are bold," said he and gave a shout, and it seemed five voices answered him with the echo in the coves below. Then I saw the rabbits running, tails up and ears back, and in a moment there was not one to be seen save an old one as grey as a badger.

"Isn't it strange the grey one didn't stir?"

"Ah, my boy, that's an old soldier at the end of his life and he is well used to that shouting."

"I wonder what length of life is appointed for them?"

"Only three years, and I assure you they work those three

years for a livelihood as hard as any sinner. But here we are home again," said he as we came in sight of the village.

"You are very good at shortening the road."

"Upon my word, Mirrisheen, I would be better still if I were seated up on a horse-cart for it is hard for an old man to be talking and walking together."

Seven

———▶◀———

A SHOAL OF MACKEREL

I saw three or four men with their oilskins coming down
the path to the quay.

"By my soul, Tomás, they are going mackerel-fishing
tonight."

"So they are. As soon as I have finished my dinner, I will call
for you. We will have great sport in the curraghs while they
are boarding the nets."

"We will. Make haste now and don't be long."

My father was at home before me and his nets ready for the
night. I began swallowing down my dinner in haste.

"What's the great hurry you are in, foolish boy?" said my
grandfather.

"Tomás Owen Vaun and I are going down to the quay."

"Musha, my pity for your head, it would be better you
would eat your food properly."

"I should think they will get plenty of fish tonight?"

"It would be no wonder if they did with all the gannets were
about today," said my grandfather, thrusting his pipe into the
ashes. "There was never such a day for them. They were right
up to the mouth of the quay!"

Tomás came in chewing a chunk of bread. "Hurry," says he. "Musha, crow, don't choke yourself," said my grandfather with a laugh.

I got up from the table and we hurried down to the quay.

I went into my father's curragh and Tomás into his. I was very happy, looking down into the sea and listening to the glug-glag of the water against the boat. After a while I put out an oar and I was dipping it gently when somehow I gave it a pull. The curragh gave a leap and her bow struck a rock, the way the two men who were standing on the thwarts, boarding the nets, were thrown down. "Your soul to the devil, what have you done?" cried Shaun Tomás who was near me. He caught me by the head and heels as if to throw me overboard. When I saw the sea below me I screamed, thinking he was in earnest, but he drew me in again quickly. After that I stayed as quiet as a cat and my heart beating like a bird you would have in your hand.

Some of the curraghs were leaving now, moving out west through the mouth of the Strand. When my father was ready they put me out of the curragh and she moved away. I walked up to the top of the slip. There I met Tomás.

"Do you know where we will go now?" said he. "Back to the top of the Strand and we will have a great view of the curraghs fishing."

There was not an old woman in the village but was already there, sitting on her haunches looking out at the curraghs. The evening was very still. It was a fine sight to look out towards the shore of Yellow Island at the shoals of mackerel and the curraghs running round on them like big black flies.

There was no understanding the old women now who were foaming at the mouth with their roaring.

"Your soul to the devil," cried one to her husband, "throw the head of your net behind them!"

"Musha, you're my love for ever, Dermod!" cried another when she saw her husband making a fine haul of fish.

One woman, Kate O'Shea, her hair streaming in the wind

like a madwoman's, was screaming: "The devil take you, Tigue, draw in your nets and go west to the south of the Sound where you will get fish for the souls of the dead. Och, my pity to be married to you, you good-for-nothing!"

"May the yellow devil fly away with you, you have the place destroyed with your noise!" shouted one of the fishermen when he heard the screams ashore.

As for Tomás and me, our hearts were black with laughing at the old women. Their shawls thrown off, waving their arms at their husbands, they called to them to come here and to come there around the fish, until the fish themselves seemed to be distracted by them.

The sea was now like a pane of glass. You could hear the mackerel splashing in the nets and others out of their senses rushing across the top of the water in an effort to escape, for the day was strong yet and they could see the nets.

Before long Shaun Fada came down from the village, and with him Shaun Michael and the Púncán.[1] They stood in the middle of the crowd watching the women.

"Achván, achván,[2] aren't they the mad crowd?" says Shaun Michael.

"They are, musha, so," agrees the Púncán, throwing out a big spittle of tobacco.

"By the devil's body, is it going out of your wits you are?" cries Shaun Fada to the women.

"Arra, your soul to the devil, my lad, what ails you?" says old Mickil, stretched out on the grass.

"What ails me is a pain in my head listening to those seal-cows of women."

"Och, the devil himself couldn't get right from some of them!"

The women were growing hoarse now, especially Kate O'Shea.

---

1. Nickname of old man in the Island.
2. Old phrase said to mean "By the white steed."

"Kate is giving out," says Shaun Michael.

"The devil a wonder, short of her having a throat of iron," says Shaun Fada.

"Faith," says old Mickil, rising up on his elbow, "I am here for half an hour now and you wouldn't find a bull-seal to bellow the like of her ever since."

"Look," says Tomás to me, "your father is drawing in his net again."

The din stopped. Not a word from anyone. You would think a hand had been laid on every mouth, everyone watching my father drawing the nets. He caught hold of one end of them.

"Musha," said Shaun Michael, "I think the net is straight down with fish."

At that my heart rose with delight. My father drew in the end of the net. There was a mackerel in every mesh.

"Upon my soul, I doubt he won't land all he has," said Shaun Fada.

"No matter for him," said the Púncán, throwing another spittle of tobacco, and a big yellow streak down his chin from chewing it.

"The devil, my lad, he will have to cut the net," said old Mickil.

"What's that you are saying?" said the Púncán.

"What I am after saying, devil."

"Och, whist so, whist so."

"Arra, devil take you, man, what do you know about fish?"

"I killed as many as you ever did," retorted the Púncán, spitting again.

"Musha, it is the few you ever killed, old crow!"

My father's curragh was now hardly an inch out of the water. He drew out his knife.

"Look now, he will have to cut them," said Shaun Fada.

"Look indeed, achván," said the Púncán.

It was then there was commotion among the curraghs when they saw my father cutting his net. They began rushing up to get the cut piece, for the man who would get it would get the fish for himself so long as he brought the piece safe to the quay.

When Kate O'Shea saw the confusion out to sea, she let out a great shout. "Musha, your soul to the devil, Shaun, keep it for Tigue!" she cried to my father.

Knowing that Tigue had not much in the world, my father shouted back to her to go and call him. She leapt up and darted out on to a spur of rock, calling her husband who was back at the mouth of the Narrow Sound. Everyone thought she would drown herself.

"My heart from the devil," said old Mickil, "what haste there is on the woman in the west."

"Achván, she is as bad as a wild sheep," said Shaun Michael.

"It's all right so long as she does not drown herself, God between us and all harm," said Shaun Fada.

"Amen," said the Púncán, not forgetting to spit.

When Tigue heard her he turned back. "What ails you?" he cried.

"Hurry on, in the devil's name; Shaun Leesh has his nets cut and is keeping the piece for you."

Without another word Tigue rowed hard to the east and my father gave him the piece he had cut from the net. Tigue drew it in and soon his curragh was as low in the water as my father's.

"That fellow has had an easy night of it," said Shaun Fada.

"I will go east to the quay before my father, Tomás," said I, getting up.

"Very well, I will wait here for mine," said he.

I went off at a run and was not long making my way. First I called at the house. My grandfather was smoking at the fire.

"Where were you since?" said he.

"I was back at the top of the Strand, and my father is coming in now, and his boat is full."

"Musha, God bless the news-teller."

"Come out till you see," said I, running out, my grandfather following me.

"Indeed you are right. Wait now till I put on the kettle and we will go down before them."

When we reached the slip the curragh was on the pool and down to the gunwale with fish.

"What are you going to do?" shouted my grandfather.

"I don't know. What had we better do?" shouted back my father.

"Back her in a while, anyway."

My father backed her in alongside the slip.

"Now," said Shaun Tomás, standing up in her, "you have good knowledge, Owen, and your teeth worn out on the sea. What do you advise?"

My grandfather looked up at the sky.

"In the first place," he said at last, "the night is very fine, and in the second place it is settled, and since you have the night for it, the best thing you can do is to make with her for the town in the east."

"I would not refuse," said Shaun Tomás.

"We had better start out so, in the name of God," said my father.

"You have time enough yet to go up and take a sup of tea," said my grandfather. "I will paddle the curragh till you return."

They went up, while my grandfather and I went aboard the boat. The fish were piled high in her, sleek and clean. Thousands of little sparkling eyes were dancing in the water.

"What would you call those sparkling eyes, daddo?"

"Sparkle fire or phosphorescence. Take in your head or you will be falling out."

Before long my father and the other two were on the top of the slip.

"Upon my word, Owen, you would stand a night back at Carrig Valach yet," said Shaun Tomás, drawing on his oilskin trousers.

"I would, by my soul, as well as any man."

Shaun took hold of the stern of the boat and lifted me out. My grandfather stepped out after me.

"Won't you take the sail? You might get a wind part of the way."

"You are right," said my father, going up for it.

"Safe and sound with ye now," said my grandfather as they moved out through the creek.

We went home. Maura and Eileen were before us with a fine red fire.

"On my oath, there is a sweat on me after that walk from the quay," said my grandfather.

"I dare say a man grows weak when he reaches your age, daddo?"

"Oh, musha, he does, my heart. Did you never hear how the life of man is divided? Twenty years a-growing, twenty years in blossom, twenty years a-stooping, and twenty years declining. Look now, I have sayings you have never heard."

"And in which twenty are you now?"

"In the last twenty, and it is to God I am thankful for His gifts. Well, it is time for bed. Let us go down on our knees and say the Rosary."

Eight

━━━━━➤●⩽━━━━━

HALLOWE'EN

WHEN the long cold nights came the boys and girls spent them in our house. How happy we were waiting for Hallowe'en, and playing the old Gaelic games—the Ring, the Blind Man, Knucklestones, Trom-Trom and Hide-and-Seek; a fine red fire sending warmth into every corner, bright silver sand from the White Strand on the floor glittering in the lamplight, two boys and two girls going partners at a game of knucklestones in one corner of the house, four more in another corner.

It was Hallowe'en, and most of the boys were in Dingle. We were expecting a great night of it, when they would come home with the apples, oranges, and sweets. Maura and Eileen had the hearth swept and scrubbed, a glowing fire was burning, the lamp alight, and we waiting.

"Aren't they a long time coming?" said Eileen, with a glance at the fire and then at the door.

"They won't be long now," said Maura, and soon we heard the clatter and laughter approaching.

The door opened and the clamour and hubbub poured into

the house. You would think they had been in prison for many a long day and had only just been let out.

The games began. A cord was tied to the rafters and a big red apple tied to the cord. One goes down to the door and takes a running leap up towards the apple. He misses it. Then another. The third succeeds in getting a bite. So they go on till the apples are all eaten. Then another game begins. There is a big bowl of water at the fireside and they are roasting beans. Every boy and girl who are great with each other get two beans, a little one for the woman and a big one for the man. They put the two beans in the fire. As soon as they are roasted they draw out the beans and throw them into the bowl of water. If they sink it is a sign that those two have great love for each other, and I tell you they are the two who would sleep happily that night.

Tomás Owen Vaun and I were amongst them, but we were too small to try for the apples. But when one of the boys would get one in the leap, he would give it to us, the way we had our bellies full all night long.

When the apples and sweets and everything else were eaten, Pádrig Peg stood up. "I am going to make a short speech," said he, "and I hope all will agree with what I have to say."

Everyone claps hands.

"Now," said he, "this is Hallowe'en, and it is not known who will be living when it comes again, so I am going to set going another plan to make a night till morning of it. We will all go in twos and threes with lanterns through the Island hunting thrushes, and when we have made our round let everyone come back here. See you have a good fire down for us, Maura, and there is no fear but we'll have a roast for the night."

"Very good," said one. "A great thought," said another. Everyone agreed.

They began to look for bottles to knock the bottom out of them, for there is no lantern so handy as such a bottle with a candle stuck into the neck. Everyone was ready to go, all except our Maura and Maura O'Shea, who were to stay in the house baking bread and cakes.

"You will come with me," said Pádrig Peg to Tomás and me, "and I promise you we will have the biggest booty, though we won't go far from home."

Off we went, the three of us with our lanterns, west to the Strand. It was a frosty night, the stars twinkling, the Milky Way stretched across the sky to the south and the Plough to the north, a light easterly breeze coming straight from Slea Head, gíog-gíog-gíog from peewits in the glen, a light here and a light there on the hillside from the others, and we on our way west to the Big Glen, for many thrushes do be sleeping in the bushes there.

"Hush now, don't make a sound," said Pádrig Peg, "for the birds will fly out if they hear us talking."

We moved on quietly, Pádrig in front on his haunches up through the glen. "There is one here asleep," said he, catching it and killing it. "Quiet now again!" said he, passing on and we following him.

We soon got another and another till we have seven altogether.

"I wonder," said Pádrig, sitting down and lighting his pipe, "where we had better turn our faces now?"

"What about the Sandhills?" said I.

"Maybe there is not a better place," said he getting up, and off with us again.

"Whist," said Pádrig, "for fear you would wake them."

He had hardly spoken when we heard gíog-gíog-gíog. "What is that, Pádrig?" I whispered. "It's a peewit blinded with the light." We began to search and before long Pádrig found it lying between two clumps of thrift.

"We are doing well," said he, taking out his pipe again.

"Arra, man, we will soon have an ass's load if we go on like this," said Tomás.

When Pádrig had had enough of his pipe he handed it to us and we smoked away like any old man. Then we turned our faces west to the Spit of Seal Cove, and got four more in the cracks of the rocks.

"I know a place where we would get twenty, if we went there."

"Your soul to the devil, let us go, Pádrig."

"But it's a very dangerous place," said he, looking into the lantern as if he was thinking deeply.

"Where is it?"

"Down in Seal Cove," said he with a bit of a laugh. "Were you ever there?"

"Oh, it is often I was," said I.

"And I, too."

"We will try it so," said Pádrig.

The cove looked mysterious in the dead of night. You would think the living and the dead were below with the roar of the waves breaking in among the rocks and the hiss of the foam through the cracks of the stones. Then the wave would sweep back again and you would think it was hurling the rocks, weighing hundreds of tons, against each other. Then another wave broke in, so high that it covered the mouth of the cove, and you would say it was afire with the phosphorescence that was running through the water. It plunged against the rocks and sent spurts of foam into the sky.

"Oh, Pádrig," said I, "isn't there an eerie look on it?"

"Not at all, man, once you would be down there. Have no fear. Catch hold of the tail of my coat and let Tomás catch the tail of yours."

He went down slowly over the edge, I with a drowning man's grip of his coat and Tomás with the same grip on mine, not a word from any of us save now and again when Pádrig would say: "Take it fine and easy. Don't be afraid."

We were just at the end of the descent when another big wage broke in, and it looked seven times worse there below. It swept in, sending flashes of light into the air. It swept against the rocks and I was sure the whole cove had fallen in with the terrible roar.

"Have no fear," said Pádrig again, "and don't speak a word now till we go across to that patch of soil beyond, for there is a big crevice there where they sleep every night."

We went across to the crevice, my head aching with the roar of the waves. Pádrig thrust his hand in and drew out a thrush. He thrust it in again and drew out another. We got fifteen in all.

The trouble now was to get up again. We crossed to the foot of the cliff and I caught Pádrig by his coat-tail again, Tomás catching me by mine. Up we climbed from ledge to ledge till we reached the top.

"Were ye afraid at all?" said Pádrig.

"The devil a bit," said Tomás.

"Do you know, Pádrig, what was troubling me? The mystery of the place. When I heard the terrible roar of the waves, it seemed as if the sea would come in to where we were standing."

"I felt the same," said he, "for it is a very lonesome spot and it's often my father told me that people had been heard speaking below in it."

"Oh whist, Pádrig," said Tomás, "don't be frightening us."

"It is time to be making for the house, for I dare say the others are come before us. How many have we now?" said Pádrig, getting up and turning towards us.

"Twenty-eight and the peewit."

"Och, the devil, we have roast for the night, so."

We made no stop or stay till we reached the house. As soon as we went in, "How many have you?" they all cried with one voice.

"Who of yourselves has the most?" said I.

"I have twenty," said Tomás-a-Púncán.

"Faith," said Pádrig, "we have twenty-eight."

With that there was a great outburst, everyone clapping us.

They were all thrown out on the table, and when everyone had added his share there were a hundred. "Let all begin plucking now," said Shamus O'Donlevy. We began plucking

the feathers, all except my sisters Maura and Eileen, Kate
O'Shea, and Kate Peg, who were busy roasting and washing
plates. The house was a pleasant sight now, everyone full of
bright laughter, Shaun O'Crihin seated by the fire playing his
melodium, four out on the floor dancing a reel, others
cooking, others eating; and as soon as each four would finish
their meal another four would take their places at the table
until all were satisfied.

Michael Baun[1] was sitting shyly at the head of the table. All
the night he had been looking at pretty Kate O'Shea. At that
moment four boys arose to dance a set. They called four girls
and Kate was one of them. I had a cat's eye on Michael, and
Kate couldn't make a step to right or to left unknown to him.
When the set was over, she sat down on the knees of
Tomás-a-Púncán. Michael's eyes flashed. He gave three or
four long sighs, stretched himself twice, and gave a yawn like
one waking from sleep. Musha, upon my soul, said I in my own
mind, the shafts of Cupid have pierced you, my boy.

After a while Kate put her arm round Tomás's neck. I was
watching Michael. When he saw her he scratched his head and
ground his teeth. Letting on nothing, I walked across to him
and sat down on his knee.

"Michael," said I, "isn't it shy you are?"

"Faith, Maurice, there's no need for a person to leave his
chair, when, if he did, he wouldn't get it again."

"Listen, Michael, did you ever hear what Pierce Ferriter
said one night when many people were gathered together,
among them the girl who had won his heart, and he saw her
sitting on the knees of another man?"

He looked at me sharply. "What did he say?"

"This," said I:

> "She I loved most beneath the sun,
> Although she had no love for me,

---

1. Fair Michael.

Seated on the knees of her own man,
It was a bitter sight and I within."

He gave such a sigh I felt myself going up into the air with the lifting power of it.

"Oh, Maurice, where did you hear that verse?"

"From my grandfather. Do you like it?"

"I like it well, for I know the way Pierce felt at that moment."

"Anyone would think the same disease was on yourself."

He bent his head, then raising it he looked across at Kate.

"That disease is on me, Maurice," said he sadly.

"The devil, Michael, tell me who she is and maybe I would coax her to you. Is the girl in here now?"

"She is."

"Wait now and see if I can make her out," said I looking around. "Kate Peg?"

"Not she."

"Kate O'Shea?"

He looked down.

"Ah, Michael, I see it is she. Does she know you want her?" I whispered.

"She does not."

"Your soul to the devil, why wouldn't you tell her?"

Eileen came over to us. "Now, Michael," said she, "turn in to the table, yourself and Maurice."

There were two plates of roast thrushes before us. Kate O'Shea had not come to the table yet. I went over to her. "Kate," said I, "come across with me now. Sit there next to Michael."

He looked at Kate and tried to speak to her, but his courage failed him. He tried again but could not.

"Well, Michael," said she, "have you any news?"

Before she had finished her question he had answered her. He looked at me, his face lit up, his lips trembling.

Nine

THE WHALE

ONE fine October morning Michael Peg and I were in the house of Pádrig O'Dála talking and conversing of the affairs of the world. After a while we wandered out into the yard. There was a light breeze from the east, rooks in plenty flying overhead and a fine settled look on the day.

"I wonder would you care to go west with me to the Inish?" said Pádrig.

"Your soul to the devil, come!" said I with delight.

"Musha," said he, looking out to the south-east. "I have some fine new pots in the sea still and if I had them ashore they would serve me another year."

"Faith, it's not better for us to be in," said Michael.

"Get ready so," said Pádrig, and Michael and I went to get provisions for the journey.

I snatched a chunk of bread and hurried back. Michael was coming down the path, his cap on one side of his head, a pipe in his mouth and the smoke going up into the air, his shoulders stooping and the stones ringing from the nails on his boots.

"By God," said he as he came down, "it will make a great day."

The curragh was afloat, each of us with his dog who knew well he was going hunting. As soon as the boat touched the water they leapt in, wagging their tails, their tongues out and barking to each other like any three men who would be talking together. We put our gear aboard and moved out along the coast of the Island to the west.

As we were making Hill Head we got a nice breeze of wind from the east. When we were far enough out we drew up the sail, and out she moved swiftly. We were very comfortable, plenty of tobacco from Pádrig, stretched out at our ease and Michael telling us the story of Robinson Crusoe. We listened intently, and so we were shortening the journey little by little.

"I suppose we are not half-way yet, Pádrig," said I.

"It's not far now, as soon as the Teeracht is visible beyond Black Head. Go on, Michael."

The Teeracht came into sight. We had a beautiful view as we crossed the Great Sound. I could see the little white buildings up in the Teeracht and the shining white road built through the black rocks from the sea all the way to the light-house. To the south were the two Skelligs bathed in sunshine, the sea full of all kinds of sea-birds, the waves murmuring around us, Inish-vick-ilaun and Inish-na-Bró growing bigger and bigger as we approached them, a group of sheep here and there on the top of Inish-na-Bró and others down in the steep, dizzy cliffs. How fearless they are, I thought, missing a good deal of the life of Robinson Crusoe on account of the beauty of the place and the depth of my thoughts.

Before long we saw the house on the Inish, its felt roof glittering in the sunlight and fine green fields around it. Farther to the west I saw a flock of goats and I thought of Robinson and of the goats he came across on an island just like this. Hundreds and thousands of birds were around, some of them flying through the air, others floating on the water, others settled on the rocks. I did not know what Michael was saying with all the thoughts that were running through my mind.

We were alongside the island now and I got the sweet smell of the fern, which grew to the height of a man. I was longing to go ashore. Pádrig lifted his cap and looked around thinking. "The first thing we had better do is to get the pots, for it is low tide now and we won't be long getting them if they are to be found at all. Then we can spend the day as we please!"

We rowed south to the bottom of the Cárhach.

"Take it easy now," said Pádrig, "there's a pot here."

I turned the curragh round on the pot, and he drew it up.

"Where does the next pot lie, Pádrig?"

"We will go south to the Moon Cave. There should be another there."

We rowed on to the south till Pádrig told us to stop. I looked in and saw a pot between me and the cave. We backed in. Pádrig got hold of the cork and began to draw.

"Why is that cave called the Moon Cave, Pádrig?"

"I will tell you. Do you see the way its mouth is turned south-east? Well, there isn't another cave in the island that faces in that direction, and when the moon does be rising over Iveragh she throws a fine light straight into its mouth."

We went on from one pot to another till at last we had five of them and I learned the name of each place from Pádrig. We went west to Merchants' Gully, across the mouth of Bird Cove, all around the Thunder Rock, till we reached Gulls' Point. There we found another pot. Pádrig was drawing it in, in a leisurely way, while he told us of the time when he was a child growing up in the Inish. Suddenly he stopped talking and looked up at a big high rock broken off from the island and about forty feet above the sea. I looked at him and could see that something was astonishing him.

"What do you see above?"

"I swear by the devil I see the queerest thing I ever saw." He was peering intently.

"What is it?" said Michael.

"Don't you see the man seated above with a hard hat on him looking out to the Skellig?"

I looked up. There he was, clearly visible, his knees crossed. Nobody spoke. Who could it be? There was no one living in the Inish, and even if there were, how could he get out on that rock?"

"Faith, Pádrig, he is there without a doubt and, if so, he is not of this world."

Michael looked at me and turned pale. I felt a shiver in my blood and a cold sweat came out on me. Then I thought I saw a mischievous look on Pádrig. I began to think. At last I remembered my grandfather telling me once of a certain rock to be seen in the Inish which was called Micky the Pillar. It looked from the sea for all the world like a man in a hard hat. "Your soul to the devil, isn't that Micky the Pillar?"

Pádrig laughed. "Upon my word, it gave the two of you a good fright."

"Indeed," said Michael, "it is no laughing matter. I was terrified when I saw it."

"You are not the first," said Pádrig, sitting on the thwart. "But this won't do, my boys," he said, putting out an oar. "We are letting the day pass and doing nothing. We will go west through the Sound of Mantle Island and then make for the Strand."

Suddenly Pádrig stopped rowing and stood up. "I swear by the devil those are tame geese in on the rocks," said he pointing in-shore. "What would bring tame geese here?" said Michael. "On my oath, a storm would," said I.

He took in his oars and remained standing in the curragh till we were close upon them. "Easy now," said he, "for fear they would fly."

We counted nine of them. We backed her in, and Pádrig had hardly stepped out of the boat when every one of them leapt into the air and flew out into the bay between us and the Skellig. We kept our eyes on them until they settled on the water.

"Back her, back her," shouted Pádrig. "Get outside them and we shall round them in before us."

It was not long before we had rounded them in, ever and ever, until they swam into Yellow Beach and climbed up on the rocks. Pádrig leapt out after them but they all flew off again except one which he caught. "Och, devil take them, they are long on the sea. Look," said he, lifting up the goose, "there's not a feather's weight in it."

He crossed its two wings and threw it into the stern.

Off we went again, blind with sweat, till we had rounded in the other birds. At last we had six of them, and indeed the evening was now growing late for a star was to be seen here and there in the sky.

We went south through the Narrow Sound and then east alongside Inish-na-Bró. There was not a breath in the sky, glug-glug, glug-glug, from the falling tide out through the Sound to the south, sea-birds in thousands on the water, porpoises diving in and out between each other on the edges of the tide, a patch of mackerel here and there, a white path of foam in the wake of the curragh, a bright shining fish taking a leap into the air with the fineness of the evening.

When we were about twenty yards from the Laoch reef I got a very nasty smell. "Poof, poof!" I cried, for it was going through the back of my head.

"What ails you?"

"Och, don't you get the smell?"

I had hardly finished speaking when Michael and Pádrig cried together: "Poof, poof!"

At that moment I happened to glance out between me and Iveragh and about ten yards to the south I saw rings on the sea.

"The devil," said I, "what is that out there?"

Pádrig gave a shout. "Your soul to the devil, it's a shark, and it is from it we are getting the smell. Row, row as hard as you can and make for land."

We pulled out, none of us speaking a word. There was nothing to be heard but the panting of the crew and the thud of the curragh leaping across a wave and the splash under her bow when she sent up a spurt of foam. We were pulling hard but had not gone far when the shark rose alongside the curragh—the biggest animal I ever saw, as long as a ship. You could see clearly its big blue gullet which could swallow three curraghs without any trouble. We were in great danger—out in the middle of the Great Sound, a couple of miles from land and that savage, ravenous, long-toothed monster up beside us, the way it had only to turn its head and swallow us up. I thought that at any moment we might be down in its belly. We were still pulling with all our strength, straining every sinew, the beast rolling along beside us, and from time to time giving us a side glance out of his two blue eyes.

"It will sink us if it moves across below the curragh," said Pádrig breathlessly. "Row on, we are not far from land now, with the help of God."

Our eyes and mouths were pouring sweat, our muscles bending with the strain, not a word spoken. I could hear the panting of the other two, the grating of the oars and the splashing of the beast through the water which kept sending spurts of foam into the curragh. And all the time the smell of its breath was affecting us. There was no escaping it.

"You had better not kill yourselves," said Pádrig, "whatever it may do with us."

He had scarcely spoken when the shark turned straight in towards the side of the boat.

"God have mercy on us, he has us now. Row! row!"

"What about throwing out one of the dogs to it?" said I.

"Arra, devil, row, or it will get you instead of the dog."

By this time we were only ten yards from Black Head. We began to take heart when we found ourselves inshore, scraping the limpets from the rocks in our haste. We rowed east till we went into the Cave of the Palm. The shark came no farther. We stopped. We were unable to speak. Our breath was gone and our mouths wide open trying to fill our lungs. Pádrig caught hold of a bottle of water that was in the stern and took a long pull out of it.

"Oh, God of Virtues," said he, "what a hacking day! The

likes of it never overtook me since I was born and God send it will not again. Arra, man," said he to me, "you were out of your mind that time, in the Great Sound, when you were for throwing the dog to the whale."

"I wonder what it would have done if we had?" said Michael.

"You and the curragh would soon have been down its gullet."

"Why do you say that, Pádrig?"

"I will tell you. When the dog had pleased it, it would have been seeking another, though it would have only been a small morsel, and it would have set upon the curragh and swallowed us all."

"What was in my mind," said I, "was that it would spend a nice while eating it and then we could escape."

"Och, that beast wouldn't have known it wasn't a fly it had swallowed."

The sun had sunk in the west, the stars beginning to twinkle, wonderful colours spreading over the sky, a seal snoring here and there in the coves, rabbits over our heads among the clumps of thrift, sea-ravens standing on the rocks with their wings outspread.

"Let us move east in the name of God," said Pádrig, putting out his oars.

"It is often," said Michael, "that mockery comes to the bed of truth. Do you remember this morning when you let on that Micky the Pillar was a man from the other world? Wasn't it a fine burst of laughter you had at the two of us? But it is no thought of laughter you had back through the Great Sound."

"Faith, I am thinking there was not a bit of fear on the two of you."

"The devil if there was much," said I.

"No doubt, for you did not know the way it was with that beast. If you had known you would have been in a yellow terror."

"We can only die once," said Michael, "and if we had died in the Great Sound wouldn't we have been as well off?"

"And why, if you are so fearless, wouldn't you leap into the water now?"

"Och, that's talk without sense."

"How so?"

"Because the day is appointed for us all."

When we reached the quay, there was nothing alive on the slip before us but a couple of waterhens picking mussels. When they saw us they flew out screaming over the pool.

Ten

THE WAKE

ABOUT three o'clock one morning I heard a knock at the door.

"Who is there?" called my grandfather.

"Me," said the voice. "Open."

I wonder, said I to myself, what that man wants at this time of night? There must be something wrong for him to be out at such an untimely hour. Listening, I heard my grandfather opening the door. "Is that you, Shaun?" said he.

It was Shaun Liam.

"My mother died half an hour ago, and I have come to call Shaun Leesh to go with me to Dingle about the wake."

"Musha, the blessing of grace with her soul," said my grandfather. "Isn't it quickly she went? Come in and sit down."

When I heard what they were saying my blood turned. It seemed as if all who had ever died were outside the window and old Kate Liam among them. If a mouse or even a beetle made the slightest stir, I thought it was she. Lifting up my head I looked out through the window. She seemed to be looking straight in at me. I was getting worse. The night was as black as pitch. Musha, Shaun Liam, said I to myself, how did you

find the courage to walk here from your own house and no one
with you at all?

The two of them were sitting by the fire talking about old
Kate, and if they were not praising her it is not day yet. Isn't
it a strange thing that everyone who dies gets great praise from
people? I wondered why. Then a thought came into my mind.
It is from fear. They are afraid, if they abused the dead man, he
would come before them in the night.

My thoughts were scattered by the sound of my grandfather
rising from his chair.

"Arra, Shaun," he was saying, "isn't it quickly she went in
the end?"

"That is the way with death," said Shaun. "I dare say if we
all knew our day there would be no knowing how it would be
with us."

"It's true," said my grandfather. "And indeed it was time for
her to go."

"Faith, I am thinking she was in and out of a hundred."

"Upon my word she was. How is the sea tonight, Shaun?"

"It is fine and soft."

I lay listening and thinking till I fell asleep. Then I woke up
and listened to hear if they were still talking. I could hear
nothing but the sound of the waves breaking wearily below the
house. Shaun was gone.

I was seized again with a feeling of mystery and hid my head
under the blanket. Then, however it happened, I peeped out at
the window. I gave a start. Two shining eyes were peering in
at me. My blood turned as cold as ice. The eyes were staring
at me—old Kate's eyes. Wasn't it well I recognized them? And
wasn't she come now to take revenge on me for stealing her
tobacco long ago when she could not run after me? But now
she could move like the wind. I tired to cry out. But my tongue
swelled in my mouth, while I could not take my eyes away
from what was in the window.

At last I let out a scream which put the whole house in

confusion. My brother Shaun was in the bed next to mine. He leapt up.

"What ails you?" said he.

"Look at the window!" I cried.

My grandfather came in. "Who screamed?"

"Look at the window!" said I again, my eyes still fixed in terror on it.

"Musha, God help you," said he, "what is it but the cat, you silly creature!" And he went up to the window to drive it away. Then I saw that it was indeed my own cat with its two ears cocked.

The next morning was fine with a light easterly breeze and a lonesome look on the village on account of the corpse being laid out, everyone idle on such a day and no school. I looked up at the Clochereeny, the hill above the village, and it seemed as if there was a lonesome look on the stones, on the sky, and on the sea. I saw an old woman approaching from the west, another approaching from the east, all making for the house of the dead.

My grandfather looked out. "Praise be to God on high," said he, raising his hat, "the day is keeping fine for the sake of old Kate, dear God bless her soul."

"It is indeed, God be praised."

"Faith, Maurice, I thought you were a great soldier till last night."

"Upon my word, if you had been lying there thinking of old Kate and had seen the two eyes in the window you would have been in as bad a way as myself."

"Och, would you believe that one night I was alone in the house and I saw three people standing at the bedside and the three of them dead for three years past?"

"And had you no fear?"

"Not at all, no more than I have now."

"And you recognized them?"

"As well as when they were in the world, they talking and I

listening, though I could not understand them. I will go east now to the house of the dead for a while," said he.

"I will go with you," said I.

A sort of tremble came into my blood as we approached the house for I had never yet seen a corpse. When we reached the door my grandfather stopped and spoke softly to me: "When you go in, take off your cap and go down on your knees beside the body and say a prayer for the soul of old Kate."

We went in.

It seemed as if I was inside a mill with the beating of the blood in my head, and when I saw the change that had come upon her, stretched out as straight as a candle and covered with a sheet, I thought she would rise up. My grandfather walked across the floor and went down on his knees. From the doorway I stood watching him. God guide me aright, said I to myself, now is the time for me to show courage. She will surely get up and eat me.

I entered slowly and went down on my knees. But it was not of prayer I was thinking, but watching the body for fear it would make any stir. Then I saw my grandfather getting up and I arose to my own feet with such a rush that I nearly tripped him over. I sat down on the long bench beside the wall.

There was a group of old women around the fire, smoking and chatting.

"Musha, I wonder now," said old Nell, turning to my grandfather with her pipe in her mouth, "what was the age of Kate Liam?"

"I am thinking she was in and out of a hundred."

"Musha, dear God bless her soul," said she again, puffing out the smoke through the house, "it is many a good day and many a bad day she saw in her time."

"No doubt of it," said my grandfather.

"Upon my soul, Owen," said she, passing her hand over her white hair and preparing for talk, "it is well I remember the first day I ever went along with her to gather heather back in the warren, and that is a long while ago. When we had the heather gathered and packed in the sheets and had sat down to rest, Kate drew a pipe from her pocket and a box of matches." And shaking her head, Nell gave a side glance at the corpse. "Musha, God send I won't send any lie on her, Owen," said she, passing her hand over her hair again. "Well, astór, Kate was smoking away comfortably and talking of the affairs of the world. 'Here,' said she, 'take a pull out of that,' offering me the pipe. But I would not take it for I had never smoked yet.

"'Ah, musha, take hold of it,' said she. 'Don't you know there is nothing so soothing as a smoke when you would be seated at your ease?'"

"It was true for her," said my grandfather.

"Musha, I don't know if she is listening to me now," continued Nell, with another glance at the body and puffing at the pipe, "but if she is, I am not putting any lie on her. Well, in the end I took it, astór."

"I am sure you did," said my grandfather.

"I did then, though I wished afterwards I hadn't, for it sent my trotters into the air," said she, and she spat into the fire.

"The devil," said my grandfather, "excuse me for interrupting your story, but it would take many a bandle of tobacco to send your trotters into the air today."

"You may well say so," said Nell, smiling. "Anyway, when the two of us were coming down Lappet Top, I had to sit down on a tuft of grass and throw up all the rubbish I had in my body on account of the pipe. Kate was sitting beside me, bursting with laughter. 'Musha, may the big fellow fly away with you,' said I to her, 'and your pipe with you, if it isn't fine the way you have nearly sent me to the other world.'" She took another look at the corpse. "Musha, Kate," said she, addressing it with a laugh, "isn't it easy to tell there's no life in you, for it is many a laugh you would make at that day yet if you were listening to me now." And with that the tears fell from old Nell.

"Faith, you have left that day far behind," said my grandfather.

"Ah, Owen, would you believe it, I was going to her very often after that, sipping at the pipe till I was an old artist at it. Look, isn't the world strange! Old Kate laid out today and I left behind after her."

"It is the way of the world," said my grandfather, getting up. "The blessing of God be with you," said he, moving towards the door. "Devil take it," he said to me on our way home, "you nearly had me over that time after my prayer. What happened you?"

"Musha," said I, "I promise you it is not many prayers I said but watching the corpse for fear it would rise up."

"Och, my pity for your pate. There is not much sense in it yet."

"Don't mind that," said I, "all beginnings are weak, and I will do better the next time."

Eileen had the supper ready.

"Isn't it strange the curragh for the wake is not coming yet?" said my grandfather, looking out towards the cliffs on the mainland. "Upon my word," said he, taking off his hat and sitting down at the head of the table, "old Kate makes a nice corpse."

"Och, whist," said I, "wouldn't it frighten anyone to look at her! I wonder, daddo, were there ever two laid out here in the one night?"

"There were, and three. I remember them myself. And what's more, they were here for three nights on account of bad weather."

"I dare say the village was mournful during that time," said I. "And isn't it strange they wouldn't have a graveyard here for themselves? Upon my word, daddo, if I were dying I would order my body to be buried above at the Tower."

"Musha, my heart, you would do no such thing. It would be another matter if others were buried there before you."

"I wouldn't mind so long as I had the fine air of the place," said I.

I went to the door and looked out.

"Look, daddo, the curragh for the wake is coming."

I walked out as far as the ditch. The curragh was approaching the quay, the coffin aboard and everyone, big and small, running down to the slip. I went down and stood at the top, looking on. The curragh was below, the coffin, with yellow clasps, in the stern, and everybody with a mournful look. They lifted the coffin ashore and carried it up. You could see yourself reflected in the polished grain of the wood. I saw the name inscribed on a yellow clasp: "Mrs. Kate Coyne, born May 2nd, 1833, died November 1913." Musha, said I to myself, I don't know in the world why they make it so fine, for in three days' time it will be deep in the clay. How strange are the ways of the world!

The next load to be brought out was a barrel of porter, then a big rough pack of bread and two boxes full of pipes. Four men were shouldering the barrel and whispering that it would make a fine night's wake. Four more were under the coffin, all making their way up the path.

On the top I met my grandfather.

"You are looking sorrowful, daddo," said I.

"It's the way with the old, my lad, for I have one foot in the grave and the other on its edge."

I noticed that the four men carrying the coffin were taking a very roundabout way.

"Why don't they go straight up the path, daddo?"

"Don't you know," said he, "that it is not right to take a short road with the coffin to the house of the dead nor yet with the corpse to the grave?"

We went home. My grandfather sat down, took out his pipe, and laid his hat on his knee. "Musha, dear God bless her soul," said he, "she was a kindly, generous, warm-hearted woman in her prime."

"Musha, I don't know," said I. "I am thinking she would get praise now she is dead, whatever she was."

"That is so," said he, thrusting his pipe under a red sod of turf, "but Kate Liam deserved praise from my knowledge of her, though it is true that the proverb cannot be gainsaid: If you wish praise die, if you wish blame marry."

"Faith, daddo, I never heard that till now."

"Och, mo léir," said he, "you have many things still to learn."

"Shall we go to the wake?"

"We will spend part of the night there," said he with a glance at the clock. "Did you ever hear of what happened at a wake in the parish of Ventry long ago? There was a woman of that parish living alone of whom it was rumoured that she had plenty of money. Well, when her last sickness struck her down she sent for the priest. He came and put the holy oil on her. As he was leaving the house she called him back: 'Musha, father, for the sake of God and the Virgin Mary, would you give me a few pence to wet my heart?' The priest gave her sixpence and departed. The old woman died that very same night, and on the morrow, when the neighbour women were preparing the corpse, one of them found a hard twisted lump in her hair behind her head. It was a purse with five pounds in it. They agreed to take it to the priest. 'What ails ye now?" said he. 'Musha, it's like this,' said the best talker of the women, telling him the story. The priest drew back as pale as death. 'Oh, oh,' he cried, beating his hand against his breast, 'after asking me for as much as would wet her heart! Go back with the money to her own house,' said he, his voice trembling, 'and make no delay till you throw it in the fire. Bad luck will come to anyone who keeps it.'

"They returned and did as the priest told them. When night came there were many at the wake, talking and conversing of the old woman's money. At twelve o'clock there came in through the door a fine, spirited, well-favoured man. Everyone looked at him, whispering who he might be. He walked over to the corpse and it seemed to the people he was talking softly. He took out of his pocket a fine white handkerchief. Everyone was watching in silence. He placed the handkerchief under the chin of the corpse and the dead woman put out the

Holy Communion she had taken the day before. Then he folded up the handkerchief and departed."

"God keep us, daddo, the people in the house must have been horrified."

"They were. When they saw the portent, some of them ran out of the house in fear; but most remained, talking eagerly, some saying that the woman was damned and it was the God of Glory who had come in—everyone with his own opinion. An hour later the door opened again and there entered a ragged, ugly man, unshaved and unwashed, with his toes out through his shoes. The people sat wide-eyed in wonder. He walked over to the body, put his hands round it and carried it off. And from that day to this no one has ever set eyes on that corpse or heard news of it."

"It is likely it was the old fellow carried it off," said I.

"Who else! God between us and evil," said my grandfather, lighting his pipe from the ashes. He got up and looked at the clock. I dare say it is time for us to be making for the house of the wake."

"Very well," said I, walking to the door.

"Wait now, Maurice, till I fill my pipe and we will be moving off, in the name of God."

I looked out towards Dunquin. The moon was high in the sky and the night very bright. I thought I saw a curragh making for the quay.

"Daddo," said I, calling in to him, "there is a curragh come in since, whoever they are."

"Musha, didn't you see the barrel coming in today?" said he, scraping out his pipe with his knife. "As sure as I am here I know those four men, for there is ne'er a wake with drink in it but those four will be there—Shamus Brack, the Tailor of Clasach, Yellow Dónal, and Shaun Egan," kneeling down before the fire to light his pipe. "Come on now to the house of the wake."

The house was full from end to end, a blaze of light from the candles on the table and and white lamp from the roof. If

a pin had fallen from the rafters it must have fallen on
somebody's head—a group of old women at the fire, the
Púncán at the head of the table cutting tobacco, Shaun Fada
filling the pipes, everyone, young and old, smoking, conversing, and talking of old Kate. As soon as a man finished his pipe,
he handed it back to Shaun to get it filled again.

My grandfather put a whisper in my ear: "How are you
pleased with the night?"

"Delightfully," said I.

In came the four strangers from Dunquin, looking shy.
Seats were found for them. "What did I tell you?" said my
grandfather, nudging me. The barrel was opened. A bucket
was handed round. On account of their reputation, I kept my
eyes on the four till the bucket reached them. A pint was
poured for Shaun Egan, the first of them. He made no stop till
he had swallowed it down. At that moment the dead woman's
son, Shaun Liam, came across to my grandfather. "Come up to
the room," said he.

We followed him, and it was there the goat was roasting as
for stout lumps of old women with pipes as long as a bandle in
their mouths. Looking up into the rafters you would think it
was a heat-haze in a hollow of the hills on a summer evening
with all the smoke they were sending through the room.

"Musha, God bless your life, Owen," said Kate Joseph, and
I think she was merry with whisky.

"Long life to you," said my grandfather, sitting down on a
chair. "How are you these days, Kate?"

"Musha, I am middling. Good health to you!" said she.
"Isn't it quickly Kate Liam went from us in the end?"

"That's the way with death. But yourself is in your third
March yet,[1] God bless you."

"Ah, musha, God forgive you, Owen, don't you see I am no
more than a shadow?" said she, handing the pipe to Maura

---

1. Reference to sea-birds which attain maturity in the spring of their first year.

Crihin. "Take that and smoke it for the soul of old Kate who was merry a year ago back from today. Musha, I wonder, Owen," she went on, drawing her black shawl up over her head, "do you remember the day when I and the woman who is laid out tonight went across to the Cosh with you in the big boat long ago?"

"I do," said my grandfather with a bit of a laugh.

"I can't remember now who were with us," said she, looking into the red flames of the fire and knitting her brows.

"Musha," said my grandfather, "it was Paddy, Pad Mór, Stephen, Pats Vicky and Shaun O'Donlevy."

"Faith, you're right," said Kate, turning round to him and drawing her red petticoat in round her feet. "It was indeed, and your brother Mickil," she cried with a sigh of delight at remembering him, "and it's great sport we had that day."

"I never saw the like of it since," said my grandfather.

Meanwhile Shaun Liam was moving around with a bottle of whisky and a glass. First he poured out a half-glass for Maura Tigue. Kate Joseph blushed and smiled as she saw the whisky approaching. She put a question to my grandfather, then glanced at the bottle without heeding his reply. Maura Tigue drained the glass.

"Well, dear God bless her soul and the souls of all the dead!" said she.

"Amen," said we all.

I was still watching Kate Joseph. I could not but laugh inside my heart. As the bottle approached, a sharp look came into her eyes. She kept fidgeting anxiously in her corner. Shaun had not half filled the glass for her when, "That's enough, Shaun, my lad," said she; "don't fill it right up. Ah, that's too much!"

She took a long draught of it, then coughed, and coughed again.

"You are choked with it," said my grandfather.

"It is pretty strong enough," said she, and you could hardly have heard her at the hole of your ear, for the drink had gone with her breath. With the second breath she tossed it all off and gave the blessing to the soul of old Kate as was meet. Then my grandfather drank a glass and, faith, I got a half one myself and drank it as well as anyone. Maura Tigue pulled out her pipe again and it passed from woman to woman till the room was full of smoke.

They were talking and smoking, my grandfather telling them of the great day they had at the Cosh long ago, when Mickil beat all the men of the place with his singing, till Shaun Liam came in again with a bucket of porter.

"Now," said he, "take a pull out of that."

They were not slow to obey him, and the woman who was sitting shyly without a word till then was now warming up in wordy dispute with her neighbour, and my grandfather as merry as any.

I got up and went down to the kitchen. A big table was laid in the middle of the floor, five or six eating, talk throughout the house, a pipe in every mouth, the young keeping each other company in one corner and the old in another discussing seriously the affairs of the world. I threw myself among my equals, but I soon grew sick of their senseless chatter. I liked better the conversation of the old and that has been the way with me always, so I went up to the room again where I found the others as before.

After a while my grandfather got up and looked out through the window. "Faith," said he, "the day is dawning. We had better go home, in the name of God."

I wanted no more than the wind of the word, for I was blind with the sleep.

"Good night to you all," said my grandfather.

"May the night prosper with you," said the old women together.

"Upon my soul," said he as we left the house, "those women don't know that it isn't a wedding feast."

Out on the ditch next morning I saw three or four little clouds between me and Grey Top. As I watched, they became entangled till they were one big cloud moving towards me from the north. It was growing black, and I watched it till it was hanging over Slea Head. I went in.

"Faith, daddo, the day is beginning to look very bad."

He put out his head through the doorway. Just then heavy rain began to fall and it started to blow from the north-west.

"Upon my soul, I am doubting Kate will spend another day here and maybe two. God help us, the sea is all in a whirl of foam."

No one stirred out that day. But next morning it was so fine you would think a bad day had never come. My grandfather opened the chest and took out a coat, the like of which I had never seen, with a long tail and three buttons behind. I watched him putting it on for the funeral.

"Musha, daddo, I never knew you had that. What sort is it at all?"

"Ho, ho, my boy," said he with a laugh, "that is the old Gaelic fashion."

I took hold of the tail of it. It was as stiff as a board of oak.

"I suppose you have had it always?"

"Arra, man," said he with another laugh, "I have not always been in the world; but it is a good age, for my father left it to me, the blessing of grace be with him, and it is likely there is no one to wear it today but myself."

I drew back from him, laughing. "Do you know what it is? To judge by your appearance, without lie or jest, you don't look more than twenty years old."

"Come on," said he, "and don't be mocking me. God be praised, isn't it sweetly that blackbird is singing?"

As we walked up towards the house of the dead, whenever I got the chance I dropped behind to take a look at my grandfather, and indeed you would have thought he was a great peer from the city of London with his striped trousers and tail-coat, the white shirt with its hard front and a high collar under his chin.

He went in among the old men and I among my comrades.

"I wonder," said Tomás Owen Vaun, "shall we be able to go out to the graveyard in Ventry?"

"Och, not at all, man, they won't let us," said I. "But look here, Tomás, if the sea were rough again today, we would get another holiday from school tomorrow."

"Arra, what good would that be, for when tomorrow came we would be seeking another?"

Four men brought out the coffin and rested it on two chairs. The old women gathering round it began to moan, sweet and soft: "Olagón, olagón!"

It was for Kate Joseph's voice I listened, for she was reputed to be like a banshee for keening.

"Oh, musha, Kate," she began with a fine tune on the words, "isn't it you were the graceful woman, and it is little profit for me to live after you, olagón! olagón! olagón!"

When they had finished their keening I saw them laughing merrily with one another.

"Musha, Tomás," said I, "do you think they are lonesome at all after old Kate Liam?"

"Yé, mo léir, no more than the seal-cow back in Bird Cove," said he.

The four men raised the coffin to their shoulders. All followed them.

"Isn't it a strange world if you look into it, Tomás? To think the day will come yet when you and I will be stretched in a coffin ourselves without a thought or feeling."

We were at the quay now, the two of us sitting at the top watching the men busy with the curragh and the oars till they had the coffin on board. They moved out through the pool, the sun shining over their heads, a white path of foam in their wake.

My grandfather came down the path with many others who were unable to go out. He stopped at the top of the slip looking out at the curraghs. We could still hear the grating of the oars.

"It is a wonder you did not go, daddo," said I.

"My sharp sorrow, there was a time when I would have gone, but, alas, not today. Ah, musha, Kate," he cried, looking out over the sea, "dear God bless your soul, you were a good companion in a market town."

The tears were falling down his cheeks.

"Look at your grandfather," whispered Tomás. "He is crying. That is the man who is sorrowful and not those fickle women."

We got up.

"I have to go for a load of turf today," said Tomás. "We have not a sod in the house."

"May the day prosper with you," said I, turning home.

Eleven

A NIGHT IN THE INISH

THE month of Samhain[1] is the time when there does be a rush for pollock in the Island.

One fine day when the ground was hard with frost, with a little air of wind from the east and a fragrant smell from the sea, I wandered out of the house and stood a while thinking. The sea-birds were flying around in quest of fish. There were thrushes in plenty hard by and they fleeing before the cold. It was of the life of the birds I was thinking and the passing of the tide from the strand.

After a while another thought struck me and I made my way to the house of Pádrig O'Dála. Pádrig was before me at the door, gazing south-east, humming a tune.

"A fine day, Pádrig."

"It is, thanks be to God, and a good day on the sea."

I went inside the house and who would be there but Paddy Tim.

"It is a fresh day, Paddy."

---

1. November.

"Ah, it is not so fresh yet, that the goats would eat it."[2]

Pádrig came in.

"Do you know what I was thinking?" said he. "That it would be a good day to go fishing for pollock on the Wild Bank."

"And spend the night in the Inish?" said I, delighted.

"I dare say we will do that," said Pádrig, "but get ready now and don't delay."

The Wild Bank lies to the south-east of Inish-vick-ilaun, a good way out in the Bay. It is a reef under water where the sea sweeps and breaks in bad weather, and it has a great name among the old men for fish.

We were across the Great Sound now, and there's no doubt but it would delight a sick man at that time to be looking north and south at the sea-birds hunting over the wild sea. Soon we saw a guillemot a little way off to the south with her young chick behind her. Above them was a great black-backed gull and he swooping down at the chick. Every time he swooped the chick would dive and go astray on him; and every time the chick came up again, the gull would make another swoop.

"Musha, isn't the gull a treacherous bird?" said Pádrig O'Dála.

"Not at all," said Paddy Tim. "Isn't it trying to fill his belly he is, and isn't it the same thing you are trying to do yourself with the pollock on the Wild Bank to the south?"

"Och, that's talk in the air," said Pádrig.

"Why so? Isn't the guillemot herself watching for something to put in her belly and isn't it the same way with the gull? Upon my word, I see no more treachery in him than there is in yourself."

I was not giving much ear to their talk but watching the gull swooping down, and the poor mother doing her best to defend her own. In the end the gull made another swoop and caught the chick by the tail. With that the mother flew at him, and

2. Glas, "fresh," also means "green."

you never saw such a tussle as there was between the two birds until at last the gull had to let go. Then the chick dived under water and the mother after it. Faith, thought I, they are after making a fool of the gull. And away he flew west over the waves.

We were making the Inish by this time and my heart beating like a watch with delight, for I was never yet up in the island. "It is growing late," said Pádrig. "The best thing we can do is to go ashore for the night and we can rise with the sparrow's chirp in the morning."

I looked west towards the island. The sea was like glass for smoothness, little fish playing on the top of the water, the sun going down behind the Narrow Sound and throwing its golden beams on the Foze Rocks which looked like a castle of gold on the horizon, shining with a supernatural light.

"Musha, Pádrig," said I, "isn't it a beautiful sight that is around and about us?"

"I swear," said he, turning to me with a laugh, "I don't know is it on myself or not, but as soon as I clear the Horse's Mouth westward it seems as if a cloud rises from my heart. Maybe it is because I was born in the Inish."

"In my opinion," said Paddy, "even if you were born above on the Muilcheann, you would love it."

The word was not out of his mouth when I heard from the island a noise which took an echo out of the coves: Gurla-gu-hu-hu-golagón! gurla-gu-hu-hu-golagón!

My heart leapt, for it is often before I had heard that spirits were to be seen and fairy music to be heard above in the Inish.

"What is it, Pádrig?" said I tremulously.

"Row on," said he with a laugh, "and you will soon see what it is."

We rowed on, our eyes on the strand, and soon we heard it again: Gurla-gu-hu-hu-golagón!

"Look in now, and keep your eyes on the shingle."

I looked in and what did I see but up to forty seals stretched at full length, sunning themselves on the strand. Pádrig let out a roar. They raised their heads. Then away with them as hard as they could go to the water. Not a spot of the strand but was hidden by the spouts of foam they sent up into the sky; and when we were within ten yards of the strand, not a seal was to be seen, the sea still again, save only the rings they had left in their wake. I looked down through the water. I could see the bottom clearly and the seals rushing out below.

"Oh, Lord, Pádrig, isn't it a marvellous speed they have?"

"It is no wonder, my boy. Did you never hear the saying: Sturgeon, ling, or seal, the three swiftest fish in the sea?"

We went in on to the shingle. I looked up at the cliff above my head as is the habit of a stranger when he comes to a foreign land. When we had the curragh on the stays and our gear in order for the night, I strolled away, wandering, taking heed of everything around me.

In the course of my ramblings I found a black stone and some old names cut into it. I could not count all that were on it, but this is the one that put the greatest wonder on me: "W. W. Wilson, Jan. 1630."

I called Pádrig: "Devil take it, would you believe there is a name here which has been made for two hundred and eighty-four years?"

"Och, my pity for your head, did I not see a man from Dublin once who found a name above in the churchyard which was made a thousand years ago?"

"Better still," said I, and at that moment a verse came into my head and I recited it to Pádrig:

> "The trout lives in the stream,
> The duck lives on the pool,
> The blossom lives on the tree,
> But lives not the hand that wrote."

"Indeed, my boy," said Pádrig, looking at me between the eyes, "there is a power of nonsense inside your head."

We turned our faces up into the island and climbed an old path through the cliff. There was a beautiful view. The Teeracht with its little white houses lay behind us to the north. Over in the west, nine miles away, were the Foze Rocks, and nothing to be seen beyond them but the sky like a great shining wall, and the sun descending big and round into the sea. Over to the east was the Bay of Dingle and a melancholy look coming over the hills with the fall of night.

We moved on together, up to our knees in the long grass. Soon I saw the house above me at the foot of a little hill with fine fields around it. We had three dogs with us, and with their ears cocked they ran off before us through the island. Hundreds of rabbits were to be seen making hurriedly for the warrens, running past as thick as ants, ears back, tails up, and the eyes starting out of their heads in terror of the dogs. In a few moments the whole island was in confusion—the sheep running wild, the goat fleeing for its life, the birds screaming across the fields northwards to the lonely reefs. What wonder! When did they last see a man of this world? I thought of Robinson Crusoe when he landed on just such an island. What would he not have given to be a goat when he saw a herd of them running together and he without a companion!

The delight in my heart was growing as I came nearer to the mystery of the island. But I grew sad as I thought of all who had ever lived there, making a livelihood for themselves like the wild goats, and not one of them alive today.

Two of the dogs came running up to us, each with a rabbit across his mouth. They threw them down at our feet, and then made off again.

"Oh, Pádrig, aren't the dogs well taught?"

"Upon my word," said he, feeling the rabbits, "there is fat on these. Have you a knife?"

I gave him mine and he soon had the guts out of them.

We walked on again but had not gone far when he saw the dogs running back with two more rabbits. "Faith," said I, "if they keep this up, we'll have spoils tomorrow."

When we came to the ditch of the field outside the house, a start was taken out of me. I stopped and listened. I hear it, said I in my own mind, the sweetest music I ever heard. I heard it again. My heart leapt. "Pádrig!" said I, "do you hear anything?"

He looked at me and listened. "I swear by the devil," said he, lifting his cap and scratching his head, "that all who ever died in the island are above in the house making sport."

I did not doubt him on account of the reputation of the place for fairies and a shudder ran up from my little toe to the roots of my hair.

Pádrig looked at me again. He was smiling. "Did you never hear of a petrel?"

"I did not."

"That is a petrel now."

"Where?"

"It is inside the ditch."

I listened again, and true enough for him I could hear it clearly now, the sweetest song ever heard by mortal ear. I would have spent the whole evening listening to it but for Pádrig making fun of me.

We went up to the house—a little, low hut with a felt roof, ruins in plenty around, weeds and nettles growing among them. We went inside. It was nice and clean, the walls whitened with lime, and a little room below. I went down to the room, to see two rabbits scampering away through a hole they had made in the wall. Pádrig came down and threw a curse at them when he saw the hole.

I looked up at the walls which were covered in cobwebs and a picture of Moses as black as soot. I took it down, but could not read what was written on it. "I suppose, Pádrig, this is here since you were born?"

"It is, and for ages before me. Let us go out now and cut some fine dry fern for the night."

Not far from the house we came upon fern in plenty

growing as high as ourselves. We began tearing it out, and soon each of us had gathered the makings of a good bed. We left it to dry at the bottom of the house and went in. One of us kindled a fire, another went to draw water, another swept out the floor—each at his own task. I opened two of the rabbits and hung the other two outside the door on a nail.

We soon got the look of a hearth on the place, the lamp alight, a fine glowing fire put down and sending out warmth through the house. We sat down to dinner, and a savoury dinner it was—a fine stew of rabbits and plenty of soup.

When we had eaten our fill: "Faith," said Pádrig, "I had better go out now and lay twenty traps or so, and maybe we will have another dozen of rabbits tomorrow."

In half an hour he was back again. "It is as well for us now to bring in the fern," said he, "for we have need of a stretch."

We soon had our beds made, each in his own corner, and stretched ourselves out after the weariness of the day.

"Don't be sleepy in the morning," said Pádrig, "for the quaybach³ is the very devil for the rabbits. Musha," said he again, stretched back contentedly in the fern with his pipe in his mouth, "it's many the day I spent here in my youth with ne'er a care nor a trouble in the world, and I tell you there was abundance here then as for milk in plenty and butter. My father had twelve cows here at one time and it's many the firkin he sold at the market. But, my sorrow! look at it today—nothing but ferns and nettles."

Before long we fell asleep. About two o'clock I awoke. There was nothing but darkness and the sound of the other two snoring. I was seized with fear when I saw where I was, thinking of all I had ever heard about the fairies. The moonlight was pouring through the window. How envious I was of the other two snoring peacefully in the dead of night! As I lay thinking, what did I see but a human hand passing across

---

3. Great black-backed gull.

the window and taking up the two rabbits I had hung on the nail.

I leapt up and tried to scream, but the tongue swelled in my mouth. I could see him clearly now. He had a horn-peaked cap and the clothes of a sailor. I could hear his footsteps outside as he went away with the rabbits. "Oh, Lord," I cried, "save me from the fairies!"

I got up somehow and went over to Pádrig and gave him a kick which lifted him clean out of the fern.

"What ails you?" said he, looking up in the moonlight.

"Oh, oh, Pádrig, it is someone I saw outside the window going off with the rabbits."

"Musha, my pity for your brass head," said he, stretching back again into the fern.

I lay down once more and at last I fell into a light doze. How long I was asleep I do not know, but when I awoke Pádrig was calling me:

"Oh, Lord," said he, "the bright day is here."

"It is not. It is only the light of the moon."

He went down to call Paddy Tim: "Paddy! Paddy!"

"Hm," mumbled Paddy at last.

"You had better stay here, Paddy, till the two of us go drawing the traps, and let you have the breakfast ready before us when we return."

"Hm, hm!" said Paddy, stretching back again.

"What were the delusions that came on you last night?" said Pádrig as he lit the lamp.

"Upon my word, they were no delusions at all, but the man was there in his own shape and I'll bet anything you like that the rabbits are not on the nail now."

"Arra, man," said he, turning to me when he had the lamp alight, "don't you know that no one dead would take the rabbits?"

"I don't know, but alive or dead, he took them."

"And where is the living man on this island?"

"Isn't that the whole matter?" I was getting a sort of courage now that the lamp was lit.

"Go out now and see if the rabbits are there still."

"Upon my word I will not, but go yourself for I have had enough of it."

As he reached the door he struck something heavy with his foot. "What the devil is this?" said he, stooping to pick it up. "Arra, your soul to the devil, it is a big tin of tobacco. Faith, Maurice, you were right. The rabbits are gone. A sailor must have come ashore and taken them, and, look, what did he do but slip a tin of tobacco under the door, as is the custom with them?"

We started out to draw the traps. The moon was moving slowly among the stars above and throwing a silver glitter on the sea through the Bay of Dingle to the east; bright points of light in the dew, which lay heavy on the grass; a dead calm on the sea and not a breath from the sky; grass and fern up to our knees and a sound like a whirlwind sweeping through the fern from the rabbits running through it with the dogs pursuing them; an odd cry from the heron with the fairness of the night; the petrel with her own song; cóch-cóch-cóch! from the black-backed gull across the island to the north; meggy-geg-geg! from the goats among the rocks; baa-baa! from a sheep in the distance; and the seal not forgetting his own olagón in the gullies far below.

We were now across the field to the south and we as light-hearted as any rabbit in the island. We heard a cry from a gull, then another, as if they were closing around something.

"Och, bad cess to them, they have the rabbits eaten," said Pádrig, leaping over a rock and I after him, ever and ever, till we came to the first trap where we found two of them tearing a rabbit asunder. "Hucs, hucs, hucs!" he cried as he drew near them. Off they flew to perch on the top of a rock near by, crying cág-cág!

They hadn't done much damage to the rabbit. We drew it out; then away with us as fast as we could by the Rock's Foot to the east and then by the Spring Meadow to the south, drawing one trap after another and a rabbit in every one of them.

Away with us again to Bird Cove in the west, till we came to the head of the Cove, and there we heard the olagón from the seals on the shingle below. Anyone who had no knowledge of them would think that the living and dead were gathered there. We sat down for a while listening, the moon shining in on us.

"I wonder, Pádrig," said I, his back to me, lighting his pipe, "would you believe that those are men under magic?"

"I have heard it, and upon my word I would believe it for they are just like old women keening. Och," says he leaping up, "the strand does not wait for milking-time."

Away he went and I after him, my heart out on the palm of my hand for I had a dozen rabbits on my back, and I could not keep up with him. Only that was not the trouble, but the island was full of holes covered with fern, the way it was often when I put out my foot I would go down a hole up to my hip and then away with me on the crown of my head and the rabbits on top of me. I was blind out, down a hole and down a hole, till at last I became so out of humour I wished the island and the rabbits to the old fellow. I had no view of Pádrig and was drowned in sweat, and I did not know east from west. I sat down, dropped my pack of rabbits on a clump of grass, threw off my cap and wiped my brow. Well, said I to myself, I am alone at last, and I might as well have taken it softly from the beginning.

I looked round. There was nobody to me or from me, and I knew not on what side of the island I had stopped. I was listening to the different cries of the birds and watching the dew sparkling in the moonlight, rabbits darting by me to the east and to the west and making black paths through the dew. Some lines of "The Midnight Court" came into my mind, and with the delight in my heart I recited them aloud:

" 'Twas my wont to wander beside the stream
On the soft green sward in the morning beam,
Where the woods lie thick on the mountain-side,
Without trouble or care what might betide."[4]

After a while I got up. I wonder am I long here, said I. Pádrig will think I have fallen over the cliff. I threw my pack over my back. I looked east and I looked west. God send me on the right road, I prayed. Where is the house now? And where is Pádrig?

I went on among the rocks, stooping low and thinking again of all who ever died in the island, and the more I thought the more afraid I became. Isn't it a strange thing I cannot think of anything else to scatter those terrible thoughts out of my mind? I would try and fail. I was glancing into every hollow in the rocks for fear there would be anyone from the other world within. Then I heard a couple of coughs such as you might hear from an old man.

My heart leapt. I stopped. There I stood poised on one foot, like the man long ago when the wind and the sun tried to see who would strip the coat from him and he standing without a stir in the middle of the road. I remained in the same posture, my two eyes thrust into a dark hole, for it seemed to me that it was out of that hole the coughing came. As I watched, a cold shiver ran through me the way I was trembling from head to heel.

Then I heard the coughing again, loud and strong. I could stand it no longer and let out a roar. When the thing within heard me, out he came with a rush, and when I saw the big white mass making towards me from the hole I let out one shout and fell out of my standing on the clump. Just as I fell I saw what it was—a big wether belonging to Pádrig O'Dála, and away he went down the hill at a gallop. "Ah, musha," cried

---

4. Percy Usher's translation. "The Midnight Court" is a long poem by Brian Merriman, a Clare poet of the early nineteenth century.

I when I got back my speech, "may the big fellow take the head from your scroggle if it isn't fine the way you are after putting the yellow terror on me!"

I stood up and looked around. Look now, said I, woe to the man without patience. And it is my firm opinion that it is thus ghosts are made for many on this island, for, for my own part, I have seen two apparitions in one night.

I put my pack on my back again and off I went. I had not got over my fright. I was still weak, but I swore to myself, whatever else I would see, it would not trouble me.

Before long I heard a hand-whistle, and my heart leapt again. Listening carefully I heard another, nearer this time. It is Pádrig in search of myself, said I, putting a finger in my mouth and whistling in reply.

"Where are you?" called his voice.

"I am here," said I in the height of my head; "where is yourself?"

"I am at the Hollow of the Eagles," cried the voice.

"Och, God be with me," said I, "where is the Hollow of the Eagles?"

He shouted again: "Where's yourself?"

"The devil I know where I am," I cried. "I'm going astray."

"Do you see the Teeracht?" he cried hoarsely.

"I do not, but I see the Foze."

"Don't stir, so, till I find you."

I sat down on a clump, exhausted. Soon he was above me.

"Come up," said he. "The devil take you, where are you all the night?"

"Arra man, I had to make shift for myself when I couldn't keep up with you."

"Faith, I thought you were up at the house long ago but when I went up myself you were not there before me."

"I will be there soon enough." But not a word did I say about the sheep for fear he would be mocking me for ever.

We went up to the house, to find Paddy Tim still fast asleep.

I gave him a kick in the side. He leapt up, looked around, and rubbed his eyes. "Are ye come since?" says he.

"Arra, man, aren't we after walking the four corners of the island?"

"It must be day, so."

"Not yet," said Pádrig, "but near it."

I put down a fire and went out to get water from the well. The windows of the day were now opening in the east, the moon sinking west of the Foze, and the red light of the sun rising over the Macgillicuddy Reeks and so westward across the Bay of Dingle, the light of day quenching the light of night.

I returned home, put the water in the kettle, and hung it over the fire. Then the thought struck me to walk out and see the churchyard. I had long wanted to see it and now was my time for it while the kettle was boiling.

It was only three hundred yards from the house. I soon found it, in nice order, and beside it an old chapel. Standing above the ruin was a cross, looking very ancient, my hand's length of moss on every stone. Look how even the stone grows old! It is said that a priest is buried there from the time when there was persecution on the clergy, though there is a great change on the world today, praise on high to the Eternal Father!

It was a lovely morning; steam rising from grass and fern as the sun drew up the dew; the goat, the sheep, and the birds stretching themselves after the sleep of night.

When I had examined the churchyard, I went into the chapel—four feet of a doorway going in and a place for an altar in the wall made out of a fine, firm block of stone. I noticed many names cut here and there into the stones. Everyone who had ever visited the place had left his name behind him. Among them I found some old writing of which I could make nothing. I was working away at it and spending my mind on it when I heard a hand-whistle. Faith, said I, I have spent the day and to say that they are calling me; and off I went at a run back to the house.

The other two were eating their breakfast before me.

"It seems," said Pádrig as I came in, "that you are running wild in the island."

"Do you know what happened? I came across an old writing in the chapel and I was trying to read it, but I could make nothing of it."

"Oh, I know where that is," said he, pouring out the tea.

"The devil, I thought no one had ever found it but myself."

"Ho, ho!" said he, turning to Paddy Tim, "hear what he says! I remember," he went on, turning to me again, "when I was but ten years old, a great scholar came here from England in search of old writings, and ne'er a stone nor a rock did he leave without examining it, and after all his examining he did not find the writing you are speaking of now. Then myself and my sister, who is in America now, we went with him one day around the island and we said to each other that we had better show it to him. So we brought him up to the place, and I tell you he was delighted to get it. There he was with big glasses on his eyes working away at it till he had taken down every word, and when he had finished he put his hand in his pocket and gave each of us a shilling."

"Well, now, wasn't he a kind man?"

"Faith, I think he was the most decent gentleman ever I saw," said Pádrig, filling his pipe.

"I suppose," said Paddy Tim, "it was the shilling made the decent man of him."

"Upon my word it was not, then, for he was decent in every way. But do you know how long it is since that writing was made?"

"I do not."

"Guess."

"A century?"

"No."

"Three centuries," said Paddy Tim, spitting on the floor.

"Twelve centuries," said Pádrig.

"And how would you know that?" said Paddy Tim.

"Arra, man, isn't the date below?"

After a while I wandered out again and there is no doubt but it was a heart-lifting day. I looked east between me and the Great Sound. The sea was black with birds, some settled on the water, others diving, and their sweet music passing through my ears.

When I was tired with the sight of my eyes I went in again. "Faith, men," said I, "it looks as if we will have a good day's fishing on the Wild Bank."

"We had better be moving off so, in the name of God," said Pádrig, rising from the table and clearing away the things.

We went down to the strand. Soon we had turned our faces to the Island and our backs to the Wild Bank, myself in the bows, the other two putting the lines in order, the sea like glass and flotsam in plenty floating on its surface.

"Do you know now," said Pádrig, with a glance to the bows, "what is the landmark you would take to be on the Wild Bank?"

"Wait now," said I, bending my head and thinking, for I had often heard that landmark from my grandfather. At last I thought of it and raised my head. "I have it, Pádrig. It is the Bank of the Gardens of the Mouth across the White Cleft."

"Quite right."

"But I am no wiser for that, because I don't know where is the Bank of the Gardens of the Mouth, nor the White Cleft either."

"You are in a muddle so, but I will tell you now where they are," said he, stretching his finger straight to the north. "Do you see that cleft in the back of Inish-na-Bró? That is the White Cleft. And about two miles straight to the north from there is a reef which they call the Bank of the Gardens of the Mouth."

"I understand."

"Be rowing on now, and as soon as you see that reef straight over the White Cleft, you are on the Wild Bank."

"Faith," said I, putting out the oars, "there is no limit to knowledge."

I was the paddler of the curragh, so I had my two eyes fixed on the horizon beyond Inish-na-Bró the way I would see the reef. I was rowing on slowly, ever and ever, till I saw clearly the Bank of the Gardens of the Mouth across the White Cleft.

"Now," said I with a shout of joy, "put out the lines, and, by God, it looks like fish."

It did, too, at that time, with all the guillemots, razor-bills, sea-ravens and kittiwakes dipping themselves in pursuit of fish, and now and then the leap of a pollock would send up a spurt of foam which sparkled in the sun the way it would put stars on my eyes. Pádrig stood up, drew out his pipe, and lighted it. I was paddling slowly round the reef, each of the others with a pair of lines out and they watching.

Soon there was a pull at one of Pádrig's lines. He began to draw, but could make no headway.

"That is no pollock, I'm thinking," said I.

"The devil a pollock," said he, "but a seal, and it will make two halves of my line."

At times it would come fine and easy and Pádrig would make a grimace, trying to keep hold of it. He was working away at it, ever and ever, till at last we could see it through the water—a big, bright eel as long as the curragh.

"The devil take you, Paddy," said I, "have the hook ready for it."

Paddy Tim took up the hook, put it neatly into the gills and hauled in the eel.

"Faith, it is a fine fish," said Pádrig, laughing for joy.

"It appears that the fish you would catch here is worth calling a fish," said Paddy Tim.

At that moment he got up quickly from the thwart for there was another fish on his own line. He began to draw, a sharp look in his eye, for fear it would get away.

"Easy, Paddy!" says Pádrig. "Back her, Maurice," says he again softly, the way you would think he was afraid to speak up lest the fish would hear him. Paddy was drawing away and panting for breath, ever and ever, till at last he landed it into the curragh—the finest pollock I ever saw.

In the end of all, the boat was down to the gunwale with fish. Then the tide turned and never a bite after it. So we turned our faces homewards, well satisfied with the hunting of the day.

There was a nice puff of wind from the west. "I suppose the sail would take us east, Pádrig?"

"No doubt. Why wouldn't it? Haul it up."

We took in the oars and I soon had the mast up and threw the jib-sheet to Paddy. I hauled up the sail to the top mast and she slipped away to the east.

We were seated at our ease without a trouble or a care in the world, though there is seldom such a thing on a man of the sea. It was a comfortable time—the boat down to gunwale with fine pollock, not a touch of stress on us as we made for home, but the curragh moving east and ploughing the sea before her, we pulling at our pipes and talking and discussing the affairs of the world.

Twelve

THE WAR

ONE evening long after that we were all on the quay
before the King in the hope of news from the mainland; the
girls maybe looking forward to a letter, a man waiting for the
tobacco he had sent for and desiring nothing more than to get
a morsel of it in his back teeth.

After handing out the letters the King sat down on his heels
and pulled out his pipe and tobacco, as was the habit with him.

"Did you hear any rumours out today, Pádrig?" asked Shaun
Michael.

"The devil," replied the King, "it is my strong opinion we
won't live much longer now."

"Achván," said Shaun Michael, "there must be a plague
coming so."

"It is worse than a plague. The two sides of the world are
likely to burst against each other any moment."

"Bad enough," said Shaun Fada.

"Arra, man," interrupted my grandfather, "why should it be
bad?"

"Your soul to the devil, who will buy the fish? Who will buy

the pig or the cow? Where will the buyers be found? That's
talk in the air, my boy," said Shaun Fada, spitting.

"You may cut off the top of my ear," said my grandfather,
looking hard at Shaun, "if buyers were ever so prosperous as
they will be at such a time."

"Have sense, man," said Shaun, turning his back on my
grandfather and walking away.

A week later we got tidings that England and Germany were
hurled against each other. Every time the King went out to
Dunquin he came home with a newspaper. The old men would
gather in his house every evening to listen to the news, and it
is often it came to a rowan-tree battle[1] between them, some of
them siding with the English and others with the Germans.

One morning the villagers were driving their cattle as usual
on to the hill, and the first man to come in sight of the Bay of
Dingle opened his eyes in wonder. Not an inch of sea but was
covered in white timber. Such a rush there was down the path
to the quay, hurry and noise, the grating of oars and ropes,
curraghs which had not stirred from the stays for six years
being thrown down to the water, and every man who had any
strength in him with his hands on his oars!

I was at school the same day with the rest who like myself
were still unable to lift the bow of a curragh from the stays.
When we came home at midday, my sister Maura told me in
great excitement that the south coast was full of wreckage. Out
I ran and met Tomás Owen Vaun on the road.

"Your soul to the devil," cried he, "have you seen the
wreckage?"

"Come south," said I breathlessly.

We ran out to the point and opened our eyes in astonishment when we saw the sea—boards, beams, wreckage of every
sort covering it; one curragh after another rounding the point,
down to the gunwale with timber, and many more in their

---

1. Reference to a legend of Finn.

wake from the west, another out in the Bay as far as you could see, another leaving the quay after bringing a load safe ashore. We found it hard to take our eyes from the sight, but time was passing and we had to go back to school.

When school was over, and long it seemed till it ended, we did not stay talking but raced home. Eileen and Maura were in before me; my grandfather, father, and brother Shaun out gathering wreckage.

I swallowed my dinner and ran down to the quay. As I looked from the top of the cliff, I started. Wherever you looked, there was nothing to be seen but white boards. I glanced back to the White Strand and my heart leapt. It was full of beams, some of them threescore feet long.

"Och, devil take it, Tomás, hurry down. The quay is full of wreck!"

"Is it so?" he cried, the eyes starting out of his head.

We both leapt into the air with delight. "The devil, Tomás, come south to the Point!"

"Hoo, hoo!" he shouted, throwing his cap into the air.

When we reached the Point, there was not a·child nor old woman in the village but were seated on their haunches on every stone looking out over the Bay of Dingle. The sea was fine and calm with a light breeze from the south and white beams floating as far as you could see over the Bay. About twenty yards from the shore was a plank of wood with hundreds of gulls settled on it picking the barnacles. Before long I noticed two of them fighting fiercely, and soon, like any other crowd, one began helping the other till they were all in the battle drifting north with the tide.

I looked south to the Skelligs and saw the curraghs making for home full of wreckage. We waited till they reached the Point, when we all ran down towards the quay, like the gulls themselves, and had great enjoyment dragging the timber up the slip. Soon the light of day was quenched and the wreck-gatherers had to put their curraghs on the stays, well satisfied with the day's work and their bones aching after all the rowing since morning.

Next day the quay and the strands were a grand sight, big timbers lying here and there and not a curragh with less than a hundred planks.

"By God," one man would say, "war is good."

"Arra, man," said another, "if it continues, this Island will be the Land of the Young."

The war changed people greatly. Idle loiterers who used to sleep it out till milking-time were now abroad with the chirp of the sparrow gathering and ever gathering. There was good living in the Island now. Money was piled up. There was no spending. Nothing was bought. There was no need. It was to be had on the top of the water—flour, meat, lard, petrol, wax, margarine, wine in plenty, even shoes, stockings, and clothes. Not a house in the Island but a storeroom was built beside it to keep the gatherings, and, without any exaggeration, when you entered one of them you would think you were in a big town, with all the barrels of flour piled on top of one another, tins of petrol and every sort of riches; and when the old man or the old woman came around, all they had to do was to make for the barrels of wine and help themselves to a draught. Buyers were coming from all parts of Kerry to buy the wood, to buy the wax and every sort of oil, so that money was being made rapidly. There is no doubt but a curragh can make a wonderful stand in a foamy sea. For from my own knowledge I can say that from that time, though storms might come, she would be out over the waves like a feather.

One Friday the King had gone to Dunquin for the post, and, as I have said already, the whole village, young and old, had to be on the quay to meet him.

"How is England doing, Pádrig?" asked the Púncán, when the letters had been given out.

"The devil," said the King, "it is likely the end of the world is coming, for they are making no stop now and England is going to send out conscription through the whole of Ireland."

"Bad indeed so, bad indeed so," said the Púncán, spitting tobacco.

"Ah, that's not the tidings we want," said another man, "but did you hear of a ship being sunk in any place since?"

"The devil," said the King, "one was sent down yesterday morning near Cork Harbour, the *Lusitania*, the finest ship the Americans ever had. They say there were millionaires in plenty on board and isn't it a terrible thing that not a sinner of them came ashore alive. If this breeze lasts from the south tonight, the coast of the Island will be full of drowned men tomorrow."

No one went to sleep in the Island that night. Many were out on the headlands, north, south, east, and west, others up at cock-crow next morning in search of the millionaires. It was a Saturday and there was no school. As soon as I got up I went south to the Point. It was a fine morning, not a puff in the sky. I sat on my heels and scanned every inch of the Bay. After about half an hour I thought I noticed something far out to sea. I could not make out what it was. I rubbed my eyes thinking it might be only a fancy, but then I saw it again and two sea-gulls settled on it. Certain of my opinion now, I ran home.

"By God, father," said I, "I have seen something, whatever it is."

"Is that so?" said he, getting up. "Go south again and I will call Mick" (his brother).

I darted back to the Point. When I got there I found Liam Tigue before me with a stoop on him, peering out to sea.

"Is there any wreckage in the Bay, Liam?"

"Indeed I think I see something between me and Slea Head," said he, pointing south-east. "Look and see if you could make out what it is."

"By God, Liam, it is one of the millionaires."

"As sure as I live," said he, getting up.

I walked up to the ditch and Liam back towards the village. With a glance down to the quay I saw my father and uncle putting out in the curragh and pulling hard past the Cliff Well to the south. When Liam saw them leaving the quay: "You rogue," said he, coming back to me, panting, "it is well you knew your father was going after it."

"Is that my father?" said I, mocking him.

"It is, and well you knew it."

My father was near it now. "Faith," said Liam, "it is a human being."

They drew alongside it. Then we saw the man in the stern leaping to the bows and the man in the bows leaping astern.

"It is a human being, indeed," said Liam, "and the man in the bows hasn't the courage to throw the rope round it."

They had it tied now and were turning home. We stayed as we were till they came towards the Point.

"On my oath, Liam, it is a human body. Do you see it standing straight down in the water?"

"You are right, for that is the lifebuoy under its head."

Shortly afterwards, with a pull from the rope, the pale face turned towards us in the sunlight.

We ran down the quay. It was a terrible sight, the eyes plucked out by the gulls, the face swollen, and the clothes ready to burst with the swelling of the body.

"What's that you had?" said Eileen to my father when they came home.

"A dead body."

"And what will you do with it?"

"Oh, we will bring it home," said he, smiling.

I went out to the door. I saw a curragh making for the quay and I thought it was peelers were in it. I ran back in excitement.

"The peelers are come to the quay," I cried, and my father got up from the table.

He went to speak with the sergeant. It was arranged to take the body to Dunquin so that the peelers could take care of it till its people would take it. They went down to the quay and I slipped into the curragh—my father, my uncle, and myself in one of them, and the peelers in the curragh from Dunquin. When we reached the Great Cliff, the body was taken out and stretched on the quay. The sergeant began searching the pockets, all of us looking on, but soon he drew back again. The smell was too strong. No one had the courage to go near it.

But there was one old man called Mick of the Hill standing beside us with his hands in his pockets. He walked up and stood over the body. He put a foot on each side of it, took his hands from his pockets, looked first at us and then at the body. He went down on his knees and began to open the coat. When he had the coat and vest open, he put his hand in one of the pockets and, drawing out a small diary, he handed it to the sergeant. I was standing by. When he opened the book the first thing I saw was the drowned man's name written like this:

HENRY ATKINSON
3 Edward Street, London, W.C.
First-class Officer S.S. *Lusitania*.

In the other pockets were found a watch and gold chain, a comb, a mirror, and three sixpences.

"Keep the sixpences yourself," said the sergeant, "you have earned them well."

"Musha, God leave you your health, my son," said Mick, putting them in his pocket.

They all helped to carry the body to the top of the cliff. Then they laid it in the sergeant's motor car and went off with it to Ballyferriter.

When I went out the next morning there was a light swell on the rocks and you would think from the look of the sky and sea that a change was coming. I was sitting, one foot up on the ditch, looking north and south, deep in thought, when Tomás Owen Vaun came running breathlessly towards me.

"Easy, Tomás!" said I, "take it softly. I think, by the look of you, you have seen something."

"Oh, Lord," he cried, "it is not that, but Shaun Lane has a big boat full of sailors!"

"Och, whist, don't be telling lies like that."

"The devil a lie. They are rounding Long-Rock Head with her."

He ran off without another word. Looking after him, I knew by the rush he was in he had spoken the truth. I ran into the house.

"The devil," said I to my father and grandfather, who were before the fire, "Shaun Lane has a boat full of sailors round Long-Rock Head!"

"Who told you so?" asked my father.

"Tomás Owen Vaun."

"Och, Tomás is like yourself," said my grandfather, rising from the chair and taking up the broom to sweep the floor.

I returned to the ditch and sat with my hand under my chin, gazing steadily at the horizon in hope of seeing the boat on its way from the west. Before long I saw the bow of a curragh beyond the Spit and the men rowing hard. I am thinking you were right about the boat, Tomás, said I in my own mind. Just at that moment she came into sight. She was full of people.

I ran in again. "The devil," I cried, "the boat is rounding the Spit."

Before you could clap your hands the news had gone through the village. Young and old were out on every clump of grass, some of the children running into hiding for fear of them, others jumping for joy, old pensioners who had not been able to leave the chimney-corner creeping to the doors to see the sight. We ran down the quay. The whole village was there, and such a crush that some were up to their knees in the sea. But little they cared so long as they got a view of the sailors.

As the boat came into the pool, the first thing we noticed was three black men on board her. There was another man, too, a Chinaman, with a small round face and a snub nose, eyes like two pins and long black hair down his back. Some were

singing, some asleep, others were talking. You would think
they were a flock of geese, some speaking English, others
Italian and I know not what. They leapt out on to the slip,
fifteen in all, some of them strong, others unable to stand.

One of them, standing just beside me, was over six feet tall,
with a long narrow face, a beard over his breast, a big fat nose
and two little black eyes under prominent brows, a scarf
twisted round his neck, a horn-peaked cap on his head and
long boots up to his knees. I wonder, said I to myself, looking
up at him, will I ask him where he is from. I tried to speak but
something came into my throat. I tried again.

"Where are you from?" said I.

He looked down at me and laughed. Then he gave out a
great rush of talk. Another answered him, and indeed, you
would go anywhere to listen to them, though you could not
understand them. Then the last man to leave the boat spoke
out and greeted the people in English.

My father spoke to him.

"I suppose you are the captain?"

"I am not, but the mate. I will tell you what happened to the
captain."

Everyone gathered round.

"We were on the sea for a week, thrown east and west on the
top of the waves. We left Buenos Aires bound for Cork. When
we were about twenty miles south-west of the Teeracht we
met a submarine. It drew up alongside. The captain spoke,
ordering us to take to the boats as he was going to sink the
ship. Five boats we had and we got them out as fast as we
could. We were not far from the ship when the torpedo struck
her and we saw her going down by the stern. Well, my good
people, we are on the sea ever since, for the weather was bad,
and, what was worse, we were scattered like the sons of Lir.[2]

---

2. Reference to one of the legends. Lir, father of Manannan, was the old Irish
sea-god. He has drifted into English literature under the guise of Lear, while his son's
name is preserved in that of the Isle of Man.

Och, it was a terrible destruction," he cried with tears in his eyes, stretching his hands to the sky. "I had three brothers in the other boats and no news nor tidings of them since."

"They are safe with the help of God," said my father; "have no fear for them."

"Indeed, I don't know," he said. "But with regard to the captain, there's no doubt he was a bad one. We had no food in the boats but biscuits. He was giving us only one biscuit a day and no water at all. He was giving me enough, but I didn't like the way he was treating the others. The crew rose against him. They told him three times if he didn't give every man his right they would throw him overboard. And then," said the mate, "do you see that big dark fellow over there?"

"The devil, my lad," said old Mickil, looking at him, "that fellow has a bad look in his eye."

"Well, that man got thirsty and asked the captain for a drink. The captain refused, and the fellow from beyond leapt from the bows and caught him by the throat and threw him into the sea."

"Ah, that was bad," said my father.

"It couldn't be helped," said the mate, "for he had a big knife ready to put into the guts of any man who spoke a word against him."

When the mate had finished his story, the sailors were brought up into the village and got what attention it was in the power of the Islanders to give them. In three hours, when they were all washed clean and shaved, with an hour's sleep, you would think they were not the same men, all but the three black men who were unchanged but for the shine on their faces after the washing.

They came down chattering to the quay, the whole village following them, for everyone was amazed at their talk, and especially at the black men.

"Great God of Virtues," cried an old woman who would not believe there were such people in the world, "why wouldn't they clean themselves?"

"Arra, Maura," said another woman, "it is not dirty they are but black from their birth."

"Oh, musha, my pity for you entirely, isn't it you who has the skull of a chicken to tell me there are people like that."

"Arra, Maura, don't be foolish. Isn't it often I heard old Andrew when he came home from America saying he saw hundreds of those there?"

We went down to the quay, for the sailors were going to Dunquin. I was standing at the top beside Shaun Michael and old Mickil. We saw them walking down the Causeway and the three black men out before the white men.

"Achván," said Shaun Michael, "isn't it a strange thing those wouldn't clean the coal from their faces?"

"The devil, my lad," replied Mickil, "all the water in Thresher's Well wouldn't clean them, for it is not dirt that's on them but a black skin."

The black men stopped near by, looking out to sea and talking in their own language, whatever it was.

"The devil, my lad," said old Mickil, "I don't like the look of the big fellow, wherever he's from."

"Take care of that one," said the Púncán, who had just come down; "he will eat you alive."

"Musha," said old Mickil, turning to him, "may he eat yourself if the spittle isn't down over your chin."

I laughed so loud that the black men looked down at me with a vicious look in their eyes, thinking that it was at themselves I was laughing.

They walked down the slip, some singing, some talking, others with heads bent as if in trouble. They all went into the boat except one who was still out on the slip, shouting and roaring, though none of us could understand him.

"Oh, Lord," said one man, "maybe he is going off his head, God between us and evil!"

He was leaping in anger.

"The devil, my lad," said old Mickil, "if that man below is not tied he will make corpses."

There was a laugh here and here. When he heard the laughter he rushed up to us in a poisonous haste, chattering fiercely. He pointed with his finger to the top of the village: "Sacca, sacca, sacca!" and then a long rush of talk. The mate shouted up to him from the boat, and he gave a bold reply. You could tell it was bold by the energy he put into his voice. Then he ran up as fast as he could to the village.

Everyone thought now that he was out of his wits.

"God between us and evil," said one man, "what had better be done with him?"

"Give him tether for a while," said another, "till we see is he dangerous."

"Upon my word, maybe he would do away with himself on the cliffs and we had better run after him."

We watched him running till he went into the house of Liam Tigue. The next minute he was out again with a bag in his hand.

"Your soul to the devil," said Shaun Michael, "it is the bag. He left it behind him."

"You are right," said Shaun Lane. "That was the sack-sack he was seeking."

He ran down the path and passed us on his way to the slip. Then, turning round towards us, he cried, so it seemed to me, "Gurlamacras, gurlamacras!"

"May your journey prosper with you!" answered old Mickil.

"Gurlamacras," said he again with a smile.

"The devil, my lad," said Mickil, "it wasn't gurlamacras with you just now when you had forgotten your bag."

He leapt aboard. The boat moved out through the pool, the men waving their handkerchiefs till they were out of sight.

Thirteen

THE SHIPWRECK

ONE Tuesday in the month of May I washed and cleaned myself with a heavy heart for school. Then I wandered out and sat down at the end of the lane to wait for my comrade, Tomás Owen Vaun.

Before long I saw the master coming down the glen. I was smitten with the weariness of the world. How envious I felt of the old men who were driving up their cattle into the hill, even of the bird that would float above my head, with nothing to trouble it but it singing to itself when it wished, and flying off when it wished, and going asleep when it wished. When shall I be a man? When shall I be free from the oppression of the master I see coming down the glen?

Tomás came up. "We'll be late," said he. He was smiling.

"Do you not feel at all lazy before school, Tomás?"

"Ah, musha," said he with a frown, "if anyone is as bad as I, I don't know what to say."

"As bad as you! Oh, Tomás, if you are as bad as I am, I am content, for I thought there was no one in the world so wretched as myself."

We went inside and sat down on the bench. The master

took up a book. "Now," said he, "we will do some dictation."

"Oh, Lord!" said Tomás, giving me a prod in the thigh.

"Long, long ago," dictated the master, "there was a man living in the village of Ballyboy."

But he had only read so far when we heard a clamour outside. I looked out of the window and saw the Púncán and the King going down the Causeway with thole-pins and ropes, three or four hurrying after them, all with the same gear. "Your soul to the devil, Tomás, more wreckage!"

The master went out to the door. He stayed there a while and then walked up to the mistress.

"Something wonderful is after happening," said he; "go out and see what it is."

"The devil take you," I whispered to Tomás, "the dictation is over."

The mistress came back, looking pale.

"What has happened?" said the master.

We were all listening.

"A big ship has gone down in the Sorrowful Cliff."

He opened his eyes in astonishment. "Look after the school till I come back," said he.

"Look now," said Tomás, "we'll have the day under the hedge."

We were all in the hurry of our lives for twelve o'clock, making the noise of the world without any thought of the dictation, for we had no fear of the mistress. She herself was in and out the door all the time, ever and ever, till twelve o'clock came. Away we ran joyfully as fast as our heels would carry us.

Great King of Virtues, it was a marvellous sight—tins, barrels of flour, big black boxes, big white boxes, big boxes of bacon, not a living being to be seen nor a curragh on the stays.

"The devil, Tomás, come west to the Spit of Seals' Cove. It's there the whole village is gathered!"

Away we ran leaping for delight. As we approached the Great Glen we met Maura Andrew with three cardboard boxes. "Oh, my heart, a big ship is gone down on the Lóchar Rock and the sea is full of all sorts of riches," said she.

We ran off wildly and darted like birds along the lane to the west till we went down on to Shingle Strand. Everything was in confusion—boxes and chests of every shape and colour, not an inch of the sand but was covered in wreckage.

"Oh, Lord," cried Tomás, throwing his cap into the air, "we are rich for ever!"

As soon as I set foot on the shingle, I saw Mickil Shamus on my left with his head in a barrel, Dermod O'Shea beside him and his mouth stained with drink.

"What is in the barrel, Dermod?"

Mickil Shamus drew out his head. There was the same stain on his mouth.

"Now is the time for you to blow out your waists," said Dermod.

"What is it?"

"Cod-liver oil."

I put my head over the barrel.

"Ah, don't be sniffing it, crow, but swallow it down. It will put marrow into your bones, a thing they lack now."

I took a mouthful, but if I had got a thousand pounds I couldn't have taken more. I spat it out.

At that moment I heard a shout from Tomás: "Oh, the devil, Maurice, look east at the King with all the chocolates!"

He had opened a big chest which had a number of small boxes inside it, and he was laying them out on the shingle. "Now, my lads," he called out, "if you have good teeth!"

He gave each of us a box. Thanking him, we ran east among the rocks and sat down without a word of talk till at last we were sick of the taste of them, for they were very strong.

"Your soul to the devil, Tomás, isn't it well we came!"

"Your soul to the devil, it is true for you."

A great din was being raised from one end of the Strand to the other, for as each curragh came in, everyone was hard at work rolling the boxes and barrels above high-water. We were half-way across the Strand when we saw one with Big Peg and Maura Maura Owen. It was all they could do to move it. We stopped to help them.

"Musha, love of my heart for ever," cried Peg, "youth is good. And as the wren said long ago when he pulled the worm out of the frost . . ."

"What did he say, Peg?"

"'Ah,' said he, 'strength is fine,' and that is the way with the two of us."

We were pushing away at the barrel, laughing gaily at Peg and her nonsense, for she was a great talker, till the barrel struck a big stone.

"My love to God," said Peg, "if it were in our power to get it over that stone, we would be on the pig's back.[1] Shoulder to shoulder, my friends!" said she with a shake of her shoulder-blades, moving in to the barrel.

We played our whole strength on it and got it over the stone. We didn't know yet what was in it; but we were not long in ignorance, for when the barrel fell down on the far side of the stone the hoops burst and it fell asunder. In a moment fine red apples were leaping out of it and hopping like balls down the Strand.

"Och," cried Peg, "that's done it."

Away she ran, herself and Maura Maura Owen, gathering up the apples. But everyone was now taking part in the snatch for them, Peg in the east and Maura in the west throwing every devil and demon at the others to leave the apples alone. And indeed when they had done, those they had were easily counted. As for Tomás and me, we were not behind-hand in the hunt, and we hid all we gathered at the east end of the Strand.

On our way west again we noticed two men up in the Cave of Shevaun de Lóndra doing something secretly. We followed

---

1 Reference to the death of Diarmuid in the legend of Diarmuid and Gráinne.

them. They had not seen us yet. They had a pretty, decorated box, not another like it on the Strand. It was full of watches.

"Oh, Lord," cried Tomás, "look at the watches!"

They overheard us and shut the box quickly.

"Be off with you!" cried Pats Lane, running after us to drive us away.

When we had gone a little distance we stopped. "Hucs!" cried Tomás, "we know what you have."

"Get out of my sight!" shouted Pats Lane menacingly, picking up a stone.

"Hucs, hucs!" we cried together and ran away west along the Strand.

In the end we were weary looking at all the wreckage.

"What about going to see the ship?"

"Oh, Lord," said I, "you are right."

When we came to the mouth of the path from the Strand, we found Shaun Liam and two others opening a big box.

"Wait till we see what they have here," said I.

They were not long taking off the top with an ax. There was a big roll inside, twisted up together like glass.

"Wait awhile," said Maurice Pad, taking a box of matches out of his pocket.

He put a match to the stuff. It took fire at once, the flames running through it with a terrible roar.

"Oh," cried Liam, "draw back quickly for it will do harm!"

"My love to God," cried Big Peg, "the devil is done and the little village burnt!"

We all fled into the Cave of Shevaun de Lóndra waiting for the explosion. But it did not come. We crept out again. The flames were roaring up into the air.

"God give us the grace of patience," said Peg, "for I had no thought but it would send the Strand and all on it in shreds into the sky."

Just then the master came down the path panting, for he was big and fat.

"What burnt the box?"

"Arra, musha," said Shaun Liam, "we had no thought but it would explode on us."

"What was inside it?"

"The devil I know, master."

Tomás and I were scraping among the ashes which had been left after the blaze. I found a piece still unburnt. I handed it to the master. "Ah," said he, examining it, "it is a great pity it was burnt. It was gelatine, very costly stuff."

"Och, God be with us," said Shaun Liam, scratching his head, "isn't it a great pile of money we have destroyed!"

"My love to God," said Peg, raising her hands, "what I have to say now I think no fault can be found with it; that if men knew what was the purpose of each thing, what it was good for and what it was worth, not one of their seed would be poor for seven generations."

Tomás and I climbed the path. When we came above the Sorrowful Cliff it was an astonishing sight. Nothing but wreckage! Without a lie, you could have walked out from the Spit of Seals' Cove and gone ashore in Inish Túiscirt without wetting your foot, with all the cotton-bales, chests, boxes, and appurtenances on the sea.

"Oh, Lord," said Tomás, "how did any ship carry all that?"

"By God, it passes understanding."

Soon we were in sight of Lóchar Rock where the ship struck. The two masts and the funnel were still above water.

"There is no doubt she was big enough, Tomás. Look at the bay of sea between the masts!"

The old women of the village were sitting on their haunches on the cliff's edge looking out, a curragh coming to the quay with a load and another leaving, the coves ringing with the sound of blows on the boxes out to sea. Every curragh had an ax, and when they found a box too big to bring ashore they split it open on the spot, and when a seal would put up his head to take the air he would only have his snout out of water when he would hear the blows and down he would dive again in alarm.

Before long we saw a curragh rounding the bottom of Well Point, followed by a boat in which were two sailors. We all made for the quay. When they came ashore, the King spoke to them in English. One of them answered. Glancing into the boat I saw another man stretched out on his face without a stir. "Oh, Lord, Tomás, look at the sailor dead in the boat!"

Tomás O'Carna and Shaun Tomás went down and lifted him out. He was alive, but could not stand. They helped him up to the house of Mickil Nell.

"It appears," said the King to the sailor beside him, "that the man above is very weak. How did the ship happen to go in there last night?"

"I am the captain and this is the mate, and the man above is a seaman. We left New York with a cargo of all sorts for London. On our journey we got a message that a submarine was on our route before us."

"I understand you well," said the King, shaking his head.

"What I did then," said the captain, "was to change my route and turn north-east. Then the mist fell and I didn't know where in the world I was. I was blind out."

"It is no wonder," said the King, shaking his head again.

"I turned the ship south-east then and that is how she struck in there. And, would you believe it, half an hour before she struck she grazed on a rock?"

"I believe you well," said the King, "for you couldn't help striking Tail Rock in the direction you came."

"It was about three o'clock in the morning. I ordered the crew to take to the boats. We left her safely, three boats in all, but I don't know where the other two are gone."

"Oh, upon my word, they are alive, for they were seen going up the Bay of Dingle today."

"That is good," said the captain. "I thought then," he went on, "that it might be possible to go ashore where the ship struck. The seaman who is after going up told me to make fast a rope round his waist and out he leapt."

The author in uniform, ca. 1934. Courtesy Mrs. Maura Kavanagh.

The Landing at Gt. Blasket   Beyond the most westerly point of Europe.

Photo: G. Chambers

Postcard of the landing at Great Blasket, ca. 1920. Courtesy Mrs. Maura Kavanagh.

The author with friend and translator George Thomson,
Dublin 1928-29. Courtesy Mrs. Maura Kavanagh.

The author with E.M. Forster, ca. 1933. Courtesy Mrs. Maura Kavanagh.

"Myself, Mickil, and Tomás Owen Vaun when we went for the ass."

Drawing by Maurice O'Sullivan. Blasket Centre / Courtesy Mrs. Maura Kavanagh.

"An bhficeann tú an simléar bán úd shiar ar sise, sin í anois an bairric?"
"Do you see the white chimney over there, says she, that there is the barracks."

Drawing by Maurice O'Sullivan. *Blasket Centre / Courtesy Mrs. Maura Kavanagh.*

"After a while we heard the sounds 'ding dong, ding dong.' Soon after when the fog cleared, Magréad saw the lights. And what did we notice but a big steamer."

Drawing by Maurice O'Sullivan. *Blasket Centre / Courtesy Mrs. Maura Kavanagh.*

"Staidhsiún an Daingean. Tuigeach dam go raibh ins an traein ag cur na súl triam."
"Dingle station. I suspected that everyone on the train was staring fixedly at me."

Drawing by Maurice O'Sullivan. Blasket Centre / Courtesy Mrs. Maura Kavanagh.

"Oh, Lord," said the King, "and I dare say it was dark at the time?"

"You wouldn't see a finger put into your eyes."

"Well, well," said the King, shutting his eyes in pity for them.

"He swam in, we holding the rope. But after half an hour in the water he had found no place where it was possible to get ashore, and there was a great sweeping swell on the rocks. We thought then that it was some backward country with no one alive in it. But, upon my word," said he, glancing around, "you are here—fine, well-favoured people, mannerly, intelligent, generous, and hospitable."

"Indeed," said the King, "we are very thankful to you for the praise. But I promise you, since the war began, it is many a sailor has been saved here from the sea. And as for attending them well, they get what we have. But you must be cold and wet standing there. Come up into the village."

The sailors spent two or three hours with us. When they had eaten and rested, they said farewell to the people of the Island and departed for the mainland.

From that out there was plenty and abundance in the Island—food of all sorts, clothes from head to heel, every man, woman, and child with a watch in their pockets; not a penny leaving home; everything a mouth could ask for coming in with the tide from day to day—all except the sugar which melted as soon as it touched water.

A week later there came a heavy storm from the north-west and every sea-bank began to break and sweep foam up on the green grass, the waves thundering on the Strand, dogs howling at night on account of the gale, as is their habit, a whirlwind whistling through every alley the way you would think it would snatch the roof from the house. Everyone was waiting in expectancy, for there was no telling what might come out of the ship if the storm broke it up. They took little sleep, but spent their time keeping a watch on the strands and the coves and going into the hill to look down at the ship.

It was a Monday. Tomás and I were talking at the bottom of the lane with no thought of school but of the wreckage.

"What would you say to going west to Shingle Strand," said I, "to see if there is anything thrown in?"

"Your soul to the devil, come on," said he eagerly.

The gale was shrieking across the Pass of the Hill-Slope from the west. When we reached the Sandhills we had to cling fast to each other to keep our feet. We went down towards the Strand. The din was terrible. An enormous wave would break in and sweep the shingle up to the foot of the cliffs. Then it would churn up the stones as it receded. We had to put our fingers in our ears to stop the noise.

"Oh, Lord, Tomás, let us not go down. We'd be drowned surely!"

"Do you know where we'll go? Out on to the Spit of Seals' Cove to see the wreck in the Sorrowful Cliff."

We made our way in the teeth of the howling wind, each with a drowning man's grip of the other. From time to time a gust would throw us to the ground. "I think," said Tomás, "we had better not trust ourselves out on the Spit."

The words were not out of his mouth when we were both covered in a spurt of foam which soaked us from head to heel and sent us sprawling on the grass. We lay there for several minutes before either of us could speak.

"Where are you, Tomás?" I cried in the height of my head.

"I am here," he shouted.

I rubbed my eyes.

As I got up it seemed as if there were a ton weight in my body with the water. "Get up, Tomás," I cried, "before we get the same again. It is lucky we were not to go any farther for we would surely have been thrown from the cliff."

We walked up to Donlevy Spit. The sun was strong in the sky, so we stripped off every shred we had on, wrung the water out of our clothes and spread them out in the sunshine. Our teeth were chattering with the cold.

It was five o'clock when we turned our faces back to the

village. We were aching with the hunger. From every house came the smell of flesh roasting. When I reached home I looked on the floor. It was covered with leather, long strips of it and big cowhides.

"Oh, King of Virtues, where did you get it?" said I to my father, who was eating at the table.

"Aren't all the strands in the north full of it?" said he.

Every man and woman was now keeping watch for the low neap-tide, leaving home at the chirp of the sparrow, searching every cave, cove, cliff, and crevice, and coming home in the evening with big bundles of leather, rain-coats, shirts, strips of cloth, and caps in plenty. Whenever you looked out to the Pass of the Hill-Slope, or to the top of the road, or to the road west, you would be sure to see someone returning home with a bundle on his back.

A week and a month passed with no school nor any thought of it, and, as the proverb says, that which is long absent grows cold. The ship's cargo was at an end now and nothing to be had on the sea, but everyone was making for the strands and coves to gather in the cloth and the leather. Tomás and I were too young and weak to go to the strands in the north, but even so we were not behind with the plunder, though we were only searching Blind Cove, Boat Cove and the Shingle Strand.

Fourteen

THE WANDERER

THE next Sunday evening my grandfather and I were sitting by the fire. My father and my brother Shaun were gone since morning to Mass; and my sisters were walking through the village as is the habit of the girls on Sunday when the weather is fine.

My grandfather was telling me stories of old times. While we were talking, my father and Shaun returned and a stranger with them they had brought from Dunquin. My grandfather got up to welcome the stranger and gave him a chair beside the hearth.

He was a short sturdy man, well-favoured, shy-looking, with the length of my hand of moustache. He sat staring straight into the middle of the fire as if his thoughts were elsewhere. After a while he took an old pipe, as black as soot, from his pocket and thrust it into the ashes. He had not a word to say but as we would question him.

When Eileen had the tea ready: "Now, stranger," said my father, "come over to the table. Do not be backward but make yourself at home as long as you are here."

"Thank you," said he.

"If you don't mind me asking, where are you from, stranger?" said my grandfather, when we were all sitting in.

"I was born in Cúl-na-gapóg on the east side of Dingle," said he when he had swallowed down the mouthful he was eating.

"And where are you spending your life since?"

"Musha, I have walked the world twice over, good people."

"Faith, that's good news," said my grandfather, "for he who travels has tales to tell."

When he had eaten his fill (and he seemed in need of it) we moved back to the fire, a fine red fire which it was the wont of my grandfather to make up at the fall of night. Maura and Eileen went out again to stroll from cottage to cottage. I decided to stay at home in the hope of hearing stories from the stranger. My father lit the lamp. The stranger was puffing at his pipe, my father and grandfather the same.

"Isn't this a fine, nice place," said he at last, a look of contentment coming on his face.

"Hm," said my father with a laugh, "it looks all right now but you would not say the same if you were here in the winter."

"I suppose so," said he, spitting after the pipe.

"I dare say," said my grandfather, "it is many wonders you have seen on your travels?"

"Musha, I assure you it is many a savage dog and a bad housewife the likes of me comes across, and I have passed through many hardships since I gave my heels to the road."

"Ah, musha, that's a true saying," said my grandfather, looking at him with compassion.

"But so far as my own experiences go, I will tell you all to pass the night."

"Very good," said my grandfather, settling himself to listen.

"As I have said already, I was born in Cúl-na-gapóg. I had two brothers but, if so, death soon carried them off."

"Ah, that is the way of the world."

"We had a fine piece of land, but, as folly strikes many, I sold it out when my father and mother died and I turned my breast to the great world. I went to America. And the strangest thing I ever saw, it is there I saw it.

"A Clare man and myself were lodging for three years in the one house in the city of Springfield, and were working in the same employment. When the day's work was over we would wash and clean ourselves and take a stroll into the city. Well, one Saturday evening we wandered out into the street without a trouble or a care in the world."

"I suppose so," said my grandfather, uncrossing his knees and recrossing them the other way.

"We were not far from the street when the Clare man gave a leap and shouted, 'What the devil is that dog doing between us all the night?' I looked and, sure enough, there was a big black dog walking along with us. We began trying to drive it away but it would not stir. 'Wait,' said the Clare man, picking up a stone, 'I will soon make him scamper.' 'Stop,' said I. 'Don't touch him.'

"Well, old man," said the stranger, turning to my grandfather with a piercing look, "would you believe it, I was lifted clean off the street, and how it happened I do not know but I awoke inside a graveyard the like of which I had never seen before."

"By my baptism," said my father, "that was a queer thing."

"No doubt of it," said my grandfather.

"I got up and looked round me," continued the stranger. "There was not a house nor any dwelling to be seen. I rubbed my eyes. Great God of Virtues, I cried, where am I? Am I dreaming? Where is the Clare man? I swear by the book I was like a man who would be out of his senses."

"On my soul, it was no wonder for you," said my grandfather, eagerly listening. As for myself, my heart was leaping with delight, the way it seemed I was there myself at that moment.

"Well, men," he continued, "I was trembling hand and foot. Twelve attempts I made to get out of the graveyard, up to my hip in grass and shrubs. At last I succeeded, but I was as blind as ever as to where I was—a great green meadow all round me and not a light from God above. I was walking on and on, a small, narrow path out before me, until at last I saw in the distance many lights. My heart opened. Faith, said I to myself, that is the city, wherever I may be at present. I went towards it and soon I saw it was a big, beautiful castle. If it is no better let it be no worse, said I, but where am I going? What was troubling me most was the man who had been with me the evening before and the strange black dog. What were the delusions which had come over me and how on the earth of the world had I parted from them?"

"Upon my word, it would confuse anyone," said my grandfather.

"No doubt of it," said my father.

"Well, I made towards the light, for I said to myself that wherever I was the people of the house would direct me. It was approached by the most beautiful path sinner's eye ever beheld, a nice stairway up to the door and flowers of all hues bordering it on every side. The lights of the castle were dazzling me. Before long I ran straight into a tree and was thrown backwards. 'The devil, you are a queer tree,' said I, looking up at it. I continued on my way along the path. By now I was getting a sweet smell and could hear the sound of meat roasting.

"I went up the stairs. There was a man before me standing outside the door, his two hands under his arm-pits, his sleeves turned up. I tried to speak with him but all he did was to bend his head, like this." (The stranger got up, put his two hands under his arm-pits and bent his head.)

"I swear by the devil, when I saw what he was doing I felt very queer and a chill came into my blood. I looked in through the door. There was a room before my face. At the far end I saw a fine handsome girl sharpening knives and talking rapidly. I put a listening ear on myself and it seemed to me she was Irish. On my left was a big table laden with riches, six men seated at it, everyone with a knife and fork, eating and conversing together. But as soon as they saw me they stopped, put their hands under their arm-pits and bowed their heads. And as sure as I am here tonight, old man," said the stranger, striking his fist on my grandfather's knee, "I recognized every one of them, all of them dead for years before."

A cold spasm ran up through my body.

"Well, well," said my grandfather, "it is a wonder the soul did not fall out of you."

"The devil it is," said my father.

"Indeed," said the stranger, "I had my courage then as well as I have it now, but I felt very queer when I recognized the six. I wanted to speak to them but my tongue would not let me."

"No wonder for you," said my grandfather.

"He made a good stand," said my father, relighting his pipe.

"Go on, stranger," said I, for I seemed to be seeing the six men with their heads bent down and I did not want the story interrupted.

"Well," continued the stranger, "when I got no heed, I wandered out again. The man at the door was still there and in the same posture. I took no notice of him but walked past for I thought he was of the other world.

"I was walking on and on again with no sight of the city of Springfield yet nor any tidings of it to be had. On I wandered, not knowing east from west, until at last I turned into a lane no wider than myself—a big wall of cement ten feet high on either side. I was walking along the lane for half an hour when I heard a bell ringing behind me. Looking back I saw a bicycle coming towards me like the wind. I could not get out of the way. It was impossible. God save my soul, said I, he will split me. I looked back again. He was nearer now, a big lamp of light on the bicycle and no slackening speed. I looked up at the wall to see if I could climb it. But at that moment the bicycle passed me like a whirlwind. That was the strangest thing of all. I did not feel him and the lane no broader than myself. Musha, said I, may the great King of Glory guide me aright. Where am I going? Or is this the path of eternity? I walked on very slowly."

"I should think so," said my grandfather, his hand under his chin, "especially since you thought you were on the path of eternity. Musha, God help us all on the day of judgment," said he, lifting his hat and putting it on again.

"I was going on for an hour when I seemed to hear the sound of talk behind me; I looked back. It was still a long way off. I was rambling on till it came nearer. I looked back again, and, by God, it seemed to me it was the milkman."

"Begging pardon for interrupting your story," said my grandfather, "but what is a milkman?"

"A man who goes round with milk from house to house each morning," said the stranger. "And we know each other well. I stopped. Sure enough it was he. I greeted him.

" 'Devil take you, Dónal,' said he, 'what ails you to be out so early in the morning?'

" 'What time is it?' said I.

" 'It is not four o'clock yet. I suppose you were out drinking all night?'

" 'Arra, man,' said I, 'let me alone. God alone knows about that.' "

"Praise be to Him on high," said my grandfather, baring his head again.

" 'What place is this?' said I to the milkman.

"He laughed aloud. 'Do you mean to say you don't know where you are?'

"I looked round and my two eyes opened. I was standing in the middle of the street where the moment before was the path of eternity. I knew the street well. Why wouldn't I when I was only a hundred yards from my own house! I was left without a word, thinking at once of the Good People, that it was they who had deceived me.

" 'Get into the cart,' said the milkman.

"When I reached home the woman of the house looked at me compassionately. 'Oh, Dónal, what did you do with your companion last night? He is upstairs in bed and cannot live,' said she.

"The Clare man was stretched out, every bit of him as black as coal. He could not speak to me and so I went for the priest. 'Is he in danger of death, father?' said I. 'He is indeed, and it is not a natural death either.' So I told him all that had happened. 'I believe you well,' said he, 'and it was that big castle and the six men you knew in it who saved you from the black dog.'"

"Well, well," said my grandfather, drawing a few sods of turf from the corner and putting them on the fire, "it is wonderful the distress you have suffered!"

"God forbid I should ever go through the like again," said the stranger, putting his hand in his pocket to find his pipe.

"Amen, O Lord," said my grandfather.

"Amen," repeated my father. "Apparently," said he, when he had his own pipe going as he wished, "they have a good time of it in the other world."

The three of them were now sending smoke through the house, myself listening and hoping for another story. My heart was snatching at just such another from his mouth. When he had smoked his fill: "Here, take a pull out of that," said he, handing the pipe to my grandfather. He stretched back in his chair, stroking his mouth with his hand.

"On my soul, old man, I have passed through hard times since I was born, but do you know the place that killed me entirely? The red army of England!"

"Upon my word, I should say that is a bad place!" said my father.

"It is indeed," said the stranger, spitting. "A couple of years before the war with the Boers I was so vexed with the world that I left America and went to England. And what did I do there but enlist in the red army though I soon wished I had not."

"Ah, wisdom comes after action," said my grandfather.

"True," said the stranger; "for wherever the yellow devil

may be it is there he was surely. After three weeks of drilling I swear by the book my bones were sore from my little toe to the roots of my hair!"

"Upon my word I often heard people saying the same," said my grandfather.

"Oh, my sorrow, it is I who know it. If you did anything wrong there was nothing for it but a beating without pity or remorse."

"I suppose so, my son."

"But, by God, I thought of a shift—to take my half-pound of soap and swallow every bit of it until I was as sick as a dog. The doctor came and ordered me to the hospital."

"No wonder!" said my father with a laugh.

"I suppose you were not in danger of death?" said my grandfather.

"Not at all, my son. Well, off I went, glad to have that much peace, but, I tell you, as soon as I would begin to recover I was to go back again at once. For two days I lay stretched on my back and while I was there I became acquainted with an old man who was stretched in the bed next to my own. Like any two who became acquainted in a strange place, we had great confiding in each other so that we had a long talk every day together on the ways of the world. In the end I told my own affair to the old fellow, and he gave a fine, mirthful laugh when he knew all."

"He would indeed," said my father.

"'Faith,' said he as soon as he had stopped laughing, 'dirty Dónal is a brother to tattered Tigue!'

"'Why do you say that?' said I.

"'Because I myself spent a bit of my life in that army and I had the trouble at the world trying to get out of it.'

"'Musha, what shift did you think of to be rid of them?'

"'If the shift I thought of will do you any good I will do my best to help you, for I know your affliction well and so I have great pity for you.'"

"Upon my word," said my grandfather, "he was a nice, good-natured man."

"It seems so, indeed," said my father.

"Well," continued the stranger, "the old man gave me his advice. 'When I was like you,' said he, 'I was vexed and tormented with the world, and my curse on drink—that was the cause of it.' 'Ah, you are not the only one drink made a slave of,' said I. 'I know it,' said he. 'Anyway I enlisted in the red army like yourself and I need not tell you the way it is with the rookie at first. There was a rub here and a rub there and, by God, in the end I would rather have been drowned. I got the advice of an old soldier to eat the soap and I ate it. But as soon as I was well they took me in again the way I was as bad as ever. So, do you know, Dónal, what was the shift I planned but to let on I was as deaf as a stone and gone queer in the head and, faith, they had to let me go in the end. But if you play the same trick have no fear but they will give you enough to do. They will try this on you and they will try that on you. But don't yield. By your ear, don't yield.'"

"Faith," said my father, "it was a great shift."

"It was indeed," said my grandfather.

"Well, three days after that I left the hospital and the first morning I went out drilling I put a big hump on my back and every queer look on myself. 'Straighten your back!' shouted the officer angrily, but I took no notice. Arra, my love among friends, at that he made at me with the butt of his gun in the small of my back and took a good shake out of my limbs. I leapt up as if he had taken me by surprise. 'I beg pardon, sir,' said I, 'I did not hear you!' 'What's that you say?' said he, scowling."

"How would it have been with you then," interrupted my grandfather, "if you had gone up to him nicely and struck him on the bridge of the nose?"

"Mo léir, if I had done that they would have torn me to pieces, my son."

"By God, I would have done it," said my grandfather with an impudent look on his face.

"Upon my word you wouldn't," said my father; "that's only fireside talk, my boy."

"Well, I straightened myself up until the officer gave another command. ''Shun!' he cried, but I did not stir. Over he came, looking like the devil, God forgive me for saying it. 'What ails you?' said he. Not a word out of me. 'What ails you?' he shouted, giving me a push. I jumped. 'I am deaf, sir,' said I. He pulled me out of the ranks. Soon he brought along another officer taller than himself. 'What's the matter with you?' I did not answer. The two officers stood talking. Then a man came up behind my back and another before my face. But I had learnt my lesson well from the old soldier and knew what was to come. The man behind fired a shot over my head but I remained as firm as a post."

"By God, you made a great stand," said my father.

"They kept me there for a couple of days trying every trick on me. I cannot help laughing when I think of the other dodge they tried. I was told one day to go for a walk. I went out through a narrow passage where on either side were storehouses. But, if so, I knew it was not for my good they gave me leave to go walking. What happened then, astór, but some of the officers were inside the houses and now and again one of them would throw out a penny to see if I would turn for it. I walked on and the money ringing in my ears after me, but that is all the heed I gave to it. To make a long story short, they had to let me go in the end, and that is how I got out of the red army."

"Musha, may you be better a year from today,"[1] said my grandfather, looking at the clock. "How pleasantly you have shortened the night for us!"

"Ah, there is no limit to the man who travels," said my father.

---

1. A blessing.

"It is true," said I, making my voice heard as well as the others.

The next morning as soon as I lifted the cloth from the window, the sunbeams poured in, dazzling my eyes. I was not long looking out when school came into my thoughts and scattered the fairness of the morning for me. Oh, Lord, said I to myself, isn't it quick and care-free I would go into the red army rather than to school!

When I was washed and cleaned I sat down to breakfast. My grandfather was already there, the stranger beside him.

"Faith, Maurice, there is nothing better you could do today," said my grandfather, "than to take the ass and bring home a load of turf from the mountain."

My heart rose to my mouth with delight. "I will do so," said I, my lips trembling with happiness.

I did not eat half my fill but went out and west to the Sandhills leaping like a goat. Back at the gardens of the Storm I met Shaun Fada with his two asses.

"I wonder, Shaun, did you see my ass back towards the Sandhills?"

He stopped and looked at me, then out over the Sound. "My soul from the devil, I saw him with the tide through the Sound to the north and a sea-gull on his back."

"Long sea-gull on yourself," said I, going west to the Sandhills where I found my ass back on the Point of Seal Cove. I leapt on his back and we were not long, I and my little black ass, when we came up with Shaun through the Great Glen to the east.

"Faith, you have found him since," said he, taking an echo out of the glen.

"Get out of my way," I shouted, my ass at full gallop, I lashing away at him as we overtook Shaun.

"The devil take you!" he cried, and I going past him like the wind, "what is the haste or do you want to kill all before you on the road?"

I did not answer him but gave another lash to the ass and away I went in delight.

When I had him harnessed I went into the house to get my stick. "Maybe you would like to see the hill of the Island?" said I to the stranger.

"Faith, it is not well for me to stay in the house," said he, getting up.

We went up the Causeway. The village children were on their way to school, Tomás Owen Vaun among them, his bag of books under his arm. When I saw how glum he looked I smiled.

"It is fine for you to be going into the hill," said he, but that was all he said for he was shy before the stranger.

"May the day prosper with you, Tomás," giving a lash to the ass and departing up the road.

"Is that Iveragh?" said the stranger, pointing his finger to the south.

"It is."

"On my soul it is a fine wide prospect."

"Oh, it is a great sight when the sky does be clear."

We went on as far as Fearee-a-Dúna. There we sat down.

"What is the name of that great rock in the north-west?"

"The Teeracht, where the lighthouse is."

"Is that the Teeracht now? It is a long time since I heard a man in New York singing a song about it and when he had finished he cried out, 'My thousand sorrows,' said he, 'that I am not near it today.'"

"It seems he knew it well."

"He did indeed. Wait now, I think I remember it, the verse I got from him that day." And the stranger began to sing:

"On a fine fair day and I plying the sea to the west
I came upon the Teeracht far out into the bay,
Where was music of birds flying over the green grass
And little fish in hundreds frolicking in the nets.

"I think it is a verse from 'The Little Heather Hill.' From the day I heard it, it remained in my memory."

"I understand that, for it is very beautiful and especially to hear it in a foreign land from a man of your own race."

"The devil a lie you have spoken," said he, drawing out his pipe and lighting it.

I was delighted to see the pipe for I was very fond of smoking now, as much as any old man. And so I began a great talk—not a hill or mountain, cove or cliff, rock or strand did I leave without giving its name to him, hoping he would give me a smoke. When he heard the name "Bay of Dingle," he gave a laugh. "Musha," said he, "do you know what happened to me after leaving the red army? It is the Bay of Dingle put me in mind of it. When I came home I had not a house nor a dwelling but a night here and a night there and not a ha'penny in my pocket."

"It was very hard on you," said I, my eye on the pipe.

"Well, I came into Dingle one market day and I paid a visit to the quay. There was a steamboat stretched alongside and the devil if the captain wasn't short of a man. 'Is there any man there,' said he, 'would work his passage to England?' I cocked my ears and walked towards him. 'I will.' 'Very well. Come aboard now, for the boat is due to leave.'

"The work I had to do was to keep up the coal in the boiler, and that place was the devil itself for heat. Every half-hour I had to throw off my shoes to let the sweat out of them."

"Oh, Lord, and how long would you be at the task?"

"Four hours at a stretch."

"Och, it was too long," said I, looking again at the pipe. It was out and he seemed to have no inclination to give me a smoke. So I was not too well satisfied. I tried to ask him for it, but I had not the courage. At last I thought of a plan. I took out of my pocket an old clay pipe and struck it on my palm. "Faith," said I, feeling in my pocket, "I have forgotten my tobacco. I must have left it at home." (I had no such thing at home, but I wanted to show the stranger that I was fond of a smoke.)

"Oh, don't have that to say, my boy, there is plenty of it here," and he drew out a big lump of it. "Help yourself to that."

"Thank you," said I, as pleased as a duke. "Well, go on with your story."

"I promise you," he continued, "when I had made my way across and set my feet on English soil, I left the ship and the captain and took myself off. I spent a couple of days there, loitering. The intention I had was to escape to America in one of the liners from Liverpool.

"One evening as I was rambling along the quay and I in old rags the way nobody would notice me, I saw three liners alongside ready to leave. One thing only was troubling me—I did not know where they were going and I did not like to creep into any of them for fear it was not to America she would go. I spoke to a man who was standing near, without letting anything on, you understand?"

"I understand well," said I with a dog's life at the pipe.[2]

"I spoke to him nice and gently. 'Those are three fine ships,' said I.

" 'They are good ships without a doubt,' said he, looking at me keenly.

" 'I suppose they are all going to America?'

" 'They are not, only the middle one.'

" 'I suppose she will be leaving at once?' said I, putting the question nice and innocently.

" 'She is due to go at six in the morning.'

"Well, when I had got all my information I slipped aside, and when night came I slid down on the quay again, a bag of bread under my arm and I like a mouse ready to creep aboard. I kept an eye on every nook and corner till at last I got an opportunity to slip on board unknown to the sailors."

2. *I.e.* enjoying himself.

"And in what part of the ship did you hide?"

"Arra, man, I went aforeships into a big dirty pipe. But I did not mind so long as I would get across. Well, I was in there, without sight of day or night, but it did not matter. Everything went well till I came to the end of my provisions. It was then I lost heart."

"It was no wonder for you."

"It was not," said he with a shake of the head, filling his pipe again. "Well, that was where the trouble was, hunger coming over me and not a bite to be had. I lost patience. I had to find something or be starved to death. So I was thinking and reflecting, and the end of it was that I remembered the boats above to be full of biscuits as was usual. So it was my intention to creep up at nightfall and get into one of them for I would never be seen inside, since those boats do be always covered in canvas.

"When night came I rose up cautiously and looked around. All was still save only the whistling of the pulleys and the sound of the waves alongside the ship. I crept out sideways and stood up, and, if so," said he, striking his palms on his knees, "I could scarcely stand upright on my feet, my legs were so weak beneath me. There was no one alive on deck at the time and I was from step to step until I went up into one of the boats. I raised the canvas and crept in and sat down comfortably between two thwarts. But the devil take it, Maurice," said he, striking his hand on my shoulder and making me jump, "when I opened the box it was empty!"

"Och, God be with us, wasn't that bad luck for you!"

"Don't speak of it, and God send that such a misfortune may never overtake me again. It was all one to me then whether I lived or died. I was spent with the hunger and making no headway."

"Were you far from land at that time?"

"Arra, man, wasn't she stretched alongside the quays of New York the following morning?"

"Oh, man dear," said I, smoking away to my heart's content.

"Well, now was my trouble how to get ashore. It was now my heart was a-flutter with fear and a shiver going through my body when I heard the sailors talking and walking round and thinking every minute they would lift the cover from the boat. That day seemed a year to me, and what wonder with ne'er a bit nor a sup had gone into my guts for two days before! Night came at last. I had some knowledge of the officers' duties, so I knew there do be five minutes with no one at all on the deck. But what good was that to me when I was not carrying the time? So all I could do was to make a guess and there's no doubt but it was hard for me. Well, at about two o'clock in the morning I fancied the time had come, for it is then they do take a rest. Carefully I lifted the cover and put out my head. I glanced round. No one alive was to be seen, but lights in plenty and a fine view of the quay. I said to myself that it was the time of the rest surely. I arose and put out a foot very carefully, for it was nailed boots I had on. When I was out of the boat I did not leave an inch of the deck without examining it minutely. Not a soul nor a sinner was to be seen. But the worst of it was there was an iron staircase down to the lower deck and I had to get down that staircase however I managed it. Twelve rungs it had, and you would need to be strong, agile and nimble to climb down them."

"I suppose so," said I, "and you, yourself, were not so at that time."

"You may say so," said he, shaking his head. "Well, said I to myself, God guide me aright, will I make the attempt? My courage came to me then and I moved to the head of the stairs. I started down from rung to rung. But when I had passed the seventh, the devil if I didn't slip and fall down in a heap on the deck and take a ringing echo out of the ship!"

"Och, man, wasn't that a great pity, and wasn't it strange you didn't think of taking off your nailed boots?"

"It is true," said he pitifully, "but wisdom comes after action. Well, I tried to get up, but I was too weak, and the flutter of the world was on me for fear I would be seen.

"I was not long there when I heard the walk of shoes towards me. I knew I was caught. God save my soul, said I. The words were not out of my mouth when the officer was standing before me. He looked at me, caught me by the shoulder. 'What brought you here?' said he angrily. 'Musha, I am one of the sailors.' 'And what brought you here?' said he again. 'Musha, I was seized with sickness in bed and I came up on deck to take the air.'

"He stopped for a while, looking at me keenly, and my heart leaping with the hope that he would leave me. At last: 'Come along,' said he.

"He brought me out into the light and, my sorrow, it was easy for him then to see what sort I was. I was foul and dirty and my clothes all awry. He turned me this way and that. 'I guess you are a stowaway. Come on!'"

"Oh, man, wasn't it a thousand pities and you alongside the quays of New York?"

"Oh, you don't know half, since you were not in my shoes," said he, his tears falling.

"It is true, and you in the place where your heart was."

"Isn't it that which was killing me entirely, but there was no help for it. They kept me in prison for twelve days until the ship was due to leave again. When she returned to England they let me go and I am wandering here and there ever since."

"Long life to you," said I, "you have shortened the morning well. You can wait here now till I return. That is my heap of turf to the west," said I, pointing towards it.

It did not take me long to fill the load. When I came back the stranger was stretched his full length on the grass.

"Isn't it fine and healthy air on the top of this hill?"

"You may well say so."

We reached home very hungry the way every morsel went to our satisfaction.

Fifteen

THE LOBSTER SEASON

As I have said already, I had let school drop for some time on account of the wreck. I was growing up now without a care or a trouble in the world. I had no home lessons at night to sicken me, nor did I spend Sunday night waiting fearfully for Monday morning. I was free from the oppression of the master.

In the month of May 1919 my father came to me. "I wonder, Maurice, would you be loath to do a lobster season with us this year?"

"Indeed I would not," I cried eagerly.

He laughed, a laugh which seemed as if he were saying in his heart, Upon my word, you will be loath yet, my lad.

How happy I was now, a grown man fishing lobsters with my father! I longed for the month of June, to be out on the sea. Soon we began making the pots out in the booly, stripped to the shirt, working away at them while my grandfather sat on the green grass putting tops on the twigs for us.

"I dare say, daddo," said I, "it is many a day since you made your first pot."

"It must be near twoscore years ago now."

"Is that all?" said I in surprise.

"That's all indeed, for we hadn't the knowledge before then."

"How did you get the knowledge?"

"I will tell you," said he, throwing aside the twig he had finished topping.

"It was some Englishmen who came to Beg-inish," and he looked out to Beg-inish as he spoke. "They had a big boat and they used to spend the week there fishing. That is why the old ruin is to be seen on the island still. Well, Maurice, one day we were going out to Mass—the King, Shaun Fada, and I—and we were rowing at our ease past Beg-inish to the north when my oar caught in a rope. 'Draw it in,' said Shaun, 'to see what is the meaning of it at all.' I began drawing it up, and faith, on every fathom of it was a cork. I thought that very strange and before long I felt a big weight on the rope. I was drawing and drawing till I had it up to the gun-wale. What was it but a pot with a big red crayfish inside, though none of us knew what a crayfish was at the time.

"'My heart from the devil,' cried Shaun Fada, 'it is the devil himself is in it. Throw it out quickly!'

"'Don't throw it out,' said the King, 'but we will take it to the English people for I dare say this is the fish they are hunting for, whatever it may be.'

"Well, the trouble now was to get it out of the pot, for whenever I put in my hand to catch hold of it, it would give a leap and make a great clatter inside.

"'Your soul to the devil,' shouted Shaun again, 'throw it out, pot and all, for it is the old fellow surely that's in it.'

"'Don't throw it out,' said the King.

"I was playing it, ever and ever, till at last I got it out and now it was crawling backwards and clattering about in the curragh. It crawled under Shaun's feet. 'My heart and body from the devil,' said he with another shout, 'it will do harm,' and he leapt up from the thwart.

"'Take it easy,' said the King, 'it won't kill you.'

" 'Musha, upon my soul you don't know what it would do with the devilish haste it is in. Don't ye see all the spikes and horns on it?'

" 'Take it easy,' said the King again, 'till we row in to Beg-inish and then we will learn what it is.'

"We went in and two of the Englishmen were before us on the shingle. They greeted us and we greeted them, one of them with Irish as fine and fluent as our own. 'Where did you get the crayfish?' said he.

" 'Faith,' said Shaun Fada, 'that's a name we never heard before, my good sir.'

"We told them how we found it and the wonder we were making of the pots, and we spent the day in their company till in the end they told us how to make them and the people of the Island are fishing lobster ever since."

"Faith, daddo, I never heard you tell that before."

"That is how it happened," said he, taking up another twig.

When June came, it was very fine. It would gladden your heart to look out to sea, the sea-raven standing on the rock with his wings outspread, the ring-plover and sea-pie foraging among the stones, the sea-gulls picking the limpets, the limpet itself relaxing its grip and the periwinkle the same, the crab and the rock-pool trout coming out of their holes in the stillness of the sea to take a draught of the sweet-smelling air. So that it was no wonder for the sinner to feel a happiness of heart as he travelled the road.

When we had the pots ready we turned our faces west to Inish-na-Bró—my father, my uncle, and myself. It was a great change of life for me, doing a man's hunting now. We laid a pot in every crack in the rocks along the north coast of Inish-na-Bró. It was a wild backward place, great dizzy cliffs above my head in which hundreds and thousands of birds were nesting, the guillemot, whippeen, common puffin, red puffin, black-backed gull, petrel, sea-raven, breeding together in the wild cliffs; seals in couples here and there sunning themselves on the rocks, each bird with its own cry and the seals with their moan, a dead calm on the sea but for the little ripples moving in and making a glug-glag up through the crevices of the rocks.

I was sitting in the middle of the curragh, taking heed of all around me, as happy as any mother's son. Now and then I saw a puffin coming in from the sea with a bundle of sprats across its bill, and I began to reflect on the life of the birds, what great wisdom they have to provide for their young. What was the difference between the nature of man, the nature of the birds and of the seals? We were fishing lobster to nourish ourselves, the puffin providing for its chick, and the seal stretched out on the rock above after its labours. How strange is the way of the world!

When we had the pots laid in the sea, we went ashore on the island. It was a delight to be in it, the stones ready to burst with the heat, clumps of thrift on every inch of the ground, and bright flowers blooming. I sat down, the sea-birds settled round me, many more flying through the air with a great clamour as they came in from the sea, a haze floating across each hill and hanging at the foot of every cliff, a path of gold stretching out before me as far as Bray Head and every ripple glistening in the sunshine.

I got up and looked round. My father and uncle were nowhere to be seen. I turned my face straight north through the White Furrow. Rabbits fled before me on every side. I went to the top of Sailors' Strand, hundreds of feet high. I saw the birds nesting in the black cliff, others coming towards me from the sea. It seemed as if they were playing tricks on me. They would make straight towards me, then curve out to sea, then, by the same curve, in again. I looked down at the shore far below and saw the seals stretched out on every rocky ledge. I stayed a while watching and listening to the cries of the birds, the moaning of the seals, and the murmur of the waves. Then I turned up towards the Gaps, the highest hill in the island, soft clumps of thrift under my feet, and a wide open view southward to Iveragh and the Skelligs, where the gannet nests, and so eastward to the Bay of Dingle and Kerry Head. I was sitting on a fine soft clump of thrift, sinking right back into it, thinking and ever thinking of the creation of the world, when I heard a whistle. I raised my head and looked round, but no one was to be seen. Then I glanced far down to the landing-place where we had moored the curragh and saw my father, cap in hand, beckoning me. They were going out to draw the pots. I ran down the slope of the hillside, leaping from clump to clump. Half-way down I got a start, for I heard a sharp scream under my feet. I had leapt on the back of a rabbit which had been sitting on its haunches at the mouth of its burrow. I took it up, but the life was crushed out of it. I ran on, very proud to have caught a rabbit without dog or trap, a thing Cos-fé-Chrios[1] could not have done in his prime. I made no stop nor stay till I reached the landing-place.

We turned west through the Narrow Sound. Not a stir of swell on the rocks, a heron standing on the shore before me with his neck straight out as if watching a fish, a ring-plover and a sea-pie by his side; and you would think the heron was a giant beside them but it's little fear they had of him. We were drawing the pots one after another till we had drawn the last and had a nice load of lobsters after the day.

I had now spent a month on the sea, as happy as a prince returning home in the evening and setting out with the chirp of the sparrow. But one day when we were out as usual, I noticed a difference. The fine view was not to be seen, there was no gladness in my heart, the birds were not singing nor the seal sunning himself on the ledge, no heron, ring-plover, nor sea-pie was at the water's edge picking the limpets, no path of gold in the Bay of Dingle nor ripples glittering in the sunshine, no sultry haze in the bosom of the hills, no rabbits to be seem seated with ears cocked on the clumps of thrift. A gale was blowing from the south, and, where the water lapped

---

1. Foot-under-Girdle. Name of a legendary hero who was so swift a runner that with one foot tucked under his girdle he could out-race all other men.

before, the waves were now hurling themselves with a roar against the rocks, not a bird's cry to be heard but all of them cowering in their holes, big clouds sweeping across the sky ready to burst with the weight of the rain, the wind howling through the coves, the bright flowers above me twisted together in the storm, and no delight in my heart but cold and distress.

"I think the day means ill," said my father, "and we had better make for home."

We rowed straight out to Skellit Head to get above the wind in order to raise the sail. I was in the middle, holding the jib-sheet, jets of foam flying aboard, the sea heaving out from her bows, the waves thundering around us, a white path of foam behind, the pulley at the masthead whistling in the wind, and the rain falling heavily. Oh, Lord, how she darted through that sea! As each squall caught her, she heeled over so far that she shipped a great flood of foam. I was anything but easy in my mind now, the water leaping into the air and the storm blowing, ever and ever, till we came in to the quay.

It is little desire I had to be telling my grandfather of the beauty of the place that night.

"Well, Mirrisheen, you have had your first day of the struggle of the world."

"I think, daddo, there is nothing so bad as fishing."

"You may be sure of it, my bright love."

Sixteen

———⟫●⟪———

MATCHMAKING

IT is many a rumour and old wives' tale does be going around in the run of Lent, by fireside, in lane, in field, on strand and hill-top. You would see paying visits from house to house old women you would never see at any other time of the year. Many will agree with me in this, for I have not spoken without authority. I have seen them myself, suffering from rheumatics throughout the year, but as sure as there is a cross on the ass they would stretch out their old bones at the beginning of Lent and go from house to house in quest of news, seat themselves beside the fire, hand round the old clay pipe, and gossip.

Walking the road, you would see them in twos and threes sitting on their haunches here and there talking of this boy's match and that girl's match, not one of them true. But that did not matter. They would believe the leprechauns themselves for the happiness of mind it gives them to be talking in such a way.

One fine day in Lent I wandered west to the house of old Nell. She was sitting alone in the corner with her pipe in her mouth.

"God save all here," said I, putting my head through the door.

"A blessing from God on you, bright love," said she. "Sit up to the fire; the day is a little bit cold."

I sat on the fireside chair which was well polished with age.

"Musha, is there any news from outside?"

"There's not, musha, Nell, unless you have any yourself."

"Yé, my sorrow and the sins of my life, I don't know where would I get news sitting here from day to day."

"But the old women who come in to you have great mouths on them for gossip, Nell."

"Musha, it is little heed I give to them. It is the tobacco mostly that brings them here, and they do be inclined to talk when they get it."

"But I dare say if they didn't get the tobacco they would be no good."

"Ah, bad luck to them, if they had anything better to do it is not to me they would come."

"Musha, Nell, company is a fine thing, you know."

"Oh, I agree," said she, pulling back the shawl which was falling over her eyes and taking up the tongs to poke the fire. "But let us throw the old women aside. Did you hear of anyone going to marry?"

"The devil I did, Nell."

"What about Shaun-na-Tay?" said she, lowering her voice as if afraid of being overheard. "Isn't it time for that lad to settle himself?"

"Indeed his teeth are well worn by now."

Maura O'Dála came in. "God save all here," said she.

"God and Mary save you," said Nell, settling herself in her corner with a smile as if she knew that Maura would have plenty of gossip. Maura sat on her heels beside Nell, who was not long handing her the pipe, to set her talking.

"Well, Maura, I suppose you didn't hear any news on your wanderings?"

Maura did not answer at once for she was nearly being choked with all the smoke she was getting out of the pipe.

"Faith," said she at last, looking into the middle of the fire, "a match has been made since last night for the man from the mainland."

"Musha, what match is that?" said Nell, shaking herself and drawing in her skirt round her feet.

"Shaun Fitzgerald," said Maura, nodding at Nell.

"Musha, dear God bless the souls of your dead," said Nell, stretching her back and drawing a sigh.

"Indeed it has been settled," said Maura, spitting into the fire.

"Musha, who is the girl who has the good fortune?" said Nell slowly and softly.

"Shevaun Liam, upon my word," said Maura with another puff at the pipe.

"Musha, the blessing of God with you," said Nell, laying her hand on Maura's shoulder. "And do you think it is true?" she asked, taking the pipe from her.

"It's as true as you are sitting there," said Maura.

Nell began to fill the pipe again.

"Wait till I tell you," said Maura, passing her hand through her hair and settling herself for talk. "About one o'clock last night, when we were all asleep . . ."

"Just so, faith!" said Nell, making ready to listen.

"There came a knock at the door. Tigue got up in the bed. 'Who's there,' he cried. 'I am,' answered the voice. Tigue got out and opened the door. Who was it but Shaun Fitzgerald and Maurice Owen Vaun! They came inside and I pricked up my ears."

"No doubt," said Nell, putting a live ash in the pipe.

Maura turned to me. "I dare say you have heard this?" said she.

"I have not, indeed."

"Go on," said Nell.

"Well, I stayed there sitting on my heels, pierced with the

cold and listening intently. I thought at once there must be a match on hand."

"Especially at the time of year," said Nell.

"Well, my dear," said Maura with a cough to sharpen her voice, "before long I heard the cork taken out of a bottle and a glass being filled for Tigue. Then Maurice Owen Vaun came down to the door of the room. 'Are you asleep, Maura?' said he. 'I am not, Maurice.' 'Come up to the hearth, so.' 'Arra, what's going on?' said I. 'Come up,' said he.

"I put on my clothes and went up.

"'A blessing from God on ye,' said I.

"'God and Mary save you,' said they all together.

"I sat on the stool by the fire. 'Musha, if there was a young girl in this house,' said I, 'I would say there was a match being made.'

"'There is, too,' said Maurice.

"'Maybe it's Shaun?'

"'He is thinking of it.'

"'Musha, may it prosper with him, so,' said I.

"A glass was poured out for me. I refused it, but Maurice kept on pressing me until at last I had to drink half it."

"Ah, Maurice is good at it," said Nell, pulling at the pipe.

"No doubt of it," said Maura, taking a box of snuff from her pocket, putting it under her nose and then passing it on to Nell.

Maura began to sneeze.

"By God, Nell,' said I, "if Maura goes on that way, we'll have to postpone the story."

"Musha," said she, looking at me with a laugh, "we would like nothing better than for her to spend the day with it."

"Go ahead, Maura," said I.

"Bad cess to it for snuff," said Maura, "it has me suffocated. Well, I have no need to make a long story of it. When I had drunk the half-glass, Maurice spoke to me: 'Would you be loath, Maura, to go with us to the house of Liam Peg in order to make the match, for I think you are a good hand at it?'

"'Musha, Maurice, I wouldn't refuse you if you think I can do any good.'

"They all agreed I must accompany them and we went down the lane to the house of Liam Peg.

"I knocked on the window.

"'Who's there?' called Bridget within.

"'Open, Bridget,' said I.

"'Arra, is that you, Maura? There must be some great haste on you,' said she.

"'Musha, there is not then, but I am perished with the cold.'

"'Oh, musha, long cold on you, wouldn't you give me time to put on my old rags?'

"After a while she opened the door.

"'Great God of Virtues,' cried Bridget when she saw the three men with me, 'what is the matter?'

"I winked my eye at her," said Maura with a nod at Nell, "and she understood at once what was going on.

"She gave each of us a chair and put down a big red fire, smiling to herself as she bustled around.

"'Where is Liam, Bridget?' said Maurice Owen Vaun; 'he must be sleeping like a corncake.'

"'Musha, he is always so,' said Bridget, going up to the room to wake him.

"Well now, Nell," said Maura, tapping her on the knee and glancing across at me, "the man who is seeking a woman does be always in a terrible fright."

"Musha there's no doubt of it," said Nell, clapping her hands and laughing.

"I wonder, Nell," said I, "does the woman be the same?"

"The same!" said she with a frown. "She does be far and away worse than the man. Do you know the night my own match was made, I would rather have been drowned in the mouth of the White Strand."

"Ha, ha," said Maura, "don't believe her, she was in a flutter of delight that night the same as myself."

"I have no doubt of it, Maura," said I.

"Well, no more of that; but, anyway, Liam came up from the room. 'A blessing from God on ye,' said he in his soft quiet way, 'God and Mary save you,' said Maurice Owen Vaun, getting up, and he had a good drop taken by that time."

"It is his father's nature in him," said Nell.

"And it's he is the fine contented man when he has it taken," said I.

"Ah, you may say so, indeed."

"Before long Maurice opened the bottle. He poured out a glass for Bridget. She drank it sweetly. Then he filled one for Liam and another for me and I drank the half of it.

"'Oh, musha, hoarseness on you,' cried Maurice. 'Why wouldn't you drink it off?'

"'Musha, dear God bless the souls of your dead, I am not able,' said I, handing it to Bridget, and she swallowed it tastily. Then he filled another for Shaun Fitzgerald.

"'Och,' said Shaun, 'I am very sorry I am not able to drink it for I don't drink at all.'"

"Oh, musha," cried Nell with a burst of laughter, "that good-for-nothing who would drink the sup from the saddle!"

"Musha, you took the word out of my mouth," said Maura, "but if you had seen him last night you would think by the pious look on him he was the soberest man on the earth, sitting without a word, though his eyes were starting out of his head at it."

"Oh, Lord!" said Nell, taking out the pipe again and lighting it from the fire.

"Well, in the far end of the night, everyone was pretty merry, the soft word and the hard word coming together. Before long Bridget put a whisper in my ear: 'Musha, Maura, is it Shevaun that Shaun wants?'

"'It is she,' said I, 'and if so she will have a man.'

"'Faith,' said Bridget, 'I wouldn't gainsay you. It is said he has a coffer full of money.'

"'Be sure of it, and there's another thing, Bridget. Suppose Shevaun went to America. Maybe you would never see her

again, and neither you nor she would know what sort of
ragged rascal she might come across over there, for I heard
Maura Pats who came home the other day saying that you
wouldn't know what sort the fellow was till you had married
him, and that it's then the women find themselves in the
slough of adversity.'

"'Oh I believe you well, Maura,' said she. 'And another
thing, wouldn't it be nice to have your daughter married at
your own threshold?'

"'Ah, you may say so, Bridget,' said I."

"I am thinking," said Nell, "that you had her warmed by
that time."

"I had," said Maura, "and so I said to myself, if Liam were
as warmed as she, Shaun would have the victory. The four of
them were in the corner, and whatever they were talking of,
they stopped suddenly and so did we. Maurice got up and,
taking the bottle, made another round with it.

"'Well,' said he, sitting on the chair and taking Liam by the
hand, 'may God preserve your throat and let you strike up
"The Red Man's Wife"!'

"'My sorrow for the day!' said Liam, 'that I can no longer
sing it as I could twenty years ago, Maurice.'

"'Lift up your heart, man,' said Bridget, 'and let the
entertainment flow.'

"Liam coughed once or twice to clear his throat. Then he
struck up 'The Red Man's Wife,' and upon my soul, Nell, you
would go anywhere to listen to him."

"If he had not lost the voice he had once he must have been
a great wonder."

"Well, astór, we sat without a word listening to the song,
and there's no doubt but he sang it well."

"Above all," said Nell, "in the stillness of the night."

"It is true for you, Nell," said I, "for, for my own part, I
know nothing so delightful, as to listen to a good singer in the
dead of night."

"You are right," said she; "it would gladden your heart."

"And indeed," said Maura, "when he had sung the song, there was a coat of sweat on him."

"Likely enough, for he is very old now."

"He is, and what's more," said I, "he is weak."

"Maurice Owen Vaun spoke to him then. 'Musha, faith,' said he, 'it's a fine sweet voice you have still.'

"'Yé, musha, I'm not half as good as I was,' said Liam, 'except for the little drop I have taken which gave me help and courage.'

"'Well, what about yourself now, Bridget?' said Maurice.

"'Yé, don't mind a cock like me,' said she; 'it would be far better for ye to be listening to the gander than to give ear to me.'

"'Ah, come now, give us "The Pretty Milkmaid."'

"He did not have to speak another word before she struck up the song."

"Oh, musha, bad cess to her!" cried Nell, "herself and her goat's throat!"

Maura and I burst into laughter.

"Indeed, by the book, you are right entirely, Nell," said I.

"Well," said Maura, "when Bridget had sung her song, and indeed it seemed long to us, Maurice made another round with the bottle, and faith, if so, everyone was well warmed by now.

"Maurice got up. 'Well now, Bridget and Liam,' said he, 'I have always had a great affection for the two of you, and so I would greatly like you both to be contented and comfortable. Do you see that man?' (pointing a finger at Shaun Fitzgerald). 'There's a man as mannerly, well-bred, and steady as any there is in the village.'

"'No doubt of it,' said Liam.

"'And don't you think it is a good match he would make for Shevaun?' said he.

"Well, Nell, I looked across at Shaun, and he was so bashful you would think he was an angel. He would look first at Liam and then at Bridget."

"I dare say it was fear that he would get a refusal," said Nell with a laugh.

"Well," said Maura, "Liam began to cough and gave a glance at Bridget. Bridget was smiling and poor Shaun in a cold sweat with anxiety. Then Liam stirred in his chair and gave another glance at Bridget.

"'By the book, Liam,' said Bridget, 'it is a good chance for Shevaun.'

"'No doubt of it,' said he. 'He has plenty of land and the best of land, hundreds of sheep on the hills, to say nothing of all the money he has saved.'

"'And, Liam, where would she get a man as good?' said Maurice Owen Vaun.

"Liam gets up from his chair. 'Give me your hand, Shaun,' says he. Shaun stretches out his hand. 'I have always had respect for you, Shaun,' says he, still holding his hand, 'for your manners and good breeding, and, if so, Shaun, it is your father's nature in you. And I promise you, as far as my own word goes, I am satisfied to let you have Shevaun and very glad to have you for a son-in-law. What about you, Bridget?' says he.

"'The very same word!' cried Bridget, jumping up and going across to Shaun and taking his hand. 'Upon my soul, Shaun, there is not a man from the eastern world to the western world who would get her but yourself alone.'"

"Well, well, faith,' said Nell, "that must have encouraged him."

"Ah, you may say so," said Maura.

Nell handed me a lump of tobacco to cut and to fill the pipe. That gladdened my heart, for I was as fond of it as anyone. I began cutting away, and when I got on her blind side I cut a good pipeful and slipped it into my pocket. Then I filled up the pipe and handed it back to her.

"Put a spark in it and take a smoke yourself," said she. "Well, Maura, what about Shevaun?"

"The devil if Bridget did not go down and call her and

before long she came up from the room with a sleepy look on her.

"'A blessing from God on ye,' said she.

"'God and Mary save you,' said we all together.

"I looked at Shaun and I tell you, Nell, a blush came into his face and a start into his eyes."

"I am sure of it when he saw the fair maid standing in the doorway, and I would not say but he had loved her always."

"Oh, I have no doubt but he had loved her secretly and, do you know, the same blush was in her face."

"I dare say," said I, "she knew before she came up from the room that the match was made."

"Yé, mo léir, she did, my son. She sat down beside Shaun, astór, and it is they were the comfortable, smiling pair."

"'Don't you think the two will do well together?' whispered Bridget in my ear.

"'I do indeed.'

"Well, half an hour after that everything was settled."

"I wonder," said Nell, "what was the dowry he got with her?"

"Oh, don't ask me, my dear, but I heard today he got fourscore."

"Enough for him."

"On my oath, he was worth it. Don't you see the fine spacious lands he has, the finest and fruitfullest land from Dingle west?"

"Yé, not minding the land, wouldn't they live happily on all the sheep he has?"

I stood up.

"Is it going home you are?" said Nell.

"I am thinking of it."

"By God," said Maura, getting up too, "I left a loaf on the fire when I came out and it is likely burnt to a cinder by this time."

We gave a farewell and a blessing to old Nell and turned our faces homeward, Maura to the west and I to the east.

Seventeen

⟫⟫◆⟪⟪

THE WEDDING DAY

O<small>N</small> the following evening a curragh came in from
Dunquin with an invitation to the people of the Island to be
present at Ballyferriter next day, Shrove Tuesday, for the
marriage of Shaun Fitzgerald.

It was a fine evening. I was sitting on a rock overlooking the
sea. There was a light breeze from the east, frost on the
ground, hooded crows flying across the fields with a caw-caw,
thrushes, blackbirds, and starlings singing sweetly in the
meadows; and if you turned your eyes seaward, herring-gulls
and black-backed gulls diving into the water and a sea-raven
among them pursuing small fish. Out before me were Mount
Brandon, Mount Eagle, and the Macgillycuddy Reeks, clear of
all vapour and mist.

It was a lovely sight, praise on high to God who made
heaven and earth, and I fell thinking of all the happy days I had
spent in the view of those hills and recalled the words of my
grandfather: Twenty years a-growing, twenty years in bloom,
twenty years a-stooping, and twenty years declining. I looked
down over the cliff where a seal was moaning softly. I wonder,
said I to myself, are the same thoughts troubling you? Maybe

you are keening mournfully for your fair child which the sea-swell snatched from you out of your cave, or some such moan.

Night was falling. I walked up from the cliff's edge a little way and sat down. As I looked out again to Mount Eagle I saw a sickle of gold climbing up behind the hill. The moon was rising. She ascends very slowly and sheds a golden light over the shadowy glens. I seem to hear the meads and valleys utter a cry of joy as if to welcome her and she smiling down on them with a greeting to Corcagueeny. I seem to see before me, full of bright laughter, all the boys and girls who were with me when I was a child. I see them running down the lanes and hiding themselves—the game we used to play in the moonlight—and I hear old Paddy crying in the distance "Caught" . . . I arise and walk slowly towards the house.

When I came home, Maura and Eileen were busy ironing.

"Faith," said my grandfather, "you will have a great day in Ballyferriter tomorrow, for there will be a dead calm on the sea to judge by the look of the night."

I ate my supper and went off to the house of Shaun O'Shea, where the boys and girls used to gather together. They were there before me, talking of nothing but the wedding. I sat next to Mauraid Buckley, a handsome blue-eyed girl with curly black hair. I felt very happy. I could not understand it. It seemed to me that night that Mauraid was the loveliest girl in the Island. I would never have tired talking to her though we had often been together before and she had never pleased me so well.

"Mauraid," said I at last, "I am very happy entirely talking to you tonight."

A blush came into her face. "Why do you say that?" said she with her eyes on the ground.

"Because I love you, I suppose."

She did not answer me for a while.

"I love *you*, anyway, whether *you* are in earnest or only mocking me," said she at last.

My heart leapt for joy. How great is the power of the god of Love. He destroyed the city of Troy, the way thousands of men were slain for the sake of one woman, and so it is no wonder he found it easy that night to subdue me who was young and foolish. Every word that came from the mouth of Mauraid was as sweet to me as the song of the lark. How greatly I was deceived by Cupid!

"Are you going to the wedding tomorrow?"

"I am. Are you?"

"I am," said she, her eyes shining.

We stayed talking together till eleven o'clock and indeed I would have felt no sleep nor weariness if I had remained till morning.

After a while the man of the house, Shaun O'Shea, got up, shook his shoulders and opened the door.

"Off with you all now," said he, "it is time for you to be going to the white gable."

"Oh, musha, Shaun," said Michael Pad, "isn't it strange the sleep never left you? There should be no haste on the likes of you. Did you never hear it said: A man without wife or children a man without heed for anyone?"

"Faith," said he with a shrug, "you haven't found one yourself yet."

"If so, I have not walked the parishes yet in quest of her as you have done. Come home," said Michael.

We were up at six, Maura, Eileen, Shaun, and I. It was a beautiful morning, a streak of light across Cnoc-a-comma in the east and life coming into everything. The sheep which had been sitting in the furrow in the run of the night, arose and stretched itself. The folded leaf was opening. The hen which had hidden her head under her wings was crying gob-gob-gob to be let out into the fields. Bird, beast, and man were awaking to pay homage to the sun. A moment before not a sound was to be heard, but now the birds were singing, the cow, the sheep, and even man himself throwing up their snatches of song.

We were washed and cleaned and ready for the road, delight and gladness in our hearts, every minute seeming as long as an hour in our haste to go out to the wedding. How gay is youth, without a trouble or a care in the world, always full of fun and laughter! Even in the sight of two hens fighting a cause for merriment!

We went down to the landing-place. We had hardly reached the top of the cliff when the youths and maidens were coming down, laughing, from all directions to the quay. As I think of that morning I move back along the paths of thought. I see them now. I hear Red Shevaun bursting into laughter, the idle talk and the nonsense. . . . Alas, we are as far from each other today as is the star from Spain.

We put out the curraghs and rowed, stripped to the shirt, across the Sound till we were approaching Great Cliff in Dunquin. There must be some magic connected with the sea, it filled me with such delight that morning. It was low tide, without a stir in the water; red weed and wrack-weed lying still on the sand; rocks all around us warming their pates in the sun; barnacles and periwinkles loosening their hold on the stones and creeping around at their leisure; little groups of crabs coming out of their holes, a sea-raven and a diver standing on a reef with their wings outspread to seaward and their necks craned watching us.

The tide was too low to take the curragh up to the quay. Everyone was shouting at once what it was best to do. One suggested we should take off our shoes, wade ashore, and walk up. One agreed and twelve did not.

At last Shaun Tomás spoke out: "Don't you know what is best? Let us go up to Hurdle Cliff."

It is a calm, handy cove with a little shingle strand at the head. We jumped out, moored the curraghs and turned joyfully up into the mainland as is the wont of the Islander when he gets his liberty. Mauraid was along with me step by step up the road to the north and I did not know was I walking on air or earth with the delight that was in my heart.

When we reached Maum-na-Caroona I stopped and looked around. The Blasket was stretched straight west over the sea like a great ship cleaving the waves on both sides of her, the white houses packed together and smoke rising up from them, the little Blaskets around like a sow with her brood behind her.

"Faith, Mauraid," said I, "if you look into the matter, it's wonderful how we are torn out from the mainland, and I believe, if I spent three days out here, I would never go in again."

"I don't know in the world," said she, "but it is sorrow mostly that comes on me when I leave it."

"The day will come yet when that sorrow will be on you."

"Oh, whist, don't say it; how do you know I won't marry in it?"

"That is a thing you will never do, Mauraid, for the times are gone when a man and woman could marry there."

"Oh, Lord, Maurice, you are like a prophet."

"Don't you see it yourself? The most important livelihood—that's the fishing—is gone under foot, and when the fishing is gone under foot the Blasket is gone under foot, for all the boys and girls who have any vigour in them will go over the sea; and take the tip off my ear, Mauraid, if that day is far hence."

"And what will our parents do when they grow old?"

"It's my opinion that they will have to do without us."

"Ah, Maurice, that will be hard if it ever comes to pass."

"Suppose now that we stayed at home to care for them, maybe we would be threescore years of age before we would lay the last clod on them in Ventry churchyard, and then we would be too old to go anywhere and who would lay the clod on ourselves?"

"Ah, that talk is true, but God is strong, Maurice."

"No doubt, but did you never hear that God ordered us to help ourselves?

"Who is that coming down the road?" said I after a while. "Isn't it like Liam Beg?"

"So it is, though I did not think that man was able to walk up Maum-na-Caroona."

Liam came up to us, a thin worn man, nothing but skin and bones but as healthy as a herring. The front of his shirt was wide open as was the habit with him.

"My love among friends, the people of the Island!" he cried. "Have you any news from the west?"

"Indeed we have not, Liam," said I, "unless you have some yourself."

"I have not, my lad. I dare say it's going to the wedding you are?"

"We are, Liam. Is there any great gathering in the east there?"

"Musha, I don't know, but I saw a power of people passing me up the road. And listen here, boy from the Island, I met a fellow just now who hadn't a word of Irish—a poor, ragged wanderer with his bag under his arm."

"It is strange he didn't understand you so," said Mauraid, "for it looks as if he is used to the Gaeltacht."

"Yé, my pity for you, that wouldn't be enough.[1] Wait now till I tell you a story about the Irish. I saw times—but you did not see them, for you were not in the world nor any thought of you—when I was at school," cocking his head on one side, "and if the master heard a word of Irish coming from your lips, I tell you, you would be singing Dónal-na-Gréine by the end of the day. Would you believe it, I had a little board tied behind my back with these words written on it: 'If you speak a word of Irish you will be beaten on back and on flank.'"

"Musha, Liam, wasn't it a great wrong?"

"Ah," said he, twisting his lips then baring his head, "but praise and thanks be to God above, it is not so today. And if

---

1. *I.e.* the fact that he is ragged doesn't prove a man knows Irish.

so," he added quickly, "do you know who we ought to thank for it? The Soupers.²"

"Why is that?"

"Because when they were here in Bally-na-Raha with their big Irish Bibles, giving half a crown to every man who would come and read a line or two, without lie or mockery there wasn't a man in the parrish but used to be going to them every night, until they were all able to read Irish fluently. And so it is they who revived it and preserved it and raised it up—and good day to you!" And he walked off briskly down the road to the west.

Soon we had a view of Ferriter's Parish, Mórach Parish, and the Parish of Kill, the land spread out before us and Smerwick Cove running up into it; Cruach Maurhin, Mount Eagle, and Mount Brandon thousands of feet above and not a wisp of fog on their summits; hundreds of houses with their lime-washed walls dotted here and there; cocks crowing and answering one another, dogs barking and mares neighing in the meadows below, the yellow furze blooms shining in the sun and the same light glittering on the roofs of the houses.

"Oh, Maurice," cried Mauraid, "isn't there a great heart-lift in that view!"

"There is indeed," said I, looking into her eyes.

"Do you see those two houses by themselves over there to the north?" she asked, pointing to them, "what is the name of that place?"

"Which place?" said I, moving closer to her and following her finger with my eyes.

"As far as you can see, far far away to the north."

"Oh, I see them now; that's the place they call Black Bosom."

"Musha, it's no lie the name they gave it and the way it lies

2. Protestant missionaries of the Famine period, who sought to induce the peasantry to change their religion by providing them with soup.

in the bosom of the hills," said she with a laugh, a laugh sweeter to me than the music of the birds.

We were now within a quarter of a mile of Ballyferriter, great crowds of people from east and from west, for there were to be six marriages on the one day—young and old, rich and poor, beggars and tinkers, one man without a word gazing at the crowd, another merry, another mad with drink, a man here arguing, another shouting, young lads wrestling in the street, the public-houses full to the brim, Mauraid and myself beaten and bruised by the crowd, trying to find our companions.

"Take hold of my coat-tail, Mauraid, and don't let go of it, for if you do I might as well be looking for a needle in a field of wheat."

We pushed ahead very slowly, for with each step forward I was thrust a step back by the swaying crowd. There was a terrible noise and shouting, for most of them were staggering with drink the way they could not put a rein on their tongues. I pressed on, pushed ahead by Mauraid till at last we reached the public-house of Shamus Kane. But we were going from bad to worse, for we could not put our noses across the threshold. Nothing but shouting and disputing and drink flying in the air.

"Wait here, Mauraid," said I, "until I get in somehow, and if our companions are inside I will come out for you."

I went in, pushing and pushing till at last the cap fell from my head. I bent down to find it, but, if so, I could not get up again. I was groping around till at last I got it, but my trouble now was to stretch myself up, for the weight from above was too heavy on me. A big man was standing beside me. I asked him to let me get up. But all he did was to go on shouting. As he gave me no heed I got angry, so that when I found on the floor a pin sharply pointed, I thrust it into his thigh. He lifted his leg from the ground so suddenly that he kicked the man in front of him, who had a pint of porter in his hand, and sent both the man and the porter sprawling on the floor. It is then was the rushing, wrestling, and gnashing of teeth, for when the other fellow got up he didn't say a word but struck on the bridge of the nose the man who had kicked him. I struggled to my feet at last and made my way into the kitchen. But none of my own people were to be found there. When I came out again, what sight was before me! Blood flying to the rafters and some foolish fellow encouraging the man from whom it was flowing. "Your soul to the devil, don't let down City-cow-titty! Remember your ancestors! Strike the bostoon!"

I reached the door somehow, but Mauraid was not to be seen. God be with me for ever, I am alone in the end, said I. I went down the road and before long I found her standing shyly under the wall of the house of Liam de Lóndra.

The poor woman was delighted to see me. "Oh, Lord," said she, "I thought you would never come out again. What delayed you at all?"

"It was like this, Mauraid," said I.

"Ah, it is well I know that fighting. I thought they would trample me under their feet!"

"By the book, Mauraid, if they had, they would leave Ballyferriter dead!"

She gave a laugh which gladdened my heart.

Then we heard the sound of a melodium in the house of Liam de Lóndra.

"As sure as I'm here, Mauraid, it is in there they are."

"Come in, dear," said she.

When I heard her say "dear" I started up like a cat you would call to its milk. I knew now that she loved me.

We went in, and it is there was the ree-raa, the merry-making and good fellowship, dancing, singing, and diversion, all the others from the Island before us, merry with drink. Mauraid and I danced together that day in great happiness.

The two of us were sitting now, a good coat of sweat on us, a couple of sets being danced on the floor. A short, sharp-eyed, hardy block of a lad came in through the doorway. He stopped and looked round. Everyone was watching him till the dances were over. Then he ran across to the musician, put a whisper in his ear, and took a goat's-leap back into the middle of the floor. The musician struck up a horn-pipe and the dancer beat it out faultlessly. It is wonderful feet he had, not a note of the music did he miss, as straight as a candle, not a stir of his body except down from his knees. The whole company sat watching him, without a word. You could hear them drawing their breath. He gave the last kick, looked around, and cried out:

"I am the broom from the top of Maurhan,
    And where is the man who will beat out a step with me?"

No one answered. When he saw no one was rising to accept his invitation to beat out a step with him, he disappeared through the doorway.

The day was almost spent now, the sun taking to his bed, the cow coming back to her byre, even the boy and girl tired after all the revelry, and the merrymaking growing cold. My friends and I came together to settle about going home.

We set out along the road to the west, talking gaily and contentedly of the affairs of the day, Mauraid and I keeping company all the way back to Hurdle Cliff in Dunquin where we had moored the curraghs.

The Blasket was stretched out before us in the west under a veil of mist, sheep-shearings in the sky, and thousands of points of light glittering on the sea beneath the moon. We did not take long to unmoor the curraghs. Each man took his place and we moved slowly out.

When we were out in Mid-Bay we ran into the heaviest mist that ever fell. The talking and singing ceased. We lost sight of the other curraghs; we lost sight of land. We could see nothing but a little ring of sea around us. We did not know east from west. There was not a breath in the sky and the bank of fog lying upon us without a stir. We were like blind men.

Then we heard a whistle, and another. I whistled in answer. We were all whistling to each other now, but it was no help. Mauraid was weeping and crying out that we were lost for ever, I singing a snatch of a song to give her courage. But as soon as I stopped she would be as bad as ever. I was like a mother petting her child, and indeed for all my fondness for her she had me tormented at last.

Then I heard a sound like this: "Ding-dong, coo-hoo! ding-dong, coo-hoo, tee-tee!"

"Listen!" I cried with a hand to my ear.

"What ails you?" said Shaun Tomás.

"Do ye hear anything?"

Everyone in the curragh began to listen. Soon all could hear it—like irons being struck together.

"By God," said Paddy Tim, "we are approaching some city."

"Great thanks to God," said Mauraid, "that we have reached some place."

"I don't know what we had better do. Shall we stop rowing, or row ahead?"

"Faith, the best thing we can do is to make for that sound," said Paddy Tim.

"If we can do it at all," said I.

"That is the knot, how to make for it," said Shaun Tomás, "for where is it coming from?"

"I think," said Paddy Tim, "it's coming from the north."

"Indeed it is not. Isn't it south it is?" said Tigue O'Shea.

"It is my opinion," said Shaun Tomás, "that it is back behind us."

"Wait now and listen again," said I; "maybe we could make it out."

"Ding-dong, coo-hoo, tee-tee! ding-dong!"

"It's out before us as sure as I live," said I.

"Arra, man, don't I hear it in the north?" said Paddy Tim.

"It is not," said Mauraid, "it's out before us."

"You are right, Mauraid," said I.

"Och," said Paddy, "have you never heard that Maurice and Kate are one[3]?"

I sat down on the thwart again and put out my oars.

"Row straight ahead, and I promise you we will soon make land."

Before long Mauraid, who was seated in the stern, gave a joyful cry: "Oh, look at all the lights out before us!"

We all looked round. Thousands of lights could be seen through the fog, and the ding-dong, ding-dong clearer than ever.

"Your soul to the devil, it's Cahirciveen!" cried Shaun Tomás.

"Isn't it Dingle?" said Paddy Tim.

"It's the Land of the Young," said Tigue O'Shea softly.

"Faith, wherever it is," said I, "let us close in before we lose sight of it."

We rowed till we were within ten yards of the lights. It was a big ship at anchor, the biggest I ever saw. "We must be in some harbour," said Tigue.

Just then the siren was blown and took an echo out of the ship. The oars fell from our hands. I thought Mauraid would faint with the start it took out of her. "Easy, Mauraid, isn't that the siren she's blowing to tell any other ships on the line to stand clear?"

We drew alongside.

"What is the English for rope?" said Tigue to Paddy Tim.

"Faith, I don't know," said Paddy.

"Rope," said Shaun Tomás.

"Throw down a rope!" cried Tigue at the top of his voice.

We heard the captain shouting, and in a moment a sailor came to the gunwale and threw out a big stout one. The captain was looking down at us. "Will you come aboard?" said he.

---

3. Proverbial expression for lovers.

They let down a ladder by the side of the ship. We all climbed up, I supporting Mauraid for fear she would fall. Hundreds of lights were to be seen on this side and that, sailors standing here and there staring at us, some black and others white, big pipes in their mouths and they chatting together.

The captain took us down to a nice room. We seated ourselves. As soon as Tigue sat down he cried: "Glory be to God on high that we have found this place." He looked around. "Great Kings of Virtues," said he, looking at the captain, "isn't it a fine life he has?"

The captain opened two bottles and poured out a glass of whisky for each of us and a glass of wine for Mauraid.

"Your health, captain!" said Tigue, tossing it off.

"Good luck," replied the captain.

Tigue was talking away to the captain in bad English. He could hardly understand him and we were bursting our sides with laughter.

After a while Mauraid and I went up on deck. With my first glance to the west what did I see but the Blasket, the fog scattered and the stars shining bright in the sky. I ran down to the cabin. "By God, men, the night has cleared."

"The blessing of God with you," said Tigue, getting up.

We got back into the curragh, left a farewell and a blessing with the sailors, and moved away.

Eighteen

❖

AN AMERICAN WAKE

"WELL," said Maura one day while she was washing the plates.

The rest of us were sitting round the fire. We turned round.

"What is the 'well'?" asked my brother Shaun.

She turned back to the table again, smiling. Then taking up a cup she turned round again. "The 'well' is," said she, "that I have a great mind to go to America."

"Oh, you have, musha, you foolish girl?" said Michael.

"What put that into your head?" said my father, his face flushing.

"I have indeed," said Maura, beginning to cry, "for Kate Peg is going and I have no need to stay here when all the girls are departing."

"Do what you will," said my father, "no one is stopping you."

"She won't go," said Eileen, her lips trembling, "or if she does I will go too."

"Arra, fly away at once!" cried my father, waving his hands in the air, "away with you over the sea and you will find the gold on the streets!"

Next day Maura wrote to her aunt for the passage money.

Kate Peg was constantly coming to the house now and she and Maura talking of nothing but America. They would run across to the wall where pictures from Springfield were hanging. "Oh," Kate would say, "we will go into that building the first day, Maura." Then the two of them would run out on the floor dancing for joy. "You will send home pretty things to me?" said Eileen. "We will, of course," said Maura indifferently. Then Eileen too would dance over the floor.

Three weeks later the passage money came.

She was changed that evening, crying bitterly with the letter in her hands.

"What is the good of crying so, you foolish girl?" said my father, who was sitting in his chair with a mournful look on him. Kate Peg came in, her eyes as red as the rose from weeping.

"Well, Kate," said my father, "what news have you?"

"I have none, save that the passage money came for me today. I hear Maura has hers too."

"She has," said my father, "and she has been distracted ever since."

"Why are you crying so, Maura?" said Kate, raising her head. "Didn't you see Nora Pats go with no kinsfolk at all over there, the poor girl? And isn't it over there all your own people are?"

I noticed his cap far down over my father's eyes that evening as I had never seen it before. Eileen was in the far corner crying to herself.

"Faith, it is a fine prospect in store for you," said my father with a long sigh, bending over the fire to put a live cinder in his pipe.

After a while Maura stopped crying, only a sob coming now and then as she put the kettle on the fire.

"Had the King any news when he came in, Kate?" asked my father, crossing his knees.

"I did not hear any except of the crowds that are going across to America this week."

"God help the old people, there will be none to bury them with the haste that is on the world."

"There's no doubt but there is a great change in the times."

"Upon my soul, Kate, I remember when there was no thought of America any more than the chair I am sitting on, and they were fine happy days."

Maura was crying every day now. "Musha, I don't know in the world," she would say when she washed the plates, "will the day ever come when I will be washing these again."

It was the same when she would be sweeping the floor. She would look at the broom and the tears would fall. Then she would run across to my dog Rose and catch her up in her arms. "Musha, Roseen, isn't it many a day the two of us were west on the White Strand, I throwing stones into the water and you swimming out after them!" and Rose would wag her tail and bark for joy for Maura to be playing with her.

Time was passing and the appointed day approaching. A mournful look was coming over the very walls of the house. The hill above the village which sheltered the houses seemed to be changing colour like a big, stately man who would bend his head in sorrow. The talk throughout the village was all of Maura and Kate going away.

On the last night young and old were gathered together in the house, and though music and songs, dancing and mirth were flying in the air, there was a mournful look on all within. No wonder, for they were like children of the one mother, the people of the Island, no more than twenty yards between any two houses, the boys and girls every moonlight night dancing on the Sandhills or sitting together and listening to the sound of the waves from Shingle Strand; and when the moon would wane, gathered together talking and conversing in the house of old Nell.

The dust was flying from the floor under the heels of the sturdy young men and girls. I went out to the grassy bank. The moon was high in the sky and the Milky Way stretched out to the south-east. I heard the lonely murmur of the waves breaking on the White Strand. It made me mournful.

Maura came out to me. "Oh, Mirrisheen," she cried, throwing herself into my arms and bursting into tears, "what shall I do without you?"

"Be easy. Don't you see everyone is going now, and soon you will see me beyond like the rest of them. Hush now, let us go in and dance."

She let go of me and sat down on the bank.

"Lift up your heart," said I again. "Come in with me now and the two of us will dance a set."

When we went in: "Musha, my love for ever, Maura," cried Peg Oweneen, embracing her and bursting into tears, "my life will not be long after you."

"Strike up a tune, Shaun," said I to Shaun Pats, who had the melodium. He began to play. Four of us arose and I called my sister for the dance.

The day was brightening in the east. We washed ourselves and made ready for the road to Dingle to give Maura a last farewell. The sun was rising in splendour and the cocks crowing all over the village. When nine o'clock came all the old men and women were coming down towards the house. All was confusion.

We moved down to the quay, Maura and Kate Peg in front of us and the whole village following.

The old women were crying aloud. "Musha, love of my heart, Maura, isn't it a pity for ever for you to be going from us."

"Oh, musha, Maura, how shall I live after you when the long winter's night will be here and you not coming to the door nor your laughter to be heard!"

We got free of them at last. We were out in Mid-Bay, looking back at the people of the village waving their hands and their shawls.

We spent the night in Dingle. Next morning we went down to the station and gave them farewell and our blessing with sorrow and tears.

The train whistled. In a moment they were out of sight.

Nineteen

THE STRANGER

I T was a fine sunny day in the year 1923. I was looking after a sheep on the hillside above, the sun yellowing in the west and a lark singing above. I raised my head and listened. Indeed, little bird, small as you are you have me beguiled, said I to myself. Just then the earth shook beneath me. I looked up and saw five or six lambs gambolling together. I heard a clatter. I heard it again, like shingle being thrown into the sea. I looked down over the edge of the cliff and saw a shoal of mackerel breaking water with a great noise below.

A spring came into my blood and I leapt up. What ails me at all? The darkness is falling and I haven't found my black sheep yet. I walked west along the ditch, whistling softly to myself. I had gone about twenty yards when I thought I saw a man approaching me, a man whose like was not in the Blasket. I stopped, looking intently. By God, said I to myself, you are there sure enough, and if it is from the other world you have come you seem to me not to be poor. Now is the time for me to stand my ground, for maybe I will get riches out of this; that is, if you have as much power as the leprechauns in olden times. I thought I saw a smile on his face. Faith, there is no bad look on you, anyway.

He was now only forty yards away, a man neither too tall nor too short, with knee-breeches and a shoulder-cloak, his head bare and a shock of dark brown hair gathered straight back on it. I was growing afraid. There was not his like in the Island. Where had he come from and he approaching me now from the top of the hill in the darkening of the day? I leant my back against the bank of the ditch. I drew out my pipe and lit it. Then I turned my gaze out to the south-east, thinking no doubt he would pass me by on his way, so that I could take his measure and say I had seen a leprechaun.

I heard a voice behind me. "God save you," it said.

I looked round. He was smiling.

"God and Mary save you, noble person," said I.

He sat down on a stone beside me and drew out a box of cigarettes. "Will you have one?" said he in English.

"I will not, thank you," said I in Irish.

I was taking his measure well as we spoke and he looking out to Iveragh. We both remained silent for a long time. Then he tried to say something in Irish, but failed. So he turned again to the English.

"What do you call that place over there?" said he in a very hard accent.

"They call it Valencia Island," said I in English.

"And how would you say that in Irish?"

I told him. He took from his pocket a little book and a pencil and wrote down quickly what I had said. Faith, my lad, said I to myself, this is not the first time you wrote Irish anyway. When he had finished I spoke to him.

"Where are you from, may I ask?"

"Repeat that, please."

"Where are you from?" I repeated very slowly.

He bent his head for a moment, muttering the words under his teeth. Then he answered in English. "I am from London, and I came to the Blasket today," said he with a laugh. (The laugh of an Englishman, said I to myself, isn't it often I was told to beware of it!)

He asked my name. I told him.

"Mine is George Thomson," said he in Irish.

"I'm thinking you have Irish too," said I.

"A little," said he with another laugh.

It was growing dark and we moved east towards the village. He was questioning me about this word and that word in Irish, and I giving him their meaning. When we came to the top of the boreen: "Where are you staying?" said I.

He stopped for a moment to think: "I am in the house of Michael Guheen. Is that right?"

"It is," said I, "and as I said before, you will soon improve in the language."

There is no doubt but youth has great ability. George and I spent the next six weeks walking together on strand, hill, and mountain, and after spending that time in my company he had fluent Irish. If everyone in Ireland were as eager as he for the language, the people of old Ireland would be Gaels again without much delay. But, alas, it is not so; for if one is eager there are twelve who are not, though there is a kind of awakening in the language now, great thanks to God.

One fine morning my father and I were at breakfast. A sunbeam was pouring through the window, the murmur of bees all around, the cat on the window-ledge making dabs with her paw at a bee which was walking up the window-pane. I noticed a spider's web between the side of the window and the wall and himself sound asleep in the middle of it. It happened that the bee touched the web. When the spider felt it he awoke from his sleep and made a dart for the bee. The cat cocked her ears watching the two of them, as if greatly amused. Then she pounced and killed both the bee and the spider. And that was the end of the fun.

"Faith," said my father, "it would be a good day to bring home those two sheep that are west on Red Ridge."

As we walked up the Causeway we met George coming down.

"Where are you going today?" said he.

"I am going into the hill with my father to bring home two sheep."

"I will come with you."

"Ah, you won't, for you would fall from the cliffs."

"I will not," said he, turning on his heel and accompanying us.

The day was fine and sultry and we had stripped off our coats. We walked into the hill, as happy as children, talking and conversing, giving words of Irish to George till we reached Red Ridge. We sat down to rest, looking south to the Skelligs.

"Isn't this place very different from the city of London?" said my father.

"It is indeed," said George, passing his fingers through his hair.

"It is a pity I am not in the city of London now," said I, "for it is a fine view I would have."

"What's that?" said George, turning to me with a frown of surprise. "Indeed you would not, but the heat killing you and your health failing for want of air. And as for the view, you would be looking at the same thing always—people walking the streets with nothing in them but only the breath, and believe me if one of them could see this view out before me now, he would give his riches for it."

"You are right," said my father, getting up. "Faith, George, maybe you are getting hungry to be fasting so long."

"Musha, words do not fatten the friars," said he.

"By God," said I, "you are as well worded now as any old man in the village. The two of you had better wait here now until I go north to Halberd Hollow after the old ewe."

"Very well," said my father.

I went north through the Scórnach and down through the fern, up to my waist in heather and wild flowers, a dizzy ravine above and beneath me and the sea far below dashing against the rocks. Many sheep were around me here and there, but my own old ewe was not among them. She was easy to recognize for she had not been shorn. She was a good climber, so I made my way to the cliffs. There was nothing beneath my feet but the blue sea, and the slightest stumble would have sent me headlong as sauce for the crabs below. I stopped again to watch the flocks of sea-birds nesting in the cliff, some flying around and others on the surface of the waves. By God, George, said I in my own mind, if you were here now and saw this view, you would never go back to England again.

Suddenly I felt the earth shaking beneath my feet. Looking up, I saw the sky blackened by a big black mass of turf. God save my soul, I cried, it will strike me surely. I leapt aside. Each time it struck the cliff it rebounded into the air like a football. It rushed past me with a terrible whirl. I watched it hurtling down the cliff till at last it struck the water. A spurt of foam leapt into the air and fell down again with a splash which made the whole cliff ring. In a moment the birds were in a tumult, darting with wild cries out to sea and chattering excitedly like any nation of men fleeing for their lives from an earthquake.

I moved west across Fern Bottom, glancing from side to side, till I reached Bun-a-Dóiteáin. There I saw my old shred of a ewe down on the lowest ledge. I went down towards her, and I climbed down to places that day which I would not have the courage even to look at now. When I was twenty yards from her I stopped and shouted. She lifted her head slowly, but that was all the heed she gave me. I shouted again and again, but it was no use. I took a stone and threw it at her. It whistled down through the air and struck her in the middle of the back. Away she ran up the cliff. I followed breathlessly after her. She was wild with fright, and what wonder!—a sheep which had not been caught for three years and had spent all that time among the ravines, only fit for the birds of the sea. I kept her in sight till at last she tripped up and came tumbling head over heels like a snowball. Oh, I cried, she will go over!

She landed in a furrow of fern. Ah, it is ever said, I cried joyfully, that an inch is as good as all Ireland.

I went up to her. Her four feet were in the air kicking wildly. Faith, you look very uncomfortable, said I, catching her and lifting her up. She gave a leap but I kept my grip, though it was a dangerous one to try to keep on the side of the cliff.

I was between two minds now. Would I keep her or let her go? If I keep her, I said to myself at last, both she and I will be thrown into the sea. So I let her follow her nose through the cliff, I running behind her. She made for the Fearee. But I was as quick as herself to reach the top. Then she made off to the east, I following, coated with sweat and blinded with fern. I shouted hard but it was of no avail. She was drifting down again, as is the way of sheep when they are weak, and this one was weak indeed on account of her age, for you could hear the crack of her old bones as she ran. Again I started off after her. Birds, sheep and rabbits fled in terror to see the madman shouting through the fern. At last I ran her down. She stopped. I stopped too. We looked at each other. She fixed her eyes on me like a beaten man as if to say, Won't you let me go? I threw a stone. "Up with you," said I.

Off she went again, I throwing stones on each side of her. Now and then she stopped and looked back at me pitifully with her tongue hanging out of her mouth. She was tiring. She moved slowly on through the ravine till she reached the top. By now she was so exhausted she could hardly put one leg before another.

Musha, how my heart opened when I got a draught of the fine sweet air which was flowing across the summit from the Skelligs! I took the fill of my belly of it and sat down on a clump of grass, tired out.

I looked round for my father and George, but I could not see them. I put a finger in my mouth and whistled. Then I saw George getting up out of the fern, smiling as usual. He came up to me.

"Oh," said he, stretching himself, "the sun has me killed," and he threw himself into the fern beside me.

"It is very sultry," said I, "but what about the man who has been running ever since, up and down the cliff after his sheep?"

"I dare say you are accustomed to it," said he, taking out his pipe and tobacco.

I did the same and we sat there smoking and discussing the world together, I with an odd glance at the old ewe for fear she would make for the cliff again. But she stood very quietly, though she was still too frightened to take grass.

As I turned my head I saw my father down at the Yellow Banks after the other sheep. I leapt up.

"Listen," said I to George; "don't stir out of that, and whatever you do don't let that old ewe north again."

He got up in surprise. "Where are you going?"

"Don't you see my father? He's finding that sheep too much for him and I am going to help him. We'll be up here in a moment. But, devil, don't let that old ewe north."

I went down the hill towards the Palm. I ran the sheep down and the two of us drove it east as far as the White Stones. When we had taken a rest: "I wonder," said I, "could you keep her here till I go and bring the other from the north?"

"Very well," said my father.

I went back to the place where I had left George and the old ewe. When I came in sight of the Scórnach, what did I see but George, coat in hand, running as fast as he could after about two hundred sheep across Red Ridge. I stopped and looked at him. Wasn't it a great and wonderful work he had in hand to bring those two hundred together! I scratched my head in amazement. Oh, Lord, said I, the ewe I am after bringing from the north is among those as sure as I live, and that is why he is pursuing them.

I looked up to the place where I had left the ewe, and there she was still! I was lost in wonder. What in the world possessed him to run after those? I whistled and whistled again, but he gave no heed. I kept on whistling, but he was running after them still with no thought of stopping. As sure as I live and there's a cross on the ass, said I, it is over the cliff you will go, I shouted in the height of my head. Just then I saw him throwing his coat after them. Then he went head over heels into the heather.

My heart leapt. "You must be hurt," said I, running towards him. When I was within twenty yards of him he got up and looked around. When he saw me he gave a fine hearty laugh.

"Is there any injury on you?" said I, my heart beating.

"There is not, faith," said he, looking away towards the sheep.

"Upon my soul, George, you are the man who slew a hundred."

"Oh, Maurice, I had to let them go."

"Arra, man, what came over you or what order did you get to keep a watch on those shorn sheep?"

"Didn't you tell me yourself?" he asked in wonder.

"I did not. I told you to watch the ewe I brought from the north."

"Oh, I see, and where is that ewe now?"

"There in the same place still."

"That's all right, so, but I thought those sheep were all yours and that you wanted to bring them in."

"I dare say but for the fall you got you would be running after them still, and observe that it is not the smooth pavements of England you have here, my boy."

"Oh, Maurice," said he with a laugh, "observe yourself how I compelled the earth here to kiss me."

"Musha, it was the earth compelled you to kiss it, but come now till we drive the wild ewe east, for my father is waiting for us at the Scythe Rocks with the other one."

We got the two sheep together. Then we sat on the top of a rock looking out over the Bay of Dingle at the trawlers fishing and the sea-birds flying around in search of fish.

I arose and looked up at the sheep. "I dare say it is time for us to be making our way to the east before night comes on."

We set out, up to our knees in fern and rushes, I above, my father below, George between us, and the dog on the top above me. When either of the sheep would take a step astray Rose would be at her hind legs and put her straight again. We shortened our road with talk, walking on at our ease till at last we reached Shingle Strand where the sheep do be rounded up. Rose was out before us, barking furiously, till she had driven the two into the Cave of Shevaun de Lóndra.

I told George to stand at the mouth and, if either of the sheep tried to escape, to seize it.

"Very well," said he, stretching out his arms to each side of the cave.

I made a dash for the sheep. I caught one and threw it, but the other got away. I looked round and saw it making for the sea with George clinging to its tail.

"Your soul to the devil," I shouted, "let her go or she will drown you!"

He let go of her at last. Rose swam out and rounded her in. When I returned after getting her into the cave again, George was sitting under a rock. He had taken off his shoes and was wringing the water from his stockings.

When we had the sheep shorn: "Well, George," said my father, "you must be hungry now."

"I was never so hungry in my life."

"Isn't it hard work we have here after the sheep?" said I.

"No doubt of it, and it is a great wonder no one falls from the cliffs after them."

Twenty

MY LAST JOURNEY TO THE INISH

A GREAT change was coming on the Island. Since the fishing was gone under foot all the young people were departing across to America, five or six of them together every year. Maura was not gone a couple of years when the passage money was sent across to Shaun. A year after that Eileen went. Tomás Owen Vaun was gone already for some time and he writing to me from over there. My brother Michael was working for a tailor in Dingle and there was nobody left now in the house but my grandfather, my father, and myself. George used to be visiting us every summer and the two of us always together.

I remember well a fine airy morning in the year 1926 when I went out on to the ditch. White streaks of foam were passing up through the Sound to the north and they nicely gathered together on the surface of the sea. Then they would turn in on each other till not a trace of them was to be seen. There was a wonderful stillness. The mountains were clear before me, nodding their heads above in the sky. Isn't it they that are proud to have power to be higher than the rest, thought I. But if so, that height is nothing to boast of in the dark days of winter when they have to stand up boldly before the storms of the sky.

I looked around at the little wisps of smoke arising from the houses and the air without strength to scatter them, but the blue sky, of a hue that could not be painted, sucking them upwards. I looked at the reflection of the rocks which was clearly visible in the sea, and when a sea-raven would dip himself he would send little ripples spreading out in a circle ever and ever till they were lost from sight.

Soon a steamship rounded the Gob from the south, steering close to the shore. She let out a shriek which sent the village dogs wild with barking and aroused the sea which till then had been calm and still. She rent it on every side, sending big ripples inshore till they made a glug-glag up through the crevices of the rocks. Then the sea calmed again the way you would think it had never stirred.

Meanwhile my father and my uncle were making themselves ready for the Inish. I put my head in across the threshold.

"Do you know, dad," said I, "what I have planned to do but for myself and George to go with you to Inish-vick-ilaun?"

"It is not good for you to be in," said he, "if George will go."

"Very well. I will go up now to see if he has any desire for it."

When I went up to the Smith's House (which is the name given to the house where George always stayed) he was eating his breakfast.

"God save all here," said I.

"God and Mary save you," they replied with one voice.

I sat down on the settle.

"Would there be any desire on you today?" said I to George after a while.

"What for?"

"Would you like to make a journey to Inish-vick-ilaun?"

"It is what the woman of the house was saying to me before

you came in that it would make a fine day back in the islands, and so I have a great desire to go, for it is said to be a fine and airy place."

"It is well for me to make up food for the journey for you so," said the woman of the house.

"Do so," said I, "for it is a place will give him the appetite of a quaybach."

When we had everything in order we moved down the path. We saw my father below on the quay beckoning us to hurry. Before long we were away, passing alongside the Island to the west, George and I rowing, the sea dead calm and a great heat on it; and when I looked south-east between me and Slea Head there was nothing but a path of sparkling light from the sun which shone without spot in the sky.

We were well back at the Palm now, seals stretched in pairs above on the reefs and they crying and keening.

"Aren't those very like people in on the stone?" said George.

"On my oath," said my father, "it is said here that many people were put under magic long ago and perhaps those are some of them. Some years ago a man went from here hunting seals, about the month of Samhain it seems, because the young seal was born. It was back in Bird Cove it happened."

"Where is that cove?"

"It is on the south side of the Inish," said my father. "When he came out of the boat he saw a young seal up in the head of the cove. He went up after it, stick in hand as was their wont when they went seal-hunting."

"I understand," said George.

"Well, as I said, up he went with the stick, but, if so, the cow-seal leapt straight at him with open mouth, snarling. But he succeeded in clambering up on to a ledge on the side of the cove, and when he had reached it, would you believe it, George, the cow-seal spoke out to him. 'If you are in luck,' said she, 'you will leave this cove in haste, for be it known to you that you will not easily kill my mackeen,'[1] and she went back again to her young one. The man was trembling hand and foot. 'For the sake of the world,' he cried out to the man in the boat, 'back her in as quick as you can.' And from that day, George, till the day he died," said my father, "that man never saw a day's health."

"Faith," said George, "that is a story I never heard."

"Upon my word," said my father, "there is many a story you would hear in these islands you would never hear tell of in the cities."

We rowed ahead. I gave a glance to the north when we were half-way across the Great Sound to the west. What did I see but some animal giving a tailor's leap out of the water into the sky! "Oh, Lord," said I, "do you see what is there to the north?" We all looked northward. When it fell down again it sent the water high into the air.

"I do, my boy," said my father. "Did you ever hear tell of the sturgeon?"

"I often heard of it," said George.

"Well, there it is for you now, and the place where it leaps like that there do be many more below."

Before long we reached the strand of the Inish and the two of us turned our faces up into the island. The sky was cloudless, the sea calm, sea-birds and land-birds singing sweetly. The sight of my eyes set me thinking. I looked west to the edge of the sky and I seemed to see clearly the Land of the Young—many-coloured flowers in the gardens; fine, bright houses sparkling in the sunshine; stately, comely-faced, fair-haired maidens walking through the meadows gathering flowers. Oh, isn't it a pity Niav of the Golden Hair would not come here now, thought I, for it is readily I would go with her across the top of the waves.

I was not long in those thoughts when I heard George

---

1. Young son.

calling. He had thrown off his jacket and was sitting on the top of the rock looking down at me.

"What do you see in the west?" said he.

"Upon my word, George, it was at the Land of the Young I have been looking."

"Faith, you are like Oweneen of the Birds."

I climbed up on to the rock and we sat together without a word, looking out over the great sea—the Skellig out to the south and white foam around it, the Teeracht to the north-west and the high road up to the lighthouse clearly to be seen, the Foze straight to the west below the edge of the sky and nothing beyond them but air and water.

"Would you believe it, Maurice," said George after a while, "that I am lonesome to be going tomorrow."

"I believe it well, and it is myself will be lonesome after you."

He looked at me between the two eyes and after a while he spoke gravely:

"Well, now, there is no one but the two of us on this lonely island and so I hope you will put courage in my heart."

"I will do it if it is in my power. Let you put the question."

I knew well what was the question he had to put to me.

"The question is, have you cast America out of your head?"

I got up without speaking a word. It was often before that George was urging me not to go across to America but to stay in Ireland and enter the Civic Guard. But there was the reluctance of the world on me to do as he said, and I was trying to put off the matter always. But the last day was come now and both of us knew that if I did not agree with him that day I would be gathered away before the summer was come again.

I looked west at the edge of the sky where America should be lying, and I slipped back on the paths of thought. It seemed to me now that the New Island² was before me with its fine

---

2. America.

streets and great high houses, some of them so tall that they scratched the sky; gold and silver out on the ditches and nothing to do but to gather it. I see the boys and girls who were once my companions walking the streets, laughing brightly and well contented. I see my brother Shaun and my sisters Maura and Eileen walking along with them and they talking together of me. The tears were rising in my eyes but I did not shed them. As the old saying goes, "Bitter the tears that fall but more bitter the tears that fall not."

I was too long in that silent thought without giving an answer to my friend. What answer would I give him? Would I tell him that it would be more to my liking to go among my companions beyond than to set out for the capital city of Ireland along with him?

I turned to him. He was looking south-east towards Iveragh the way I could only see his cheek.

"George," said I after a while.

"What is it?" said he, turning towards me.

"What is your advice?"

"My advice to you is that it is not on the streets of America you will get money, as many think."

I looked out over the sea again.

It seemed to me now that Maura was raising her fist to me and saying aloud, "Don't mind him, but come out here where your own people are, for if you go to Dublin you will never see any of your kinsfolk again."

I looked at George.

"Many entirely are the thoughts which are passing through your mind. But listen here," said he with a gesture of his hand; "if you want the history of America look at the Yank who comes home; think of the appearance of him. Not a drop of blood in his body but he has left it beyond. Look at the girl who goes over with her fine comely face! When she comes home there does be a colourless look on her and the skin furrowed on her brow. If you noticed that, Maurice, you would never go to that place."

We were talking that way until I agreed with him at last and said I would go to Dublin. "But if so, I will not be with you tomorrow anyway."

"You have plenty of time yet. But do not go to the place beyond. That is my advice to you."

When we had everything talked over we moved down towards the Strand where the curragh was awaiting us.

"The devil take you," said my uncle, "the night has fallen. Where were you since? I would say you had the island walked four times over."

"Ah, here a while and there a while," said I, leaping into the boat, and away we moved slowly, tired and reluctant after the journey of the day.

I gave a glance to the east across the Bay.

"Oh, Lord, isn't it many the stroke of the oar is before us yet before we reach the house?"

"It is ever said," said my father, "that however long the road there comes a turning."

We reached the quay.

"Well, George," said I on our way up, "you will be leaving us tomorrow, and I suppose it is as well for us to spend the last night pleasantly."

"Faith, it is, and let you bring up your fiddle."

"Oh, little fear," said I as I turned back from the boreen and George going up to his own dwelling.

When I had eaten my supper I took the fiddle down from the loft.

"It seems there will be dancing up in the top of the village tonight?" said my grandfather when he saw the fiddle in my hands.

"By my book, daddo," said I, "if I were in need of a priest I would go up tonight."

"Why so?"

"Won't George be going tomorrow?"

"Achván, if that is so it is well for you to spend the night joyfully together, in the name of God."

When I went into George's house he was seated on the little stool, his two hands under his chin, staring into the fire.

I struck my palm on his shoulder.

"You are in love, my boy."

"Why do you say that?"

"Because I have ever heard that he who looks that way into the middle of the fire does be heavily in love."

"Don't mind Tigue's nonsense," said he, "but put the fiddle in tune."

I had to laugh when I heard the answer he gave me. "Musha, George, it's a fine, rich Irish you have now."

"And if it is, it is you should be thanked, for isn't it from yourself I learned all I have?"

Soon the strains of the music were reaching the young men who were outside, and before long they were lightly dancing on the floor, George stripped to the shirt like themselves for the night was soft. It would delight you to see the boys and girls at that time, joy and mirth in every step they took, and even the old women who had any vigour in them gathered in, in pursuit of the music.

About ten o'clock George and I walked out a short distance of the road talking together.

"Well now, Maurice, I shall be leaving tomorrow and, if so, I shall be expecting you every day from this out. Don't forget when you reach Tralee to send me a telegram and I will be before you at the station in Dublin."

"Very well," said I with a heavy heart and the reluctance of the world, thinking of the long road which lay before me. While George was describing the journey to Dublin, my own thoughts were of the fine days I had spent hunting on the top of the hill and fishing on the sea. I seemed to see a rabbit out before me and Rose after it. Ah, how would I ever leave the Blasket?

George touched me with his elbow. "Wake up," said he.

"Ah, there is great mourning on me, George, to leave this place. I cannot help it. The parting is too hard."

"Look at me who left England and came to Ireland without acquaintance of anyone alive."

"You and I are not the same, for I was never yet beyond Dingle to the east."

We went back to the dancing. It was in full swing now, music going into the air and we spent the rest of the night in gaiety.

On the morrow it was sharp and cold from the north. I went out and looked around. The day had a threatening look, swell on the stones, showers falling on the edge of the sky, and the Bank of the Black Rock breaking and tearing from the north. Faith, said I to myself, the Paorach will have another day.

The word was but out of my mouth when I saw coming down the Causeway towards me George and the King and others after them. My soul from the devil, said I, he is going out.

I noticed now a thing I had never seen before. I did not see the smile on George's mouth. It was enough. He had his fill of sorrow and my own heart blackened likewise.

He came down to me and went into the house to say good-bye to my grandfather. When he came out again, we walked down together to the quay where the curragh was afloat, waiting for him.

"Bestir yourself, George," said Shaun-a-Ree,[3] putting out the oars.

We looked at each other and shook hands without a word. Then he smiled and he looked at me between the eyes.

"Farewell for a while," said he.

"May your journey prosper."

---

3. Shaun, son of the King.

Twenty-One

I LEAVE HOME

A FEW days afterwards a letter came from my friend with nothing from beginning to end in it but talk of the fun we would have in the capital city of Ireland—to keep up my courage of course.

A day passed and two days. Then I wrote to him to let him know I had made up my mind to take on myself a different way of life. But, if so, my reluctance was growing, for it was a great change for a young man who had been cut off from the great world with no knowledge of its affairs.

One day when I was in beside the fire and nothing to trouble me in the rainy world but the long unknown journey which lay in front of me: "Well, father," said I, and he on the other side of the fire reading a letter which had come that day from America, "what is your opinion of the great, long journey that is now before me?"

"What journey is that?" said he quickly, raising his head and looking at me over his glasses.

"It is not long now until you will see the Guards' uniform on me."

He looked into the fire, thinking. At last he looked up. "Are you in earnest?"

"I am indeed."

"When will you be going?" said he with a sigh.

"Tomorrow."

"Well, I give you my blessing, for so far as this place is concerned there is no doubt but it is gone to ruin."

"It is, long since; and even if it were not, what is there in it but fishing, hunting, and fowling, and according to the old saying they are the three most unprofitable pursuits going."

"It is true," said he sadly, and he returned to his reading.

The next morning was fine and soft. It was a Tuesday—the 15th of March 1927. I got myself ready early, for it was the day for the King to go out to bring in the post, so I was in the yard watching out for him for fear he would go unknown to me. There was everything in readiness with me, my mind at rest, my holiday clothes on, and no one knowing my destination but only my own people.

After a while I saw Shaun Fada approaching. He stopped and looked me over from top to toe without speaking a word.

"I see there is some intention in your head today, son of O'Sullivan," said he at last.

"I am for taking the leap."

"Whither are you travelling?"

"Yé, where would it be, Shaun, but to spend a week in the town of Dingle. Amn't I tired of this place?"

"My heart from the devil, you are right, for when I was young I used to be spending half my life in that place. Yerra, the devil take it, there are young people here and without lie or mockery there is the look of the cinders on them."

At that moment I saw the King coming down the Causeway. "Faith, Shaun," said I, "here is the King going out. It is as well for me to be moving."

"It is as well for you," said he, going east.

The King soon came up with me on the top of the quay.

"Are you going out?"

"I am resolved on it."

"If so," said he, looking at me, "it seems to me that you will not be coming back."

"Ah, maybe I would spend a week on my wanderings," said I.

Soon we were on our way out from the pool, my back to the Island of my birth and my face to the mainland. I heard barking behind me. I knew well what it was. Looking back I saw Rose out on the bank howling as she saw me departing from her. I crushed down the distress that was putting a cloud upon my heart.

We reached Dunquin at last. I walked slowly and heavily up the path. I stopped. I stretched myself and looked back at the Island. Little I thought once of forsaking it, but, my sorrow, that day was come at last. I looked around. There was nothing to be heard, only the sound of the waves below. I was thinking and pondering and no one to heed me but the God of Glory in Whom I trusted to guide me on the right road to the capital city. I looked south at the Slea Head road and then north at the Ceann Sraha road, then again at the Clasach road; and I thought of a story I had read a while before of a widow's son who turned his breast to the great world and the cross-roads confounding him.

I heard a voice behind me: "Are you there still?"

I looked back and saw the King. "Faith, I am," said I, shaking myself. "There is no great hurry on me."

"I suppose you will be going to Dingle tonight?"

"I will. Is the road to the north the shortest?"

"Without doubt it is."

We said good-bye and parted. I set out on my road, and the King on his way up towards Bally-na-Raha.

I was alone now, groping my way to the north and a west mist over the road. When I came to the top of the Carhoo I stopped again and sat down to take a rest. I lit my pipe seeing I had no other comfort. I looked again at the Island. It was the last sight I would get of it back from Maum-na-Carhoona.

The first spot that struck my eyes was the summit of the Cró, the highest hill in it, and this verse came into my head:

> Thou art there, beautiful Cró
> With thine ancient heather summit,
> And he who once raced on thee
> Looking back on thee in sorrow.

Well, said I, getting up, however long the journey is before me, I have no cause to let the night catch me here.

I stepped out, ever and ever, until I came down into Ballyferriter. It was necessary for me to get a certificate from the priest there and I made my way to his house. A girl came to the door. "Is the priest inside, if you please?" said I. She did not answer but looked wonderingly at me between the eyes. "Have you Irish?" said I. Again no reply from her, so I spoke to her in English.

"Oh, he is. Come in here a while."

I went into a little room with many books and papers in it. Well, thought I, isn't it a strange thing to meet already a girl without Irish!

I was looking round at the pictures on the walls but, if so, no one was coming and the day passing. It is fine for me, said I to myself, and the long journey I have before me into Dingle.

At that moment I heard striding footsteps coming towards the room. The parish priest came in. I bowed to him and he greeted me courteously. He asked me my name and my business. When he had given me the certificate, I gave him a farewell and a blessing and went on my way.

I was going on and going on when a thought came into my mind—the road before me seemed to go very far up into the hill. I took out my pipe and lit it. There was not a trace of the Island to be seen now. God help me, said I, where am I? Will there be an end to this road tonight?

I got up and looked round me. There was a by-road turning east and a by-road turning west. Soon I saw an old man in tatters coming down towards me across the hill, an old yellow pipe between his teeth, a couple of cows before him. He was making towards me and calling Sho amach! sho amach! to the cows.

When he came down to the road I greeted him. He returned my greeting in fine Irish.

"Listen here, good man, is this the right road for Dingle?"

"It appears you are a stranger in this place?" said he.

"I am, good sir."

"Oh, have no fear. Do you see those telegraph poles? Follow them and they will lead you into the town."

"A thousand thanks to you."

"You are welcome," said he, shaking my hand and going down the road to the west.

I started forward again. The evening was now well spent, the cow lowing as is her wont when she makes her way to the byre, the bird, the sheep, and the horse returning contentedly each to its own dwelling.

Soon I saw ahead of me big high houses packed together and many trees growing in their midst. It is likely this is Dingle, I thought, if I live alive. My heart was lifted with joy. Eagerly I made my way forward. I saw coming towards me a swell of a gentleman with a chain across his belly, a hard hat on his head, and an umbrella in his hand.

I greeted him.

"Is that Dingle to the east?" said I, pointing towards it.

He stopped and looked at me, looked to the east, then looked at me again. "Have you any English?" said he.

"I have," said I in English, "but I want to know am I far from Dingle still?"

"Oh yes, yes," said he, taking out a little handkerchief and wiping his brow, for I think he was sweating with the walk, "that's it over there among the trees."

"Thank you very much," said I, going east.

I looked back at him and, by God, he put me in mind of my

grandfather the day he wore the tail coat, for it was a coat of
almost the same make the gentleman was wearing now.

After that I made neither stop nor stay till I reached the
house of Martin Kane in the town, myself and the star
together.

I strolled into the kitchen and my heart full of delight to
have accomplished the journey of the day. Martin rose from
the chair.

"Where did you come from?" said he, "or who are you at
all?"

I was surprised when I saw he did not know me though
indeed it was long since I had been in Dingle. I went up and
gave my two heels to the fire.

"Faith," said I, "I am no Irishman anyway."

"You are not?" said Martin in astonishment.

"I am not indeed, though I have Irish blood in me."

Both he and his wife were now looking at me intently.

"When did you come to Ireland, so?"

"Today."

"And how the devil then did you pick up the fine Irish?"

"Arra, my dear sir, isn't it we who have the best Irish?"

"It seems so," said he, looking at me between the eyes, "but
if you are not an Irishman what are you?"

"I am a Blasket man, my boy," said I.

Martin laughed. "I swear by the devil that is an answer I
never heard before and it is many come to me. By God, you
may well say it and it is well I recognize you now."

When I had eaten my supper I questioned him about the
train and especially the time it was to leave in the morning.

"Do you mind me asking you, where is your destination?"

"Ah, to take a week in the capital city."

"Faith, I knew you had the spirit in you."

"But don't let the yellow devil keep you from calling me in
the morning," said I, going up the stairs.

"Have no fear."

Twenty-Two

FROM DINGLE EAST

I DID not sleep much that night, ever pondering over the difficult journey which lay before me. I was soon in a nightmare. Railway tracks are running across one another. I see the people like ants and myself among them. In comes the train and my heart is seized with panic. Soon it begins to move. I leap in. I slip. A man cried out, "Oh, he is dead!"

I awoke with great comfort and contentment of heart to find myself stretched in the warm bed. Three nights I lived in that night.

About six in the morning there was a knock at the door. "Get up," said Martin, "or you will be late."

I was not long making myself ready. When I had eaten my breakfast, I said farewell to Martin and his wife and set out for the train.

I looked down the street and up, people in plenty passing me in every direction and everyone seeming to have his eye on me.

I looked back and noticed an old man hurrying breathlessly behind me. Faith, said I to myself, maybe you too are making for the train.

I waited for him.

"God save you, sir," said I.

"God and Mary save you," said he in Irish.

"Will you tell me, please, where is the railway station here?"

"Follow me, my good lad. I am going there myself. From where do you come?"

"From the Blasket."

"For America, I suppose?"

"Not so, but for Dublin."

"And you were never there before?"

"I was not, and likely it is a pretty difficult journey?"

"No doubt for him who is unaccustomed to it. You would need to keep your eyes open."

We were soon at the station.

"It is as well for you now to go into the office and get your ticket," said he; "the train will soon be leaving."

I went in. There were many before me. I waited. By God, said I to myself, to judge by the progress I am making, the train will go without me. I ran out on to the platform and met a man with a horn-peaked cap on his head. I saw that he had something to do with the train.

"If you please," said I, "is it long till the train will be going?"

He took out a watch. "In ten minutes more," said he.

I leapt back into the office. The others were now ready and I got my ticket and came out again.

I stopped, looking all round me. Oh, Lord, where did the people come from? A man catching a bag, a woman running, another woman after her, chatter and confusion everywhere. They seize hold of a handle on the outside of the train to open a door, but the door does not come. They run to another door, men and women running together.

Well, said I in my own mind, it is not the windy day is the day for scallops. If I don't make a better show than this I will find myself on a stranded rock. I caught up my bag and away with me. I had only gone a few steps when an echo came back from the whole town of Dingle with the whistle the train threw out, and as for myself I was lifted clean from the ground. I looked round to see if anyone had noticed the start it took out of me, but nobody had. Everyone was inside the train but myself.

Off I ran, but I could not get an opening anywhere. As I was fumbling with it, I heard a voice at my back. I looked over my shoulder. It was the old man again. He opened a door.

"Go in there, and remember you have only two changes to make, one in Tralee and one in Mallow. Good-bye now." And he shut the door behind me.

I sat down on the seat and soon the train began to move. There was no one in the compartment but myself. I was gazing out through the window—fine green fields and trees everywhere, houses in every glen and ravine, the Blasket Island and the wild sea far out of sight. They were gone now and I a lonely wanderer, and as the old saying goes, "Bare is the companionless shoulder."

After a while a jolt was taken out of me and the train stopped. I looked out through the window and saw many people leaving the train. We are in Tralee, said I to myself, taking up my bag and stepping out. I ran straight into a horn-capped lad pushing a truck with a box on it.

"I beg your pardon, but is this Tralee?"

He stopped and looked at me. "Arra, man, you are only in Annascaul yet. About twelve o'clock you will be there."

"A thousand thanks to you," said I, and in I went again.

I sat down. What good luck I had to come across that man! I began looking out of the window again, but before long I had a twist in my neck so I stretched myself at full length on the seat, feeling thankful to the man of the horn cap. How vexed and tormented I would have been if the train had gone on without me! Would I have tried to walk back to Dingle? Alas, I would not have walked it tonight. It was so I was turning over the thoughts in my mind and I stretched contentedly on the flat of my back.

The train stopped again. Again I looked out. And again

many were leaving. As they leapt out they would stop to look back at the train, and, faith, it seemed that every one of them was putting his eyes through me and saying to each other, "Why isn't that fellow coming out?"

I slunk back and caught up my bag. It is likely, said I, the train will go no farther, and that worthless lout I met on the station just now was mocking me. I got out and looked round. Musha, if this is Tralee, said I, the devil if it is much of a place to look at. I saw another man like the one I met before. I went up to him. "When shall we be in Tralee?"

"In another hour," said he, leaving me in haste.

I got back into the carriage more than ever pleased to find I was going right. Drawing out my pipe, I took a good smoke from it. It did me good, and why wouldn't it with the long journey I was making which had been tormenting my mind for a week with the mere thought of it.

Well, when the time came I was landed at Tralee. The train stopped. I got out and again I spoke to one of the horn-peaked caps. "I suppose this will be Tralee," said I.

"It is," said he. At the same time I felt he was a nice man to talk to, so that I took a liking to him. We fell into conversation and I picked from him the time the train was to leave for Dublin. He said good-bye and went his way.

I had four hours to spend in the city, but, if so, though I had been told that the train would not start till four o'clock, I had no intention of leaving the station, for I had no trust in the train but that it might go at any time.

I put my bag against the wall and kept my eye on it always. I was walking up and down at my ease. As I looked around I saw first one woman, then another, putting their bags in through a window. They were given some kind of red ticket and then departed. I saw two men doing the same. Faith, said I, it looks as if that is a place to keep the parcels. I caught my bag and went up to the window. Inside was a man working busily at the bags. He asked me my name and wrote it down quickly in a book. He put some figures on the bag and handed

out to me a little red ticket. I was well pleased with myself
now, and why wouldn't I, and every knowledge coming to me?

I wandered out again on the platform and whatever way I
looked what would I see but "Telegraph Office" written in big
letters over a door. My heart grew as big as a cow to see it and
I went in to send a telegram to my friend George in Dublin.
A girl was sitting on a chair before me reading a book. I
greeted her. She lifted up her head and looked at me sourly,
with a sallow face on her and an ill-tempered expression.
When I told her my business she got up and handed me a
paper, then, sitting down, she began to read again. Very well,
my girl, said I in my own mind, and I began to write at my
leisure. When I had finished my task I handed in the paper,
but, if so, even yet she did not speak a word.

"There is no fear, my girl, but you are a stiff one," said I in
Irish, knowing she would not understand me.

"Good-day to you, sir," said she in English.

Would you believe it, I felt great esteem for myself when I
got that answer from her. It seems, said I to myself, I must
have the look of a gentleman and she to be calling me "sir."

My heart was now rising continually the way I was getting
knowledge of everything. Only one thing was troubling me—
my poor empty belly. I was considering now would I make an
attempt into the city, for the hunger was oppressing me and as
the proverb says, "When it's hard for the hag she must run."
Well, now was the time to try it.

By God, I will try.

I walked out of the station. But, musha, I was not far when
my courage was failing. Putting up my hand I scratched my
head. There was a cross-road to the east and a cross-road to
the west, another above and another below. Wherever I
looked there was a cross-road. My soul from the devil, said I,
if I go any farther I will be like a blind man wandering through
the city. I will never find the right road back again. But, God
save my soul, I will be perished as it is, if I go on fasting like

this, for the soul will fall out of me on the road. And then again if I go up into the city how shall I come back?

Well, I walked ahead, but, if so, the farther I went the more the cross-roads were confounding me. I stopped. The devil another step will I go, said I. Whatever I will do without food, I have no need to send myself astray in the city.

I turned on my heel and went back to the station. I sat down on a big, long bench stretched up against the wall. Two little lads were running past me, up and down, playing ball. They sent me back on the paths of thought to the time when I was doing the like on the top of the sandhills, myself and Tomás Owen Vaun. After a while another thought struck me. I called them up to me. They stopped playing, looked at each other, and giggled.

"Would you mind to go up into the city for me?"

"We would not," said they, looking down at their feet bashfully.

"Good boys!" And putting my hand in my pocket I gave them some money, "Here now, keep that for yourselves, and let you buy me a pound of bread and butter with this."

They ran away without another word, and in ten minutes they were back again with my food for the journey done up nicely and little packets for themselves. When I had thanked them they ran off into a quiet corner and soon I could see them chewing busily.

When I had eaten I arose contentedly and began walking up and down the platform again. There was only another hour to pass before I would be moving off towards the capital city. In my walk I noticed a young man and a girl coming on to the platform, carrying a couple of bags. The woman was about thirty years, so far as I could tell, and the man about twenty-five. I knew by the way they cast an eye here and there they were without knowledge of the way. By my baptism, said I in my own mind, I think you are a pair of blind travellers like myself. After a while the young man came over and greeted me. We soon made acquaintance. He was one of the O'Connors back from Annascaul. Like myself he was going into the Civic Guard, but without a word of Irish. He made me known to the girl, a sister of his, who was going to Dublin with him.

It was a great comfort to me to have made friends with the two of them, for now, thought I, I have found good guides for the journey.

"I suppose it is well you know the way to Dublin?" said I to the girl.

"Oh, I do so. It's many the day I made the journey," said she boastfully. "Do you know it well yourself?" said she with a little laugh, the kind of laugh a person makes on becoming acquainted with you for the first time.

"Indeed, good woman, this is my first time on the platform where I am standing now."

At that moment a train coming in let out a loud whistle which took a jump out of me, but I thought of myself in time. The train stretched up alongside of us.

Oh, Lord, what a din!

"I suppose that is the Dublin train," said I to the girl.

"I think it is," said she.

Oh, the confusion on the platform, my head split with the terrible roar throughout the place, boxes thrown out of the train without pity or tenderness, big cans, full of milk as I heard, hurled out on to the hard cement. Very good, said I to myself, isn't it often I was complaining of the fishermen at home making a rush to leave the quay when there would be a heavy sea, but, indeed, there is the same rush on them here though there is neither swell nor breakers. Why all the haste or where is the tide coming on them? Great God of Virtues, the chatter and gabble of the people! And not a word of Irish to be heard! I don't know in the world what brings strangers into the Blasket to learn Irish, for, so far as I can see, when they come back to this place after leaving the Island they have it thrown under foot. Look at myself now! What would I do if there was not a word of English on my lips? Wouldn't I be a public show? Where is the man or woman would give me an answer? Will the day ever come when Irish will be poured out here as English is poured out today? I doubt it.

Those are the thoughts which were passing through my mind; no thought of the train or of Dublin, but yielding to the sight of my eyes, the rush and the roar, the chatter and laughter, the welcoming one with another, big fat bucks of men along with lean and lanky spindleshanks, and the women likewise.

In the midst of my reflections I was struck a blow in the middle of the back. It was O'Connor. "Hurry!" said he, "the train will be going now."

"Is that so?" said I in a flutter.

"Have you no bag?"

"Oh, the devil take it, I forgot." And I leapt towards the window where I put it in. "Hand me out my bag, please," said I to the man inside, but in my excitement I spoke to him in Irish.

"What's that?" said he in English.,

When I repeated my words in English to him: "Where is your ticket?" said he.

I began searching my pockets but it was not to be found. I was now very anxious thinking I would never get the bag without it. "I am afraid the ticket has gone astray on me," said I, "but *there* is my bag." And I pointed my finger towards it.

He went inside and handed it out to me quickly. I thanked him and ran off, but, if so, my boy and girl were nowhere to be seen. Everyone was now in the train and my anxiety was growing. Up I ran and down I ran. Nowhere could I get in. Then O'Connor put out his head through a window: "Come in here," said he, and in I went quickly.

It seemed to me that everyone had his eyes on me. My soul to the devil, said I to myself, sitting down in their midst, anyone would think there were two heads on my shoulders the way you are all peering at me.

I turned to the boy again and we began talking.

"I suppose you are pleased to be going into the Guards?"

"I am surely. I am to be up at the Depot at eight o'clock in the morning."

"Ah, God help you, isn't it hard for you?"

"Why so?" said he.

"Arra, man, before you reach Dublin won't you be as worn out as an old woman?"

"I don't care about that if I will only pass. Are you going into them, too?"

"Not at all. It is to spend a week in Dublin I am going."

He looked hard at me. "It seems you are a pretty independent man."

"Ah, I have enough to do that much for myself."

He laughed.

"Upon my word," said I, "you are a queer fellow if you have all that fondness and affection for money. Arra, man, while you have it make use of it. What good are you unless you travel and study the world while you are in it?"

At that moment the man of the horn-peaked cap thrust his head in through the window. "All tickets ready, please," said he, and I could hear him repeating the same thing as he passed down. Everyone began to search and take out his ticket, and a shudder seized me for fear I would not find my own. I was searching and searching and it was not forthcoming, but as luck would have it I found it at last in the corner of my pocket. I sat down again and before long the man entered.

"Tickets, please," said he, and put a hole in each of them and departed.

The train began to move and soon she was passing rapidly across the country to the east. I got up and put out my head through the open window. There was not an inch of the sea to be seen now, but fine broad fields and green leafy woods and birds flying over the trees in terror of the train. Before long I noticed the train making the worm's twist round a turn in the railway. Oh, Lord, said I to myself, as I saw the length of it, what is drawing it at all? Is it possible to understand its weight, to say nothing of all the people in it? I gave another look ahead and what did I see but it passing under a bridge. When I came to the bridge myself I had no thought but that my head had been torn off with the start which was taken out of me. Quickly I crouched back inside the carriage. I looked round at the people but, if so, I was not at all pleased with the way some of them were smiling. I looked out again to see what had become of the others who were looking out at the same time. They must have had their heads torn off, said I, if they were not as quick as myself in crouching back. But musha, when I looked they were there still. Before long I saw another bridge, but this time I drew in quietly, without letting on anything, and I sat down next to O'Connor and the girl. I had another spell of talk with them and did not feel the time passing till the train drew up at the station.

The men of the horn-peaked caps were running up and down, taking an echo out of the place: "Change for Dublin! Change for Cork! Change for Dublin!"

O'Connor nudged me. "You are asleep," said he.

"I am near it. Is this Mallow?"

"It is. Let us get out."

My eyes opened wide to see men and women, their bags in their hands, walking across a bridge. What a great work! What hand of man made it? But I let on there was no wonder on me.

"What shall we do now?" said I to the two.

"Oh, follow me," said the girl with assurance, walking on. She led the way up the stairs, across the bridge, and down the other side. Another train was there before us. "This is the Dublin train now," said she, "get inside."

In we went comfortably, sat down, and away with us once more.

I was soon deep in thought, looking out through the window at the fields and valleys which were darting by, and looking in at the people, wondering who they were, from where they had come, or what business had taken them from home to send them rushing through the middle of Ireland. I sat meditating on the world. Look, it is many a thought comes to the man who goes alone. With the power of his mind he brings the great world before his face, a thing which is not possible for the man who is fond of company. I believe it is in solitude that every machine and work of ingenuity was created.

I fell asleep. I do not know how long I was so when I awoke, the train at a standstill and the ticket man before me.

"Tickets, please!" said he.

I showed him mine. He looked at me. He put a whisper in my ear: "Where are you going?"

"I am going to Dublin."

"I think you have made a mistake. You are half-way to Cork."

He went across to the other two and it was the same with them. Writing something on our tickets he returned them to us and went his way.

I looked at the girl who had been so self-confident. She was lit up to the tip of her ears. I looked at my ticket. The writing on it was hard to decipher but at last I made it out. After a while the girl raised her head and asked me what was written on it. I was unable to crush down the ill-will I felt towards her.

"Isn't it a queer thing for yourself to be unable to read it?" said I, "and you so smart at making your way to Dublin?"

There came the size of my fist of a snout on her and she turned away from me without saying a word.

I turned to O'Connor. "Isn't it a bad matter for you, who have to be up at the Depot at eight in the morning?"

"It is indeed," said he is vexation, "but what is to be done now? We must go ahead. What is that he wrote on the tickets?"

"'Here in error,'" said I sourly.

By now I was like milk and water. I couldn't remain any longer where I was and to have to be looking at the two of them. I went out into the corridor, my head bent, walking up and down, thinking and ever thinking of what I ought to do. Would I have to spend the night in Cork? Would I have to pay again for my passage to Dublin? If so, it was a great sin for ever. Och, wouldn't it be a fine thing to be back in the Blasket now! What prompted me to leave it at all?

The train was whistling from time to time, and with every whistle anxiety was growing on me. Through the windows of the corridor I could see, now and then, noble gentlemen talking together and laughing merrily. I wonder, thought I, if you knew there was a poor traveller like myself gone astray, would you give him any help? I suppose you would not, for as the old saying goes, the fat does not notice the lean.

The day was now almost spent. Glancing out of the window I saw lights here and there. One more whistle, and in a few minutes the train was at a standstill once more.

Oh, Lord, isn't it there was the gathering! As soon as I leapt out, ten hotel-porters began to tear me asunder, like a swarm of bees you would see humming round a hive on a fine summer evening. Running up, a man would make a grab at me. "Come to Buckley's Hotel! come to Buckley's Hotel!"

"I am not staying here tonight."

"Aren't you going to America?"

"I am not. It is to Dublin I am going."

With that he would leave me, still shouting.

Up came another man and seized me by the shoulder. "Come to St. Patrick's Hotel! Come to St. Patrick's Hotel!" The same reply I gave him and away he went. A ragged lad ran up, sending his voice out higher than the rest: *"Evening Echo! Examiner! Evening Echo!"* There was yet another man, pushing a truck and my head splitting with the din he took out of the place. Two, three, and four here and there among the crowd and they whistling. Oh, wasn't I envious of them, without a care or trouble in the world! Isn't it a pity I am not an emigrant now! Isn't it fine and safe I would be, taken up by the hotel people!

I looked back again. O'Connor and the girl were nowhere to be seen. My heart leapt. I looked on this side and on that. But, if so, it would have been as well for me to seek a needle in an oatstack as look for those two among the crowd passing by like the dark clouds that come out of the sky from the east on a winter's day. Oh, God send me on the right path, said I. What good is it for me to stand still here like a stock, looking round, ever thinking and doing nothing. Remember it is not on the top of the Strand you are now, ready to run along the road to the east towards your house, but in a place where you must have an eye in the back of your head as well as the two that are out before you.

I took up my bag and moved on, putting people from me on every side. Then I noticed coming down towards me a man who was got up very fine as for yellow bands on his sleeves and a horn-peaked cap on his head ornamented with gold. Faith, thought I, it is likely if I went talking with you it is yourself would give me every information about the train.

I went up to him quickly. I showed him my ticket and told him what was after happening to me since I left Mallow. "Ah, don't be troubled," said he, "that ticket will take you to Dublin. The train will be leaving in three hours at nine o'clock exactly, and it will land you in Dublin at half-past three tomorrow morning."

"A thousand thanks to you," said I leaving him, and as pleased as any other mother's son from here to Halifax, as an Islander would say.

One thing only was troubling me now. There would not be anyone before me on the station in Dublin. In the telegram to my friend I had told him I would arrive at half-past seven. Then as luck was in it, with a glance I gave to the left I saw "Telegraph Office" written over a door. I went in rejoicing and wrote another telegram telling George I had gone astray and to be before me on the station at half-past three in the morning without fail.

I wandered out and courageously I turned my face towards the city. I walked down through a great broad street and my heart filled with delight when I saw on my right hand hundreds of masts beside the quay. "Oh, your soul to the devil," cried I aloud for joy. Recollecting myself I looked round at once to see if anyone were listening. There was no one. But what did I see but a man standing up in a corner with a very strange appearance on him—a big stick in his hand which he moved from side to side as if he were feeling the place with it, his face turned upwards, some kind of board hanging down his breast and he muttering to himself. Now and then he would take off his cap and make the sign of the cross. People in plenty was passing by, but they took no notice of him. By my baptism, said I to myself, you are a strange one and it is a great wonder you get no heed from the people who are passing. After a while I walked over to him. I could see now what was written on the board: "Have a heart and help the blind!"

Oh, thought I, woe to him who would complain! Oh, God, give help to this poor blind man here.

"In the name of God," said I, "whatever I will do without money I will spare a small sum to you."

I put my hand in my picket and gave him a shilling.

I went down the street to the quay. Putting down my valise beside me I looked around. The harbour was coloured with shipping: steam-ships, sailing ships and rowing-boats, those far away very small. White gulls in plenty were flying over the water. As far as I could see were houses in hundreds of every hue, some of them of which you would say they were afire from the sun sparkling on the panes and it going down in the west. I thought of the strong lads and comely girls who had left that quay, and mourning came on me as it had come on them when they left this place and nothing to be seen out before them but the edge of the sky.

A voice spoke behind me: "I see there is grief on you, my boy."

I looked round. He was standing by my side—a bent old man well worn with the hardship of the world. There was a knitted cap on his head, a clay pipe in his mouth, a grey beard under his chin, and boots up to his knees. I saw he was a man of the sea.

"You don't mind my asking, is it beyond you are going?"

"It is not, but near it."

"Your girl that is gone before you likely?" said he, laughing.

"Musha, the cause of my sorrow is every boy and girl who was once in my company. They have all turned their backs on this quay, and I am like Usheen left alone after the Fianna."

"Ah, that is no fault in you, young man. It was the same with me." And he took out a pocket-handkerchief which had not been washed for a long time by the look of it. "I tell you I was well off once, a fisherman with a motor boat owned by myself and my four sons. But my sharp sorrow, the fishing fell under foot and my heart was sorely smitten a year ago on the place where the two of us are standing now, when my four sons said farewell and turned their backs to me out through the harbour.

"Ah, it is little I thought," cried he mournfully, "ye would leave me alone as I am!"

Hunger was oppressing me by this time for I had been fasting since two o'clock when I had eaten some dry biscuits, only enough to sharpen my appetite. So I said good-bye to the old man who was still gazing sorrowfully out, as if he were talking to the great sea. "Musha, my lad, a thousand blessings go with you," said he.

I walked on quickly through the street. Before long I was standing outside a big, high church. God of Virtues, thought I, isn't it wonderful the work of men! Who could believe that any human hand would have the power to pile those stones one on another! I was gazing up at the spire, moving backwards to see it better. A gentleman chanced to be passing and in the confusion I struck him in the back.

"I beg your pardon, sir," said I, looking over my shoulder.

He leapt aside and walked on ahead without a word or even a look at me. Isn't it a wonder the speed there does be on the people of a city! Upon my word, my lad, said I looking after him, if you had spent five hours seated on the thwart of a canoe in a foaming sea you would not be such a buck for leaping.

I turned on my heel and went into the chapel. I knelt down

to offer up a prayer, though it was not of prayers I was thinking but of the fine sight before my eyes.

I went out again, and it was a great opening was taken out of my eyes when I reached the door. Whom would I meet coming in but O'Connor and the girl?

"We are well met," said I joyfully. "It is ever said that men meet again but not so the hills or mountains."

"Where are you all the evening?" said he.

"Arra, man, where would I be but in the city of Cork. Did you have anything to eat yet?"

"Nothing at all."

"Wouldn't it be a good thing for us to get some food before we leave for Dublin?"

"It would surely," said she; but I tell you my heart was not very bright towards that girl.

We were now walking up the street. I noticed O'Connor sighing. "The devil, O'Connor, there is a great sighing on you altogether. What is distressing you?"

"Musha, man, isn't it a great affliction to have to be up at the Depot at eight in the morning and without a wink of sleep this night? No doubt there is nothing troubling yourself for you can sleep it out."

"Upon my word, that is not what you will be saying a week from today when I will see you in the Guard's uniform. It is high on your head the cap will be then."

At that moment a voice cried out: "Hello! country cauboons!"

I began to tremble from head to heel, and O'Connor the same. I looked back but could see no one behind me. "Where did that voice come from, O'Connor?"

"Begor," said he, "it is beyond me to make it out."

After a while I looked back again and I saw a stout lump of a boy seated above on the top of the wall, his legs hanging down. When he saw me looking, he cried out again: "Hello, hello, country cauboons!"

"Musha, it is to the devil I give you if I haven't the slant on you, you dregs of the city," said I aloud in Irish.

When I looked at the two they were laughing loudly.

"The devil," said I, "it is fine and soft are the shells on the two of you, but take heed of this, if that brat were before my face I would soon make his ears tingle."

"I think, Sullivan, it is in a temper you are," said O'Connor.

"The cause of my anger is to see the two of you making fools of yourselves laughing like that. Let us be off before he makes a public show of us."

Off we walked and the brat shouting after us: "Hello, hello, country cauboons!"

My blood was boiling with rage.

"Sure, anyone would know," said the girl, "that the two of you come from the country with the stoop on you walking."

"Musha, long stoop on yourself," said I, "there is a fine hump on your own back if you could see it."

I looked at O'Connor. "I swear on my oath, O'Connor, there is a great stoop on the two of us, the way the people of the city know we are countrymen. Raise your head, man," said I, stretching myself up and walking as light as a bird. And by God, when I looked at O'Connor again, he had his snout turned up like a seal you would see when bad weather would be coming. "Oh, man," said I, "don't take too much of the sky."

I had no sooner spoken than I saw the word "Hotel" written over a door.

I went in, the two following me. You would think at that moment I knew the city as well as the mayor. A middle-aged woman came out to us, her head as grey as a hedgehog and pearls hanging from her ears. She addressed the girl. Look, said I in my own mind, how one goose knows another.

She directed us upstairs. We went up and into the eating-room where were many tables laid under bright cloths, an odd person or two here and there, eating. We sat down together at a table; knives, forks and spoons in plenty upon it, and as for the bottles, they took my senses from me. As sure as I am alive, said I to myself, I am in a periwinkle shell now, for it is likely those bottles will work the wrong way with me. I cast an eye here and an eye there to watch the people around how they were working the bottles. Knife or fork I did not touch yet but talking hard, letting on I was in no hurry to begin. I glanced at O'Connor and the girl, and by God, I saw they were country people like myself for they had the same reluctance to try them.

Well, I was making a Tigue's tale of my talk,[1] and watching everyone around till I had learned at last how to work the knife, the fork, and the bottle.

"The devil," said I, seizing hold of the knife and fork, "isn't it reluctant ye are before the table?"

I had no sooner done it than the other two did the same and they with a mouse's eye on myself. When I would take up one of the bottles I would hardly have put it down again before the other two would snap it up, so that if I had taken the salt-jar and emptied it into my tea-cup, they would have done the same.

It was now half-past eight. It was time for us to hurry for the train. We left the hotel and walked straight on our way till we reached the station.

Lights in hundreds here and there, the same ragged lad walking up and down with the same cry selling papers.

In a short time the train gave out a whistle. One jerk and away with us.

---

1. Proverbial expression for making a short story long.

Twenty-Three

―――――▸━◂――――――

THE CITY OF DUBLIN

I STRETCHED back on the sofa and was soon sound asleep. I do not know how long I passed in that slumber till the whistle of the train awoke me. I leapt up. O'Connor and the girl were still sleeping. A cold shiver struck me. My soul from the devil, said I, it is often I would complain while stretched on the thwart of a curragh back beyond Carrig Valach at such a time, and it is little I thought that if I were in a train the same cold shiver would strike me.

I thrust my head out through the window. The night had a lonesome look. It was sharp and cold, nothing to be heard only the duga-ga-dug, duga-ga-dug of the train and now and again the fairy music of the wind as it ran in against the window-panes. It is far away my thoughts were at that moment—far west in the Blasket. I see the curraghs back beyond Carrig Valach and hear the glug-glag of the ripples on their sides. I see others off the strand of Yellow Island and yet others down to the west of the Tail, the nets stretched back out of the sterns and phosphorescence around them. I see again the old crew—Shaun Liam, Tigue O'Shea and Tomás O'Carna down at the Tail, their nets in the sea and they talking. Look how they strike their arms together to keep themselves warm! I hear the cág-cág-cág of the black-backed gulls hovering in the air above the nets and see them swooping down at the phosphorescence as if it were mackerel. I see a seal snarling behind the nets and hear Tigue O'Shea throw a curse at him: "Blindness and darkness on you, we won't have a fish alive in the nets tonight!" Now I can hear the grating of the oars as the fishers make for the quay and not a fish in the bottom of the curragh. I can see them going in through the pool, not a sound to be heard but the lonely murmur of the ripples through the clefts of the rocks in the dead of night, a dog barking in the distance, and the whole village sound asleep.

Duga-ga-dug, duga-ga-dug, then another whistle from the train. The other two were still asleep. I shut my eyes close and soon the village appeared in perfect likeness before my face, for "with eager desire I was making my fullest endeavor to see my love," as the poet said long ago.[1] So great is the power of the solitary man.

Now the train was whistling again. I saw through the window thousands of lights. Going across to where O'Connor was stretched on the other sofa I looked at the little watch on his wrist. It was a quarter-past three. I roused them. O'Connor sat up and rubbed his eyes.

"Wake up, my boy," said I, "we have made land."

"God help us," said he, "and if we have it is time for it."

"Arra, man, you have slept enough now to go up to the gates of Paradise."

He stretched himself as if the same gates were not to his liking.

"Upon my word, it is little more sleep I will tonight," said he, "for likely I won't find a house to let me in."

My heart was in my mouth now, for it was so late my friend might likely not be before me. The train was entering the

---

1. Carolan.

station, my heart beating. It stretched alongside the platform. There was no one alive to be seen, only a big fat policeman covered well up under his chin. I took my bag and stepped out, and I tell you I hated the thought of that city.

As I leapt out who was before me but George!

"God save you, Maurice, you have brought home your load at last."

"I have, George," said I, shaking him by the hand.

I cannot describe my relief of mind at that moment to see my friend. My thoughts changed so that I was like a bird for joy.

"Well, we had better be going," said he. "The motor car is waiting for us."

The other two were standing behind me.

"I wonder, George, could you find a hotel for these two who were with me?"

"Very good." And we moved out with him.

The motor was not gone far when it stopped outside a big house. We got out. George put his finger on a little button beside the door.

"What is that, George?"

"You have only to press that button and the people of the house will hear a bell ringing within."

Cause for laughter from God! said I to myself, if I happened to be alone and to come to that door, it is the toe of my boot it would get and, if so, it is likely I would be arrested for it. Soon we heard strides down the stairs and the door was opened. We said good-bye to the two and went back to the motor.

Oh, wasn't my heart delighted when the car moved out through the street; wasn't it a great change of view; wasn't it a wonderful prospect in the dead of night! I looked out. I was blinded by the hundred thousand lights, lights on every side of me, lights before me, and lights above my head on the tops of poles. Soon I saw a small light coming towards me like a star through the mist. In half a minute it was gone by. It was another motor. Then came another after it and yet another, our own making rings round the corners and blowing the horn without ceasing. I don't know if I am in a dream. If not, it is the Land of the Young without a lie.

"I think you are not contented," said my friend.

"Oh, it is not that, but that I cannot believe the sight before my eyes. Great God of Virtues, isn't it a spacious city?"

"The place we are going to is the house of a friend of mine—Furry Park it is called. She has invited the two of us to stay there for a week."

"Are we far from it?"

"It is not much farther as we are approaching Killester now."

I looked at him in wonder.

"I don't know how on God's earth you can make out where we are and the motor darting hither and thither like a bird."

He laughed. "You, too, soon will know it when you will be accustomed to the city."

"That will be one of the greatest wonders that ever happened, if you will see me passing through this city without guidance from anyone."

"Upon my word I shall see it, Maurice, and in no long time."

Soon the motor stopped outside a big castle, a magnificent lamp alight above the door, the walls covered in ivy, up to twenty windows in it and they big and broad.

I stepped back a little way and looked round. Apparently I was in the middle of a wood, for I could see the stars twinkling in the sky through the trees, and I could hear the lonely music of the wind in the leaves, a sound that would put a man deeply into thought.

"Come in here," said George. "Softly now, for fear we would wake the people of the house."

He unlocked the door cautiously and we slipped gently in. "Sh, sh," said he, his lips pouting.

I thought at once of robbers, but, mo léir, we were walking like mice, for the floor was covered with big, soft rugs.

He went up the stairs, I following him.

"Sh, sh," came from him again, ever and ever, until we entered a big, richly furnished room, pictures of noblemen long dead hanging on the walls, ornamental furniture here and there and wonderful curtains hanging down over the big, long windows.

It was now four o'clock. We were worn out. It was not long till we were asleep.

About eleven o'clock the next morning the sunbeams were pouring in through the curtains and the two of us awake, talking and conversing of the affairs of the Island. There was a knock at the door. In came a girl, young, handsome, brightly laughing. I saw she was of the flower of nobility. She gave me a thousand welcomes, sat down and began to pour out tea for us. Soon we were talking at our ease, especially of my journey to the city.

After awhile she went away. "Isn't that a handsome girl?" said I to George.

"She is, indeed."

What was my wonder when I heard that she was married!

About the middle of the day I walked out among the trees, where there was comfort and delight for the singing of birds in the branches above my head, the sun sparkling through the leaves and the leaves shaking in the little air of wind was coming from the west. I walked in among them, and the thrush singing above me fine, soft and sweet. I looked up at him. He seemed to be singing in order to delight my own heart. He made me think of the great world, of things I had never understood before. I could see the city clearly at the edge of the sky, great high pillars standing here and there and wisps of smoke from them rising upwards. I was deep in thought considering the life of men. I looked east towards the castle, covered in ivy and sparrows quarrelling amongst it. Isn't it a fine life is given to some rather than to others! I don't know what in the world could trouble the man who lives there, though I have often heard it is they who are the worst for discontent. It is a great lie. He would need only to sit outside his castle listening to the music of the birds for all sorrow to be lifted from his heart.

I arose again and walked down a pleasant path where the trees were coming together in close grips above my head, and a sweet smell from the flowers around me. I walked through the wood till I came to the east corner, where the crows were chattering in the branches above. I stopped and looked up. A sort of shame came on me when I saw them looking down at me, crying cág-cág-cág and jerking their beaks down towards me as if to drive home what they were saying. I thought at once of that brat of a Cork lad who had called us country cauboons. Was it any wonder for him to guy me when the rooks themselves are mocking me.

I wandered down to the bottom of the meadow where three or four cows were lying in the grass, each as big as an elephant and with a gloss on their hides from the fat of their bodies. I walked back again in the direction of the castle. I had been out for three hours, though it had seemed no more than half an hour to me. There was great wonder on George and Moya (that was the name of the woman of the house), for they thought I must have gone astray through the city.

Late in the evening: "I wonder," said my friend, "would you like to pay a visit to the pictures?"

My heart leapt. "No doubt of it," said I.

We stopped at cross-roads near the castle to wait for a bus. Oh, King of Virtues, wasn't the street clean! It would not harm you to stretch back on it for any dirt you would have on your clothes. There were many others at the cross-roads going to the pictures like ourselves, each boy with his own girl. Isn't it they have the comfortable life with nothing to hinder them but the dry road out before them always. Isn't it a great pity entirely for the poor lads back in the Island with nothing for them to see or hear but the big rollers coming up through the

Sound and the rough noise of the wind blowing from the north-west across the hills, and often for four weeks without news from the mainland! Musha, woe to him who travels not, as the old woman said long ago on her first journey out to Dunquin.

I felt a prod in my shoulder. "The bus is coming," said George.

She comes across with a loud grating noise. The crowd moves towards her, myself and my companion among them. She moves away rapidly. Soon motors and cars of all sorts are passing each other like ants, the bus turning the corners like the wind and a tumult in my head from the horns blowing to let others know that they are coming. Isn't it great the intelligence of the drivers to guard themselves against one another! For myself, I did not know any moment but I would be splintered.

We reached O'Connell Bridge and got out. Trams and motors roaring and grating, newspaper-sellers at every corner shouting in the height of their heads, hundreds of people passing this way and that without stopping, and every one of them, men and women, handsomely got-up.

The trouble now was to cross the street. A man would make the attempt, then another, an eye up and an eye down, a step forward and a step back, until they would reach the other side.

"Oh, Lord, George, this is worse than to be back off the quay of the Blasket waiting for a calm moment to run in."

He laughed. "Here is a calm moment now," he said suddenly. Off we went in a flutter, George gripping my arm; now forwards, now backwards, until we landed on the opposite side.

We walked on and I tell you my eyes grew large when I saw above me every letter of the "Capitol" alight. "Great God, George, look at the wonder above your head!" At that moment it went out, but again every letter was lit up till the whole "Capitol" was on fire. In deference to me, George let on he was as greatly astonished, like a mother petting her little child. Well, well, said I to myself, I must change and not show my wonder at anything else.

We went in. Such a building for size! Without any non-sense it took my sense from me. Stars came before my eyes with the sight—the cleanliness and the splendour of the place within. It was impossible to comprehend it. Wonderful is the power of man! We went up a staircase as twisty as a corkscrew and my delight was so great that I thought of heaven. If it would be as fine as this, it were worth fighting and getting sudden death for it. Before long a girl came to us, dressed in a sailor's suit as it seemed to me, a light in her hand. She showed us to a seat and departed.

Before me now was the fairest sight a sinner's eye ever beheld, and strains of music as sweet as fairy music itself. Two big curtains slowly parted the way I saw a wood and a wild desert with great hills covered with snow above. A man comes towards me through the wood, growing bigger and bigger until he is the size of a giant. He stops—a bright suit on him and a long black beard under his chin. He looks out at the assembly and leans his shoulder against a big tree. Then he opens his mouth and begins a beautiful song. Oh, Lord, it is he had the sweet, trembling voice. I thought I was in a dream. And what wonder, with the great change which had come into my life so suddenly.

No sooner was the singer gone than the curtains opened again. What would there be but about twenty people with every kind of music and a man before them with a stick in his hand. As he raised the stick the music would rise. When he lowered it the music would fall.

When it ceased the curtains were let down again. A blaze of light was sent throughout the building so that I could see all round and the smoke rising up to the rafters from the hundreds of cigarettes that were alight around me.

"How did you like the music?" said my friend.

"The way it is with me, if I were here always I think death could not come near me."

"You will change yet, Maurice."

"I suppose you are right," said I, and he spoke truly.

The curtain rises again and I tell you it was now I was astonished to see the loveliest girl my eyes ever beheld seated on an ornamental chair, an old lady in bracelets and pearls seated beside her. The mother is advising the girl not to marry this man but that man. The girl is not content and bursts into tears. Well, there is no need for me to make a Tigue's tale of it, but at the end of the story she escapes with her own fair love, as a woman of the Island would say.

George stood up. "It is over," said he.

Twenty-Four

―――❧◉❧―――

THE CIVIC GUARD

On the 28th of April I shook my feathers, made ready my mind, washed and cleaned my body till I had the salt rubbed out of my skin, and with the sea-tan gone from my face and the look of the city swell upon me, I set out for the Depot in Phoenix Park, myself and my friend beside me.

A peeler was standing at either side of the gate. George spoke to one of them. He told us to wait till he sent in a message to the office. While we were waiting, a Guard passed with a bugle in his hand. He stood some way off, as straight as a candle, put the bugle to his mouth and took an echo out of the square. Then we saw a great company of men in Guards' uniform coming out, a sergeant walking before them and shouting: "Left, left, left!" The sergeant stopped and the men passed him in step together.

The peeler returned. "Come with me now," said he.

He took us into a big room where three or four Guards were busy writing and going through papers. Musha, I don't know in the world, said I to myself, will the day ever come when I will be as you are. My friend was talking to them, and after a while one of them came up to me. We followed him into another room.

"Take off your coat and shirt till I measure you."

I did so. He took out his tape.

"He is very thin, only thirty-four inches round the chest," said he in English.

"And what is the right measurement?" said George.

"Thirty-six."

I became anxious, thinking he was going to throw me out for the sake of two inches.

"Ask him," said I to George in Irish, "if he had been stooping every morning to lift a big heavy hulk of a curragh and carrying it on his back to the water, his ribs rattling and doubling under the weight, would his own waist be as broad? And tell him further than when I get the beef and mutton into mine it will soon be as good as his."

"Throw off your shoes now till I take your height," said the Guard.

"What is the right height?" said I.

"Five feet nine inches."

He put a sheet of paper on the floor by the wall. I did not know what was the meaning of it. "Put your heels on the paper now," said he.

I obeyed.

"And now stand straight up against the wall."

I obeyed again, but I thought it as well to raise myself on my toes to increase my height. He bent down and drew the paper gently from under my heels. I was caught in the act.

"That won't do. You must keep your heels on the ground."

I stood up straight again, and, by God, I was five feet eleven inches.

He told me I could go and to be back at eight o'clock on the following morning.

Now was the time for me to gather my wits together, to strengthen my courage, and to cast under foot my foolish thoughts, to rub the rust from my limbs, to lay aside all childishness, and to go as far as the eye of the needle.

Next morning at seven o'clock George and I arose and set out once more for the Park. Some forty young men were standing inside before me, country boys who had been called up. They looked worn and distressed, gazing anxiously around.

"Well, I had better be going now," said George, "and leave you in the company of the others."

He bade me good-bye and departed.

I had my shoulder against a pillar, looking out lonesomely, the other recruits sitting on a long bench talking merrily. The Guard with the bugle came out. He stood at the corner of the barrack and blew. In a moment Guards in hundreds were gathering from all directions. There were two sergeants in charge and before long I heard that terrible word, "'Shun!" You could have heard it a mile from home. The company crossed the square and the recruits got up to look at them. They stopped, bringing their heels together with a kick. At the same time another company came down towards me carrying all sorts of music and led by an officer. The officer raised his stick. The music began. The men marched past, the merry music filling my ears.

I turned back towards the recruits. Well, said I to myself, I had better go and speak with you. I stood watching them and soon I noticed one wearing the Irish fáinne.[1] It must be, I thought, that you are from some backward place and know the old tongue. I went across to him.

"God save you," said I.

He looked at me in surprise. "God and Mary save you," said he.

"Where are you from?"

He smiled. "From Donegal. Where are you from yourself?"

"Musha, I am thinking you never heard mention of the place, but I will give you Kerry."

---

1. A badge worn by Irish-speakers.

"Oh, I know it well."

"Did you ever hear mention of the village far west?"

"Where is that?"

"Och, you don't know Kerry, so."

The sergeant came up with a sheet of paper in his hands. He stood before us, looking at it. "Patrick Feeney, stand out here!" And so on till he had called the last man.

"Squad!" he cried immediately afterwards the terrible word "'Shun!" "Form fours! Right turn! Quick march!"

Then away we marched into the gymnasium.

Each of us seated at a table by himself, a pen and plenty of paper before him. I looked at my pen and laughed. O God above, I thought, am I not a fine gentleman at last!

An officer came in with a form for each of us and gave us sums to do. Then we were told to write a short essay on tillage. I scratched my head. Musha, I don't know in the world, said I to myself, will I do it in Irish? Upon my word I will. I will let them see I have a respect for the language.

I seized my pen and attacked the paper vigorously. I left no stone unturned nor thread unstrung but wrote down everything. I went down as far as the strand in the end till I had the crop stored.

When we had finished we were ordered to go into the city for our dinner, and to be back at three o'clock. We went out through the gate, the Irish-speaker and myself together.

"How did you get on in the examination?"

"Musha, upon my word," said he, "I found it very hard."

"Are you in earnest?"

"Indeed I am, and I am much afraid I didn't pass."

"Oh, don't say that, for if you leave me I shall be a pooka entirely."

At three o'clock we were sitting in the same place inside the gate when the same sergeant came down and called us out as before.

"Squad!" he cried, and then, "'Shun! From fours! Right turn! Quick march! Left incline!" and away we went till he led us into the Dispensary. There we were ordered to strip off our clothes. We spent an hour waiting for the doctor in that way, just as we came into the world, our teeth chattering with the cold.

My own name was called and I went into the room to the doctor, a very decent man. He took up his instruments and put one of them into my back: "Say ninety-nine, please." "Ninety-nine," said I. "Again." "Ninety-nine!" I said again loudly, for fear he might find any fault with me.

"Oh, you are as sound as a herring," said he.

"It no wonder," said I, "for I was born and bred in their company.

He laughed. I put on my clothes and went out.

It was past five o'clock before everyone had been examined. We were ordered to go into the city and return at nine the next morning. I said good-bye to the Irish-speaker for I was going to see George who lived in Leeson Street.

I leapt on to a tram. Ah, said I to myself when I was seated inside at my ease, wasn't it true for George when he told me the first night that I would soon be traveling alone through the city without guidance from any man.

I knocked at the door. The woman of the house opened it and welcomed me, for we were already acquainted. George was in his own room before me, surrounded with an ass's load of papers and books.

"God save you, George," said I.

"Musha, God and Mary save you, how did you get on?"

"By God, I don't know at all for the order we got was to be back again at nine tomorrow."

"Oh, you have made your white coat,[2] so."

"It is tomorrow I shall know that," said I.

We sat down before the hearth talking of the fine times we had in the Island long ago until the two of us were struck by

---

2. You are settled for life, said of a girl after her match is made.

the sleep of the corncrake on either side of the fire. We got up and went to the white gable.

Next morning I made my way back to the gate. The other recruits greeted me, especially the Irish-speaker.

"Well, what is your opinion today?" said I.

"The devil I know. We shall have it over anyway."

The sergeant came down, gave us the same commands and off we marched. We turned in under a big archway and were ordered to wait there till we were called. We spent the time walking up and down to keep ourselves warm, the Irish-speaker and myself talking together.

Before long we heard a voice:

"Michael O'Callaghan, come in here!"

We stopped talking at once. The boy went in. We all watched the door with beating hearts, waiting for the news he would bring. Soon he came out with a look of weeping. He walked up and held out his hand to one of them.

"Lord God, what's wrong, Mick?" said the other fellow, taking his hand.

"I did not pass," said he with tears in his eyes.

"Ah, what harm, man?" said the other. "It might be all for luck."

He shook hands with us all and went his way.

Then another was called in, and he came out in the same fashion, until twelve had been struck off the books. Among them was my Gaelic companion. He said farewell to me and departed.

Eighteen of us were left. But we said to each other that the same end was in store for us all, and so we had given up hope. I heard my own name called. My heart was in my mouth with the flutter of fright that came over me, for I had no thought, of course, but that I would get the same treatment as the rest. I went in.

"Well," said the Guard who was there before me, "you have passed, boy. Write your name here."

"By God," said I in Irish as I took up the pen, "I have made my white coat at last."

He did not understand what I was saying and looked at me between the eyes.

"Is that all I have to do now?"

"That is all."

"How did you get on?" I was asked when I went out.

"Well," I replied contentedly.

I took out my pipe and I tell you I sent the smoke flying. One by one they went in heavy-hearted and came out rejoicing.

We went off to the sleeping-rooms. Five or six of us were put in each. My eyes opened wide when I saw about fourteen small beds along the walls. Ah, it is now I was in a place where I would have to keep my two eyes well open. I was acquainted with no one.

The Clare man was there, the Galway man and the Cork man, the city swell and the country lad—the Blasket man among them.

I sat down on my bed. The other recruits were talking to some Guards, inquiring after this person and that. Whatever happiness I had felt before it all left me now when I looked at the little iron bed beneath me covered with two thin blankets. I was tired and weary, without vigour, pleasure, or mirth. I knew well I was under control again. It is often I had complained during my school-days and said to myself, if I were a grown man I would be content. But look at me now without anyone around me who knows me. I drew out my pipe, filled it and lit up. But seven times it went out, for I would forget to keep it alight with all the thoughts which were running through my mind.

I jumped up, took off my clothes and got into bed. A fellow here and a fellow there was glancing at me. "I swear by the devil," said one of them, "the recruit above means to get his sleep."

But I took no heed. I stretched back, turned on this side and that. But it was no use, for the hard thwart was piercing my back. I thought of the old soldier in the red army. No sleep was falling on me. How could it?—a man here singing a snatch of a song, another laughing, two more wrestling all over the room and now and then falling on top of me, a man playing a flute, another a fiddle. Oh, Lord, said I, it is often I would complain of the roar of the waves below the house on a rough winter's night at home, but upon my word I am in a madhouse now.

After a while a sergeant came in. The noise stopped, all without a word like mice at sight of a cat.

"Lights out!" he cried.

The lights were put out and everyone groped through the darkness to his bed. Well, thought I, it was no harm to give you that much. Maybe you will be a littler quieter for the rest of the night. But indeed it was not so, for when they were stretched out on their backs they surpassed themselves. Not a wink of sleep could I get for all the chatter and clatter through the room, and from time to time a train whistling from afar. Not a sound came to my ears that night but I heard it.

At six o'clock, not a moment before or after, I heard the bugle blowing. A man leapt from his bed. "Wake up, lads," he cried, "remember you are far away from home now!"

Oh, Lord, wasn't I vexed and tormented without a wink of sleep all night. Everyone was getting up, stretching and yawning, especially the recruits like myself whose bones were reluctant. It would have been little use for you to say that morning, "Wait a while, I will be getting up now." Ah my sorrow, you would not soon have forgotten it.

We went out and made for the wash-house, clamour and confusion, everyone shaving himself hastily. In ten minutes we were washed and clean. Then the bugle blew again.

We went out into the square. The sergeant was standing there before us, calling the roll. It was there I heard the first word of Irish. As he called out each name, a man would answer

"Annso!"[3] and, believe me, there were many who spoke it with an English accent.

There were about four hundred of us in the square now, the adjutant out before us.

"Company!" he shouted.

Everyone was ready waiting until there came the sickening word, "'Shun!"

What a wonderful throat that same adjutant had! "Form fours!" he cried again. "Right turn! Left turn! Quick march!" and away we went into Phoenix Park.

Discontented though I had been ever since I went into the Depot, a cloud was rising from my heart now when I saw the view—the earth white with snow, the foliage on the trees bending under the burden they were carrying, the wind whistling shrilly through the wood. Hundreds of crows were flying from tree to tree, and before long I saw a couple of deer galloping away from the terrible host which was approaching. Musha, did I not think at once of the Fianna, of Oscar and Conán Maol and Goll mac Mórna.

We had marched a couple of miles into the Park when we were given that strong word, "Halt!" which ran through the woods like a whirlwind. "Fall out!"

We left the ranks and sat down in rows by the roadside. I was sitting with my back against the ditch, listening to a blackbird singing above my head. Musha, isn't it many a thing it put me in mind of! The sun was climbing the sky and all the birds greeting it; sounds of all kinds were passing through my ears—the voice of the birds, the whistling of the trains, the grating of the trams, and the lonely sound of the wind in the woods.

Before long I heard a shout which went through the back of my head: "Fall in!"

I leapt up. Everyone was making for the road and standing

3. "Here."

shoulder to shoulder. I took my place among them, and away we marched again.

On our return to the Depot, we were ordered to go for our breakfast. We ran like a flock of sheep to the hall. My eyes opened in wonder to see forty long tables, twenty on each side of the hall and twelve men at each. But indeed it was a meagre portion was laid before us. Looking round I soon saw everyone laying down the knife and fork on his plate. I thought it very queer but did the same. Since you are in Rome, said I, it is as well for you to be a Roman. Then I saw the superintendent walking down the middle of the hall. He stopped:

"Any complaints?"

"No, sir," cried a hundred voices together.

It was then I understood that they had stopped eating out of homage to him.

Well, no sooner were we seated in our own room after the meal, and cigarettes in our mouths, when the bugle was blown again. God be with us for ever, said I to myself, isn't it a discontented and vexatious world when a man wouldn't get time to have his smoke!

We were turned right and turned left till we came out into the square. "The last batch of recruits, fall out here!" cried the officer.

We were put in charge of a sergeant, a small, short, haggard, rough-voiced fellow with a pale face and two eyes like candles. He stood out before us and began by giving a lecture on what we had to do, turning right and left, kicking the square as he brought up the other foot. Then he gave us a command.

"Squad!" he cried. "'Shun!" and I noticed the sinews of his neck ready to burst with the strain. "Right turn!" he shouted again. We turned right. "Quick march!" and away we marched up the square.

The sergeant remained where he was, and as we moved away from him he was like a dog barking in the distance. After half an hour's hard toil he dismissed us. We returned to our room, running with sweat, worn out, and weary.

I spent three months drilling in that fashion, until I was as thin as an eel without a drop of sweat in my body. One night in the beginning of September, about three o'clock in the morning, the boy in the bed next to my own let out a scream and told us to call a doctor. Everyone was awake in a moment and the room in confusion. The doctor came. He immediately ordered the boy to hospital. The next day we were all moved to another room that our own might be disinfected. "And you will be very lucky," said the doctor, "if none of you has caught it."

He was right. I was suddenly struck down myself and sent off to hospital. I spent a couple of days there, getting worse. Then they moved me down to the Fever Hospital in Cork Street, where I lay without wish for food or for drink, worn out with the world, nothing around me but white beds, an old man on one side and a boy with his own complaint on the other, another being brought in on a stretcher, a smell of drugs and of sickness throughout the place. How vexed and tormented I was, especially when I would see every other patient visited by his people, for no one was coming to me. My friend was over in England and the people of the castle on holiday in the west. As for my own kin they were all on the other side of the world, and I miserable that I had not followed them. Och, isn't health a fine thing! Woe to the man who would complain so long as he could walk out and take a draught of the sweet air of heaven. I would often think of the days gone by when I would be hunting with a light heart on the summit of the Cró, or fishing on the top of the waves or playing ball on the White Strand. Not a man in the Blasket then who could keep up with me in the race. Often too I would think of the night when the traveller was telling us beside the fire of the days he had spent in the red army and the old soldier he had met in the hospital. Little I thought then that I myself would be in the same case. How little any man knows what is before him!

However, I was not thinking of dying yet. I passed six weeks in hospital, four on the flat of my back and two walking in the garden. Happily and gaily and contentedly I spent those two weeks though I had nothing but the skin to keep my bones together, and indeed there were tears in my eyes when I was leaving.

Twenty-Five

CONNEMARA

IT was on the 10th of November. After a good hour's drilling in the square, we went into the schoolhouse as usual to learn points of law. We had just sat down, with our books open, when the superintendent called my name.

"Annso!" I answered.

He called another name. "Annso!" was the answer. And then he called a third. "Annso!"

"Well," said he, "I have to examine the three of you for sending you into the country."

Oh, Lord, I trembled hand and foot. I had made no preparation for it. How could I, after spending six weeks in hospital without looking at a law at all? Well, I pulled myself together. How lucky I would be if I passed today! "Your soul to the devil," a lad whispered to me, "isn't it fine for you to be leaving this devilish place?"

My heart was in a flutter when I saw the superintendent preparing to begin the examination. He took me first, and questioned me about at least nine acts. I answered each question. He stopped and raised his head. "That's not too bad," said he, "after all the time you spent in hospital. You will be going to the country any day now."

Next day I got instructions from the Commissioner that I was to leave at five o'clock on the following morning for Inverin in the county of Galway. I was walking across the room and I doubt if there was any man in Ireland at that moment as happy as I.

"Musha, it is a pity I'm not in your shoes now," said one of the lads.

"Take it easy, boy," said I, "your own day will come yet. But pay attention to your lessons," I added with a laugh.

I had nothing to do that day but to pack my belongings for the journey. Again I overheard that angry word, "'Shun!" and with a glance through the window I saw the recruits out on the square being cursed by the sergeant. I gave a fine hearty laugh.

"Don't be sleepy in the morning, Shaun," said I to the lad in the bed next to mine, "till you help me carry my baggage to the gate."

"All right," said he, "and indeed I will perish after you."

"Yé, don't mind that. They can't keep you here much longer if they do their worst."

"Ah, musha, I don't know, but I would rather than all I ever saw that I was going with you."

"There is no doubt but it's pretty hard here, Shaun."

I got no answer. "Do you hear me, Shaun?" No answer. "Are you asleep?" Again no answer. Indeed, you are in a sound slumber, said I to myself, and I laid my had back on the pillow.

I remembered no more till I was pulled by the ear. I opened my eyes and saw the man who was on guard at the gate, for it was his duty to call me. "Get up," said he, "it is five o'clock."

When I had pulled on my clothes I went over to Shaun. "Get up," said I.

I gave a tug at his ear. He opened his eyes, with a wild look in them. "Are you going?" said he.

"I am."

He leapt out of bed and put on his trousers and shoes. Then we took up my trunk, one at each end, and carried it across the square. We left the trunk at the gate and went back for my bag. When we returned, the lorry was waiting for me. I said good-bye to Shaun and was driven away to Broadstone. I bought my ticket and entered the train.

I was seated at my ease, thinking and reflecting on the world, I in Guard's uniform going out to Connemara to enforce the laws. Musha, isn't it little I thought a short time ago that I would ever go on such a journey!

My fare was paid to Moycullen, wherever that was. I got up and looked out of the window. The day was threatening and heavy snow lying on the hills. I listened to the sound of the train and thought of my first journey through the middle of Ireland.

After a while we stopped and I heard them shouting, "Change for Clifden!"

I took up my bag, went out and crossed the bridge, now as used to that work as any old dog. I went down on the other side, entered the train which was waiting, and before long it started out from the station.

There were two others in the same compartment, the queerest two I ever saw, clad in white flannel from head to heel. Before long one spoke to the other in Irish. My heart leapt with love of that language, though I found it hard to understand them, for they were speaking in the Connacht dialect.

"It looks like rain today, Cole," said one of them.

"It does indeed," said the other man.

"How far is it to Moycullen, Cole?"

"Oh, we are not far from it now."

"I dare say it is after the poteen the peeler is going," said the other fellow with a glance at me.

They looked at each other, smiling. I pretended to be reading a book, as though I did not understand them.

"I dare say they were bad enough back in your place," said Cole.

"Oh, musha, my son, the devil is in them all."

"That peeler doesn't look too bad," said Cole with another glance at me.

"Indeed there is a decent look on him, whoever he is."

"I suppose he has no knowledge of the Irish?"

"How would he? Who has Irish but the wretches of the world?"

"Well, we are in at the station now."

When I heard that I got up.

"I dare say you are from Connemara," said I to them in Irish.

"Oh, the devil!" said Cole.

"Oh, the devil!" said the other fellow. "Isn't it well we didn't say anything out-of-the-way? I tell you, Cole, no one can be trusted these days on road or on path."

"Oh, the devil a lie in that," said Cole. "Did you never hear that a peeler is not to be trusted until he's seven years under the clay?"

I leapt from the train and went into the parcels' office. "I dare say it is far from here to Inverin?" said I to the man inside.

"It's nearly twenty-eight miles."

"I wonder could I get a car here?"

"That is a thing you could not get," said he with a laugh, "but I'll tell you what you will do. It is not far up to the barracks and the Guards there will help you."

Just then I heard a voice outside; "Arra, devil, peeler, peeler!"

I ran out and saw one of the bauneens[1] who had been with me in the carriage with his head out through the window and my valise in his hand.

"Throw it out," I cried.

---

1. Bauneens: the cream woollen costume of the Connemara peasant. And hence "a bauneen," a peasant wearing such costume.

He did so and I caught it, I waved my hand to them in farewell and returned to the office.

"I dare say this baggage can wait here till I come back with the car?"

"Oh, of course."

"Where is the barracks?"

"Come out here and I will show you. That is it up there," said he, pointing towards a building with a red roof. I thanked him and went off.

I walked on till the road began to climb. I stopped and looked around. King of Virtues, wasn't it a wretched poor place! There was not a hand's-breadth of lea-soil to be seen, but everywhere rocks and stones, little untidy, unlimed houses with roofs of rushes dotted here and there. Before long I saw an old woman in her red coat coming down the road with a big black dog. She clapped her hands, crying, in Irish, "There they are below, Cos! Put them out, Cos!"

I looked down where she was pointing and could see nothing but stones, some of them moss-grown with age. Then I noticed two calves pulling at a couple of hay-cocks hardly bigger than my head.

"Oh, oh, musha!" cried the old woman, when the dog had driven them off, "blindness without light on you if it isn't fine the way neither field nor valley would content you!"

Musha, God help them, said I to myself, I don't know where is the field here to nourish them. The old woman departed. Faith, said I, I am among the Gaels again. Isn't it well they are keeping up the old ways—the costume, the language, and the houses.

I walked on again till I met a little boy, well clad in sheep's wool and carrying his bag of books. "What is your name?" said I. He did not answer and tried to slip away. "What is your name?" said I again.

He was looking into my eyes as if he was going to cry. At last he said tremulously: "Colum O'Flaherty."

"Have no fear, boy," said I, "but tell me where is the barracks in this place?"

He ran up on to the top of the ditch, and pointed up the road. "That's it above."

"Good boy," said I, putting a hand in my pocket and giving him sixpence.

"Thank you," said he and departed.

I walked up along a wet rough road till I found the barracks. Three Guards were inside. I told them my business—to get Inverin on the telephone. I spoke into the telephone myself. "Hello!" said Inverin. "Hello!" said I, and I told them to send out a car.

I took dinner with the other Guards and stayed talking of this and that, especially of the Depot, till at eight o'clock the car arrived with two Guards along with the driver. They welcomed me. I said good-bye to the men of the barracks and we drove to the station where I had left my baggage; then out to the west, with a stop here and there, till we reached Inverin late in the evening.

I carried my bag up into the room. I was very happy. I looked out of the window. The moon was high in the sky and the night as bright as day. Galway Bay lay stretched out before me and the coast of Clare lying over in the south-east. I went down and walked out as far as the gate. Children were playing up and down the road, calling to each other in sweet, fluent Irish. I heard the sound of footsteps approaching. He was within four yards of me before I saw him, for he was wearing a suit of bauneens of the same colour as the ground.

"God bless you!" said the old man.

"God and Mary bless you!" said I.

"A fine night," said he again.

"It is so, God be praised."

He passed on.

Before long another was approaching.

"God bless you!"

"God and Mary bless you!"

"A fine night."

"It is a beautiful night, praise be to God on high!"

I stayed a while listening to the sound of the wind in the trees and watching the glitter of the moonlight on the sea. Then I turned on my heel and went in.

Twenty-Six

CONCLUSION

Aᴀ̨ꜰᴛᴇʀ two years in Connemara I went home for my holidays to the Island.

How full of happiness I was when I reached Dingle! I went up to Martin's house. They gave me a bright welcome and told me all the news: this boy was gone and that boy, this girl and that girl gathered away to America.

I took a car to Dunquin and how my heart opened when I reached Slea Head and saw the Blasket, Inish-na-Bró and Inish-vick-ilaun stretched out before me in the sea to the west! I was as gay as a starling as I went down to Dunquin, and it happened that my father was before me on the top of the cliff, with two others whom I did not recognize.

"Musha, God bless your life home again, my son!" said my father with a light of joy in his face.

I glanced at the other two They were looking at me, smiling.

"Who are these?" said I.

"Don't you know Shauneen Liam and Mirrisheen Kate?" said my father with a laugh.

"God of Virtues," said I, looking at them again, "isn't there a great change in them, who were only little children when I left and now they are sturdy men?"

When we came into the quay in the Blasket I thought I would never reach the house.

"Oh, King of Angels," cried an old woman, "isn't it a fine man you have become!"

"Musha, how is every bit of you?" cried another.

"Musha, isn't it you have the great shell of flesh!" cried a third till at last I was mad with them. As for the little children, though I was putting my two eyes through them, I was unable to recognize most of them.

As I approached the house, I saw my grandfather standing in the doorway. When he saw me, he remained there standing, shedding tears of joy.

"Musha, how are you since, daddo?"

He could not speak yet, but embraced me.

"Musha, my heart," said he at last, laughing, "it's many a savage dog and bad housewife you have met since."

"No doubt of it," said I, walking in.

Rose was at the fireside before me, greatly changed, with no thought of fawning on me now. Soon my father came in. My grandfather poured out the tea.

After tea I wandered out through the village. Everyone I met on the road stopped to welcome me.

There was a great change in two years—green grass growing on paths for lack of walking; five or six houses shut up and the people gone out to the mainland; fields which had once had fine stone walls around them left to ruin; the big red patches on the Sandhills made by the feet of the boys and girls dancing—there was not a trace of them now.

When I returned home the lamps were being lit in the houses. I went in. My father and grandfather were sitting on either side of the fire, my grandfather smoking his old pipe.

ABOUT THE AUTHOR

MAURICE O'SULLIVAN (Muiris Ó Súilleabháin) was born in 1904 on the Great Blasket. He left the island as a young man to join the Civic Guard of the nascent Irish Republic, but soon found that law enforcement was not to his liking. While posted in Connemara he wrote this book for the entertainment of his friends back home on the island. He was drowned tragically in 1950, leaving behind a widow and two children.

In his postscript to the 1951 edition of this book, translator George Thomson sadly reported that the population on the island had been "reduced to five households, comprising twenty-one persons, with only one child." Today the island is completely uninhabited; the descendants of the Blasket islanders are scattered throughout the Republic of Ireland, the United States, Great Britain and elsewhere. Interest in Blasket culture, however, appears to be on the rise: books and articles on the subject continue to appear; the Blasket Centre, at Dunquin, County Kerry, maintains a permanent exhibition on the island's history; and tourists to the Dingle Peninsula can now take a day trip to the Blasket to witness the spectacular natural beauty so vividly described by Maurice O'Sullivan.

There is hope yet for the fulfillment of George Thomson's fondest wish, that "there will arise out of the infinite suffering involved in the dispersal of this fine people a new Ireland, replenished by her exiles and their children returning from overseas."